EDUARDO BALDERAS

Eduardo Balderas

EDUARDO BALDERAS

FATHER OF CHURCH TRANSLATION

1907–1989

IGNACIO M. GARCIA

SIGNATURE BOOKS | 2024 | SALT LAKE CITY

This work is dedicated to all those men and women who volunteer throughout the Church of Jesus Christ of Latter-day Saints as well as in many other churches to ensure that their fellow worshipers hear the message of faith in their own language. Also, to all those children, like myself at one time, who translated for their parents and other family members this foreign English Language.

Join our mail list at www.signaturebooks.com for details on events and related titles we think you'll enjoy.

Photographs courtesy Balderas family

Design by Jason Francis

FIRST EDITION | 2024

LIBRARY OF CONGRESS CONTROL NUMBER: 2024950471

Paperback ISBN: 978-1-56085-517-0
Ebook ISBN: 978-1-56085-499-9

CONTENTS

ACKNOWLEDGMENTS

As often said, books are not easy to write and completed manuscripts often follow days, months, and even years of research, reflection, writing, rewriting, and editing, and these can often be quite long and lonely moments. Luckily for me, there were several important people who accompanied me on this journey, sharing their thoughts, questioning my assumptions, and reminding me that the work I was doing was worth all the effort. First, and most important, is my Alejandra who for years patiently listened to me talk about Eduardo Balderas, and kept encouraging me to do the work, believing I was the right person to do this. Without her, there would be no biography.

Fernando Gómez, director of the Mormon Museum in Provo, Utah, was a great source of information and inspiration. No other person knows more about Mexican Latter-day Saint history or has collected as many sources on them as he and his dear Queta have for the museum they established mostly on their own. Eliza Eastwood Pulido, friend and author of *The Spiritual Evolution of Margarito Bautista* shared her research and also patiently listened to me as I worked out Eduardo's story in my mind. Sujey Vega, another friend and scholar shared her thoughts and expertise on Mexican Latter-day Saints, the Arizona-Mesa Temple, and about Chicano history in general. My colleague at Brigham Young University David James Gonzales also took time to discuss the project and provide important reflections on the history of the Mexican population on the US side of the border. And there were numerous other scholars, friends and ordinary Latter-day Saints with whom I spoke about the project and who provided thought-provoking feedback.

I was blessed with two wonderful research assistants, Cindy Pérez and Paul Guajardo, both undergraduates at the time, who were critical to my research as they found people, documents and secondary sources that I had no idea existed. Both are going to be great historians in their own right. Kelsie Westphal provided a thorough first major editing of the manuscript, and made some valuable suggestions.

Just as inspiring as those previously mentioned are the translators that I have seen in all my years attending Spanish language services. Most do it like Eduardo Balderas, without much training or schooling. I know how hard it is to translate words from one language to another, but how much harder it is to interpret concepts, emotions, passion, and the "spirit" in a second language. So many do so well in spite of their limitations. They truly are exceptional whether volunteers or professionals.

Finally, thank you Signature Books for believing in this project.

INTRODUCTION

One particular Sunday, as I sat on a hard bench, staring at the pale wall behind the podium in the old but beautiful—to me anyway—chapel in the West Side of San Antonio, Texas, I first noticed it. My mother, my brother, and I, along with many other Mexican and Mexican American Latter-day Saints (Mormons), had come to hear speakers during the general conference of the Church of Jesus Christ of Latter-day Saints (the annual worldwide gathering of "saints") to be inspired through the radio transmission from Salt Lake City, Utah.[1] It was the time for my family and many others in the San Antonio Fourth Ward to reconnect with those white, aging leaders who told us our duties and spoke of the great things being accomplished around the world by people we knew nothing about, but of whom we learned to be extremely proud.[2] For a church community like ours, whose members were poor but stable, general conference was the highlight of our religious life every year.[3]

It must have been during the second session—conference had

1. I will be using the Church of Jesus Christ of Latter-day Saints, LDS Church, and the Mormons or Mormon Church interchangeably throughout this biography.

2. Ward is the name given to LDS congregations, and branch (as will be seen later) is the name for smaller congregations.

3. The church, which now has millions of Spanish speaking members, was founded in 1830 by a young man named Joseph Smith, who declared that he saw and heard an angel who told him to establish a "true" church. Over time, he added three new scriptures to the Christian canon. One of those was the Book of Mormon, which claimed to be a record of the indigenous people of the Western Hemisphere, and eventually all (today, just some) of the indigenous peoples of the Pacific islands, including Australia and New Zealand. The book held promises of a "blossoming" in the latter-days for these people. Mexican and many indigenous Latin American Latter-day Saints would become known as "Lamanites," a term the book uses to describe a people who survived multiple religious wars to become the ancestors of today's indigenous peoples.

five sessions over two days—when it struck me that all those aging white men spoke with the same tone and accent—basically, they all sounded alike, but in Spanish. I knew that the conference was translated, though I did not at the time know what that meant exactly. Admittedly, there were a few who sounded different from each other, but they were usually the "less" important speakers. I was still young, and so I did not dwell on it, but years later I learned that José Eduardo Balderas, a one-time refugee from Mexico, was doing much of the translating. And not only translating general conference but also translating most of the church's lesson and instructor manuals, pamphlets, and anything else we got from Salt Lake City.

I learned that our red hymnal was compiled by him, and the Spanish-speaking youth of the church throughout the United States, the Caribbean, and Latin America sang hymns he composed for us. We also read articles in the *Liahona* magazine, a Spanish-language periodical, which he helped establish and translated mostly by himself for years. Those young men and young women in my ward, and in hundreds of other wards and branches through the Spanish-speaking world, who went on proselyting missions were using material he not only translated but adapted to fit the dialect of the regions to which they were assigned. There was nothing that we used that did not have the familiar *Traducido por Eduardo Balderas* imprint. Most of the Spanish-speaking Latter-day Saint world knew of him even when they did not know about him.

Though he got little credit for it in the wider Latter-day Saint world, Eduardo's work proved the importance of not only translating church material into other languages but also developing professional translators and a full department to provide them the tools necessary to complete their work. His translation of the temple ceremonies made the church's most important rituals available to Spanish-speaking members and prompted the church to begin translating them into other languages at a time when some church authorities believed that the temple rituals should only be in English.[4] His travels with church authorities not only allowed

4. For Latter-day Saints, temples are their most sacred places where they make special covenants with God. More will be said about them later, but it is important to emphasize their value to the church.

Spanish-speaking members to hear "prophetic voices" in their own language but also provided them a connection to church leaders through Eduardo's proximity to them. And his translation of two of the faith's canonical works and the editing of a third opened the full measure of the Latter-day Saint gospel to millions.

Known by some as the "thirteenth apostle," Eduardo became an iconic figure for many Spanish-speaking saints, and some of them, when they visited Salt Lake City, took to driving by his house in the hope that they might get a glimpse of him, or at least know where he lived.[5] When he became a patriarch, he blessed many Spanish-speaking leaders and members in the United States, Latin America, and even Europe.[6] Throughout all of this, he remained soft spoken, humble, and approachable, a characteristic not as common among some in that era who tended to emulate some of their fundamentalist counterparts who relied on "fire and brimstone" sermons—*talks* in Mormon language—to keep the flock faithful.

For years, I understood Eduardo's importance to the history of the Mexican, Mexican American, and Latina/o members of the LDS Church—and the church at large, as I came to find out later—but I had no inclination to write or research Mormon history, and Eduardo, back then, did not interest me as a historical figure. I periodically pushed back when the idea of writing about him entered my mind. It took several decades before thoughts of Eduardo began to stay with me. I had by then written a few essays on Latina/os in the LDS Church, but not much history. I hoped that by then someone would have taken an interest in him but it became apparent that most Mormon historians had little knowledge of him, and there were literally no LDS Latina/o historians who could write about him.

Waiting for someone to write about "*Hermano* Balderas" turned into an uncomfortable pause for me. Uncomfortable, because I knew that I was one person who could write about him, and I was reminded

5. This was told to me by his daughter-in-law, Christine Balderas. See unpublished and undated manuscript, "Christine and Dan Balderas Interview," in author's possession.

6. In the LDS Church, the office of a "patriarch" is a calling within the faith's priesthood. That church officer provides "blessings" in which he tells recipients their lineage within the house of Israel and provides them a general—sometimes specific—roadmap of their lives, as well as promising them blessings through obedience to church covenants and gospel commandments.

that "discomfort" is the way most of my scholarly work begins. I identify a work that "needs to be done," wait to see if anyone else sees its importance, and then, tired of waiting, I start to write about it myself. The difference here, however, is that most of my earlier books and articles reflected my passion for social justice by men and women I admired, or came to admire after time. Eduardo Balderas, notwithstanding his importance to my people—and Mexican and Latina/o Mormon history—did not ignite that passion.

He left no important writings (at least as I interpreted "important writings" back then), he was anything but a social warrior, he never gave a zealous speech about inequality in society, and he never assumed any leadership role in the church or his community. Finally, he was too timid for my taste. Humility is fine—after all, there were Gandhi, Mother Teresa, César Chávez, and a host of other historical figures who spoke softly but figuratively carried big sticks—but try as I might, I could identify no "stick" in Balderas's arsenal. Just a pen and paper and multiple dictionaries and thesauruses.

Eventually, I got tired of waiting for someone else to write about him and decided the work had to be done, though at the time I vacillated between a long article, a series of essays on his life, and grudgingly, maybe a biography. I thought and talked about how to write his biography for at least two years while doing only minimal research. The more I learned about him, the more his importance grew in my mind, but most people I spoke to said there was "little material on him," and as it turned out, there was not even a file on him at the Church History Library.

When I started, I wanted, through him, to write about the spiritual heroics of my people as some have about the Mormon pioneers coming west—to take our land, and that of our indigenous cousins, whose faith carried them through obstacles of violence, long patches of desert, never-ending grassy plains, hostile "Indians"—mostly people trying to defend their way of life—bitter snow, and scorching sun, until they finally arrived at the mountain tops where they built Zion. The heroic faith of our "white brothers and sisters" was a staple of Sunday School lessons, sacrament meeting talks, and reenactment marches of brown people around the parking lot of our small chapel in the West Side of San Antonio. I would be remiss if I did not acknowledge that these experiences were important to my own faith and to the decisions I took in my life. My understanding of the complications of race, ethnicity, land appropriation, and so on came later, when my faith had matured and so had my knowledge of history and the Mormon past.

I yearned to understand the thoughts and the homegrown theology that people like Eduardo had developed of the Mormon gospel over the years. I saw and listened to older people in my congregation, whom I saw as wise *Mormones*—in essence our "elders"—and I could imagine there were others before them who had a particular view of how to practice the faith because of their own experiences with Latter-day Saint doctrine. What did they think? Did they write something, perform miracles, or travel their own pioneer treks? Did they fight demons, feed hundreds, resist mobs, or teach great doctrinal truths?

This led me to ask some profound questions about the celestial pecking order, though then I did not frame the questions in that way. Without a doubt, the "Spanish-speaking" saints—as they were known throughout my youth, and in some places are still referred to this way—have never played an important part in the actual pecking order of the LDS Church, though they have often been talked about as the future of the faith.[7] Nonetheless, within their bubble, Mexican and other Latin American saints created their own pecking order, developed their own local histories—though they were written down only occasionally and always as history in the peripheries—and nurtured their organic leadership.

Even as a young man, it was easy for me to see that in my own congregation we had all kinds of leaders and people with perceptive insights into the doctrine and the practice of the Latter-day Saint gospel, but I rarely saw them speak about it publicly—sometimes not even in our congregational meetings—because only our white leaders spoke "doctrinally" and "authoritatively." These white visiting leaders often spoke with sincerity and kindness, but their sensitivity to our concerns sometimes silenced our own thoughts and words, even if not intentionally, though intermittently it was to keep our

7. This comes from the promises to people of indigenous origin found in the faith's most important canon, the Book of Mormon.

practice of the gospel message within what they saw as correct parameters. When we did discuss our religious views among ourselves in classes, one-on-one conversations, in a fireside here or there, in small group chats in the corner of a hallway, or in someone's house, they were faith promoting and had meaning, but they seemed to exist in some in-between spaces. Not fully of the world, but neither fully in the church.

The story of Eduardo Balderas and the Mexican saints also has a place in those in-between spaces. His importance to the work of the church, both among the Spanish-speaking and other saints, is unquestionable, yet, besides a few articles or remembrances, there has been little effort to write about him, and in the only book about the church's translation department, he merits only a few lines. He is often lost in the triumphant story of the church's proselyting successes in Latin America and among Spanish speakers in the United States and Europe, and it is easily forgotten that the words used to convert, nurture, and prepare Latina/o and Latin American saints to embrace and live the Mormon gospel were his translations. For many years, the sound of the words that Spanish-speaking saints heard from their leaders were his.

Unfortunately, when it comes to indigenous saints and saints of color, actions similar to Eduardo's are rarely part of the official institutional record. Brown bodies have often been important mostly in terms of the numbers of their conversions, baptisms, missionaries sent out, congregations formed, and temples built. While often lauded for their devotion and embrace of the Mormon gospel, they have seldom been seen within the context of their own lived religious experiences—in other words, through their history. Eduardo, whether he fully understood it or not at the time, sought to change this by providing his fellow Spanish-speaking saints the *plenitud*, or fullness, of the Mormon gospel, hoping to increase their numbers and develop more leadership within their community. They needed to read the doctrine, make sacred temple covenants, and have a church magazine in their language, and he made all of this possible.

As my astute research assistant Paul Guajardo so succinctly declared in a panel discussion about Eduardo and his brother Guillermo, the brothers sought to create a brown space for the Spanish-speaking members of the Church of Jesus Christ of Latter-day Saints. This space was not only physical but also emotional, intellectual, theological, and spiritual because in that place, they could read the text, sing the hymns, declare the words, inspire each other, and reflect on the divine in a language they knew and understood.

Eduardo Balderas believed in the promises of the Mormon canon that prophesized that his people would "blossom as [a] rose" and take their place in the church at all levels (Doctrine and Covenants 49:24). To do this, however, they needed their brown space in which to reflect upon the Kingdom, as Latter-day Saints like to call their church. The Spanish-speaking saints had to speak the language of the church, but their dialect had to be constructed through interpretative filters that gave meaning to Sunday worship and their readings and preaching that built on their experiences as immigrants, workers, and oftentimes second-class citizens in American society, and even in a church they loved dearly.

Traducido por Eduardo Balderas were beautiful words for Spanish-speaking saints of my generation, and I believe that in my telling Eduardo's story a new generation of Latina/os in the church will appreciate his work and his significance to the church whether they speak Spanish or not.

1

COMING TO AMERICA

LIFE AS AN IMMIGRANT AND A REFUGEE

The Mexican immigrant story of the twentieth century is the story of the Mexican Revolution that displaced millions through horrific violence, destroyed much of the countryside, and sent many across the border to the giant to the north. The revolution prompted migration initially, but the voracious appetite of America's industrial and agricultural revolutions enlarged the numbers of immigrants and expanded their exiled space. Like the modern immigrant caravans from Central America in the twenty-first century, but in larger, less organized numbers, nearly a million people, young and old, traveled by foot, or on one-horse wagons from deep in the southern part of the country to the major cities and border towns, and many came across the border. These people came to escape grinding poverty and merciless killing by both revolutionaries and *federales* and because of the lure of returning to a land that once was theirs. They became what writer, artist, and entrepreneur Leonel Sosa called "the children of the revolution," and they helped build the southwestern part of this nation by laboring in the fields, factories, restaurants, construction sites and small businesses.[1]

Their coming to this land fulfilled the canonical prophecy of the Book of Mormon, a book that "record[s] ... God's dealings with ancient inhabitants of the Americas" (introduction to the Book of Mormon) and was "written to the Lamanites, who are a remnant of the house of Israel; and also to Jew and Gentile" (title page of the Book of Mormon). "Wherefore, I, Lehi, prophesy according to the workings of the

1. Lionel Sosa and Neftalí García, *The Children of the Revolución: How the Mexican Revolution Changed America* (Self-pub. 2012, distributed by University of Texas at Austin).

Spirit which is in me, that there shall none come into this land save they shall be brought by the hand of the Lord. Wherefore, this land is consecrated unto him whom he shall bring" (2 Nephi 1:6–7).[2]

This concept of being brought by the hand of God grew as the Spanish-speaking community of *Mormones* itself grew.[3] Eventually, many of these Mexican and Latina/o Latter-day Saints shed their embarrassment or guilt about coming, even without documents, to work and live in the United States. In the beginning, however, those Latter-day Saints who came, of which we know only a few, came for reasons similar to that of most refugees and immigrants: to work and to escape poverty and violence. Such was the case for the Balderas family, who at the time of their journey to *el norte* were not yet members of the church.

José Apolinar de Jesús Balderas Carranco (Apolinar as I will refer to him), the patriach of the family, was born in Rancho de Amolitos, Cortazar, Celaya, Guanajuato, Mexico, on July 20, 1883. Celaya, which lies in the south–central part of the state of Guanajuato, is part of the fertile volcanic region of the Mexican plateau just northwest of Mexico City. Little is known about his youth except that he grew up on a "farm," though more likely a small home in a rural area where the family grew as much of their food as they could and had a few domesticated animals, such as chickens, pigs, and small goats. He grew up, as most young boys back then, tending the animals, working the land with his family, and getting what schooling was available given the sparsity of teachers and schools in the rural countryside during the Porfirio Díaz dictatorship, which lasted on-and-off for thirty-one years, between 1876 and 1911.

---

2. This book is the most important book of scripture for members of the Church of Jesus Christ of Latter-day Saints (Mormons). It was once purported to be the history of people who came to the Americas from the Middle East and were descendants of the house of Israel. These people, called "Lamanites" in the book, are now thought to have been one of the many indigenous groups that inhabited the American continent. The term Lamanite refers to all indigenous converts—from South and North America and the Pacific—to the LDS faith. *Lamanita* was used to describe the Spanish-speaking converts with indigenous origin.

3. Even as a young Latter-day Saint convert, I heard Spanish-speaking members and often their leaders talk about being "led by the hand of God" to this land. Often, this was a response to those who criticized Latina/o members for coming to the United States without documents.

Apolinar's family seems to have been devout Catholics, because he remembers his father wanting him to enter the priesthood. It may also have been that the priesthood was a vocation that provided stability, safety, and education, something unavailable to children of families like the Balderases. So, Apolinar entered a monastery along with other working-class, rural young men, many of whom were no doubt sincerely seeking to lead a religious life while others were guided by their families' wishes. Apolinar, however, soon found the discipline "too strict," particularly the part about "atoning for his sins."[4] Eduardo, his eldest son, remembers his father talking about waking up at four each morning, stripping down to the waist, and "[taking] a whip and strik[ing] himself across the back."[5] It did not take long for him to decide that he'd rather have a less painful life, so he quit the monastery and moved to Mexico City. Though he went through a period of secularization, the spiritual in him—though not the Catholic—remained deeply embedded and flourished when he converted to the American religion that became the dominant influence in his life.[6]

In the large metropolis, teeming with thousands of immigrants from the countryside like Apolinar—with little education, no money, and no connections, yet still hopeful they would find a future—he met María Columba Centeno Guerrero, a native of Orizaba, Veracruz, whose family also sought to find a home away from the harshness of rural lands. They married on August 22, 1906, he at the age of twenty-four and she nineteen, at the Santa Catarina Mártir Church in Mexico City.[7] With little in hand, they set out to establish a family, and in a year, on September 14, 1907, they had José Eduardo Balderas Centeno, the first of ten children (five boys and five girls) of whom eight lived to be adults.[8]

4. Eduardo Balderas, Oral History, interviews by Gordon Irving, 1973, typescript, 1, Oral History Program, Church History Library, the Church of Jesus Christ of Latter-day Saints, Salt Lake City (hereafter CHL).

5. Balderas, Oral History.

6. Balderas, Oral History.

7. Santa Catarina Mártir Church, "Parish Records," Partida # 42, left margin. These records have José Apolinar as being from Cortázr, Morelia. In his naturalization "Decm laration of Intent," he states that he was born on July 23, 1883, which is when he was christened (No. 2353, Dec. 2, 1943, Bisbee, Arizona).

8. See FamilySearch, "Guillermo Balderas Sr (1910–91)," familysearch.org, accessed July 12, 2023.

With a dark complexion, large eyes, a Roman nose, and standing at five feet, nine inches tall, Apolinar exuded a serious confidence and strong personality that belied a humble demeanor.[9] LDS Church president Gordon B. Hinckley wrote about him years later: "There is nothing high-pressure about him. He knows he is doing the Lord's work, and he goes about it in an attitude of humility and love. Somehow people feel a confidence in him. They know he is sincere. They trust him."[10] That demeanor was reflected in the lives of his two sons, who were cut from the same tree. His other children we know less about.[11]

Of Apolinar's life in that large metropolis, where political rallies, massive labor marches, and great debates were frequent even as dictator Porfirio Díaz ruled with an iron fist, we know little. It is probable that, similar to other young couples, Balderas and his wife faced precarious times in a Mexico dominated by foreign—particularly European and American—influences, where class differences, racial snobbery, and low-paying jobs defined life for those *de abajo* (disadvantaged) and created hostile resentment against the dictatorship. Only a year before Apolinar's marriage, Ricardo Flores Magon, one of the intellectual precursors of the Mexican Revolution, launched an ill-fated military invasion from the southwestern part of the United States. It failed, and Magon exiled himself to the United States.[12]

Banned from Mexico for his insurrectionist journalism, Magon riled his readers against Díaz, a military hero turned dictator, who welcomed foreigners, and stole peasants' land to modernize his country. Mexican organizers and radicals on both sides of the border worked to undermine the regime while ferociously debating the

---

9. José Apolinar Balderas, "Declaration of Intent."

10. Gordon B. Hinckley, "The Virtues of Joseph, the Wisdom of Apollo Are His," *Deseret News*, May 23, 1948.

11. The Balderas children were reticent about including too much information about the family.

12. For a good revisionist discussion of Ricardo Flores Magon's activities on both sides of the border, see Juan Gomez-Quiñones, *Sembradores: Ricardo Flores Magon y el Partido liberal Mexicano: A Eulogy and Critique* (Los Angeles: Aztlán Publications, 1973). For a more traditional view of Magon and his activities, see John M. Hart, *Anarchism & The Mexican Working Class, 1860–1932* (Austin: University of Texas, 1978). For a brief history of the revolution, see Alan Knight, *The Mexican Revolution: A Very Short Introduction* (New York: Oxford University Press, 2016).

type of government they wanted. The breaking point for the volatile nation came after the election of 1910, when a rich landowner, Francisco Madero, challenged Díaz for the presidency but massive voter fraud led to his defeat and caused many to question the legitimacy of the president's re-election.[13]

Following his electoral defeat, Madero issued the "Plan de San Luis Potosi," which declared the grievances against the dictatorship and then launched an armed insurrection. Imagined first as a fight for the rights of Mexican elites who sought a greater voice in the government and resented foreign control of much of the nation's industry, railways, and mines, the revolution took a life of its own as peasants, urban workers, miners, small farmers, and others joined the fight for a more just Mexico.[14] The conflict pitted brother against brother, and the battles and wanton killings engulfed the whole nation, killing nearly a million Mexicans and forcing another million to head north.

It was months before the start of the more violent phase of the Revolution, however, that José Apolinar gave up on finding a better life in his beloved Mexico. By this time, his son Eduardo was nearing his third birthday, and María was pregnant with their second child. There is no record of Apolinar's occupation or economic situation, but it is likely that he eked out a life as most Mexico City proletariats did, working seasonally and for meager pay, until eventually learning the trade of a barber. As resilient and tenacious as Apolinar proved to be, he saw no hope for a better life in a poor nation about to engage in all-out war, with revolutionary forces gathering around the countryside for the short-lived violent first phase of a conflict that lasted decades in one form or another. Apolinar thus decided to flee to the United States like many of his countrymen, who fled the cities, provincial towns, and rural *ejidos* where much of the fighting occurred.

Apolinar's migration followed other smaller ones and preceded

---

13. See footnote 12.

14. For a slightly more in-depth view of the Mexican Revolution, see Anita Bremmer, *The Wind That Swept Mexico* (Austin: University of Texas Press, 1971); Federico González, *La Revolución: Mi Contribución Política-Literaria* (Mexico, 1936); and Alan Knight, *The Mexican Revolution, Volume 1: Porfirians, Liberals and Peasants* (Lincoln: University of Nebraska Press, 1990) and *The Mexican Revolution, Volume 2: Counter Revolution and Reconstruction* (Lincoln: University of Nebraska Press, 1990).

the massive one that began once the shooting started. In the "conquered lands," as the American Southwest was known to many Mexicans, massive irrigation projects opened much of the arid desert for farming, and the new mining techniques brought a need for laborers and seasoned miners. Packing and shipping businesses also sought low-wage workers. Apolinar, however, did not come for those labor-intensive jobs. We know nothing of his having any manual labor skills, though we do know that upon arrival he started cutting hair and opened his own barber shop. We don't know what he expected to find in the United States. He had no relatives in the states and no prior experience with the country. What he knew of *los Estados Unidos* most likely came from newspaper accounts, conversations he'd had, or bits and pieces of information that he heard from others.

His travel plans and expectations are unrecorded. What we know comes from his son Eduardo, who told an interviewer many years later that Apolinar took the train with no idea of where he was to go, but at the time El Paso was connected to the Mexican migration routes north by the Southern Pacific, and that is where he chose to stay. It is hard to imagine Apolinar and María, who seemed always to present a middle-class appearance, riding a bumpy, hot train full of dust and smelling of coal fuel over more than a thousand miles of mostly desert landscape. Traveling by train meant being sweaty, hot, thirsty, and hungry for days on end. Pictures of trains from those times present them as full beyond capacity, with people sometimes riding on top and others literally hanging from the doors and windows with their few possessions and sometimes even with one or two domesticated animals. It's harder still to envision the physical and emotional discomfort that Apolinar felt, how his pregnant María coped, or even how their three-year-old endured the journey.[15]

Their voyage was far from atypical, as thousands of immigrants left and continue to leave their countries by similar means today to escape violence, hunger, poverty, and disease. And like many immigrants, Apolinar and María were both hopeful and apprehensive, believing anything was better than what they left. Unlike many of their countrymen, however, they chose not to rush and stopped in

15. Balderas, Oral History, 1.

Ciudad Torreon for a "few weeks," most likely to give María, now more than eight months pregnant, some rest, and there José Domingo Guillermo was born. After a short recovery period, the family continued the journey north and arrived in Ciudad Juarez, where they stayed several weeks.[16] It is quite possible that José had saved some money, and it is also probable that while María and his children convalesced, he worked in whatever he could find, most likely cutting hair.

On reaching the border, where people were crossing by the thousands, Apolinar hired someone who today would be called a "coyote" to cross him. It is unclear why he did so. Crossing the United States–Mexico border was mostly unregulated until 1929. In fact, Eduardo remembers Apolinar telling him that the border was "quite open and free [and that he] was not challenged.... He just came in and that was it."[17] Still, it is possible there was a fee and a health inspection. Some historians even write about "kerosene baths" and the charge of 50 cents a head—a steep price for many immigrants—though that seems to have come later. It is difficult to know if the El Paso border officials (there was no border patrol in 1910) were engaging in activities beyond the requirements of United States immigration law, or whether Apolinar had something to fear. Possibly, like my own father, he had heard about law enforcement's treatment of Mexican immigrants and the overall disdain that many white Americans had toward the neighbors from south of the border.[18]

Having crossed the border, Apolinar and family moved to a "rundown tenement district," wrote one Mormon writer, who also added that "there was little beauty in the crowded flats whose front doors opened directly on[to] the sidewalk." He continued, "Neither art nor comfort had been taken into consideration in the construction of their drab walls and flat roofs."[19] The writer's negative description

16. Guillermo Balderas, "Historia," 1, Balderas Family, Balderas Family Scrapbooks, 1910–11, Oral History Program, CHL.

17. Balderas, Oral History, 1.

18. For a discussion of the border patrol, see Kelly Lytle Hernández, *MIGRA: The History of the U.S. Border Patrol* (Berkeley: University of California Press, 2020); Peter Andreas, *Policing the U.S.–Mexico Border* (Ithaca, NY: Cornell University Press, 2000); Mark Reisleer, *By the Sweat of Their Brow: Mexican Immigrant Labor in the United States, 1900–1940* (Westport, CT: Greenwood Press, 1976).

19. Hinckley, "Virtues of Joseph."

misunderstands the immigrants' desires to mitigate the dire circumstances they shared with their Mexican American compatriots in El Paso and most other border towns. These "tenement" districts arose because the people were poor, segregated, and unwanted in other parts of the city. At the same time, they provided a cultural safe zone for Mexicans who wanted to go back to their country once the strife ended. Not all went back, but many did, and others became "border crossers," going back and forth for most of their lives. In fact, these border towns became transnational spaces that took a little of both countries but never fully succumbed to the cultural or social dominance of either one. Thus, despite their limitations, these "Mexican spaces" played an important role in the lives of many of these immigrants.

The Balderas family experienced the life of refugees: fleeing war, arriving with little resources, crossing the border with the help of a coyote, and landing in a place of segregated neighborhoods and schools with poor housing, low-paying jobs, and spaces where smokestacks dominated the skies, smelly tanning and meat plants fouled the air, and open sewage met them when they stepped out of their homes. Most Mexican immigrants in the early twentieth century, regardless of their regional or even class differences—except for the most extreme cases—were lumped together and found their ethnic identity in those Mexican barrios of the Southwest. Those who had longer roots in the territory were soon overwhelmed by the massive migration to their community and were again reminded of their second-class status by the attitudes and reactions of the white population that lived near them. For most white citizens, a Mexican was a Mexican regardless of time in the country or native birth, and they resisted their presence through laws, city ordinances, segregated schools, and, at times, violence.

The Balderas family thus entered a Mexican–American world that became their contextual space for most of their lives. Their children became transnational citizens who went back and forth to Mexico and, more importantly, retained a bicultural existence even as they cemented their relationship to their new land. This cementing began with Apolinar opening a barber shop. Residents were poor but they sought to look respectable, especially those who came to be known as *los exiliados* or *los ricos*—the exiled or the rich. Most were not really rich, but they were educated, and some brought some wealth after fleeing the revolution when their side lost. They would become an important fixture in El Paso. They opened schools for the children excluded from American schools, established theaters to entertain and maintain the culture, promoted religious and cultural festivals, supported the Catholic Church with money and volunteer hours, and many became de facto leaders in their communities. They worked hard to keep Mexico alive in the hearts of their working-class compatriots while keeping an eye on conditions that might enable them to return to their country.[20]

I remember my father pointing out to me the businesses—pharmacies, herbal and barber shops, notary public offices, restaurants, small factories, and so on—owned or once owned by the "educated Mexicans" in San Antonio. He exuded pride as he revealed to his son that Mexicans, too, were educated, owned businesses, and had influence in the city. While happy for my father—a man who suffered depressions over the harsh work, his poverty, and broken dreams—those moments of his joy brought many questions to me about why our successes were sandwiched between bigger buildings and what had happened to those people. Some had gone back to Mexico. Many of their children had intermarried or assimilated so much that we saw them as "Anglos" or *agringados* and rarely saw them as part of us. Apolinar, in his lifetime, would have seen much the same thing.

Not all, and probably not most, of Apolinar's customers were well-educated individuals. In fact, many were working-class individuals who took pride in their appearance, particularly after working long hours in jobs that had them dirty and sweaty for most of the day. It was common for many of these laborers and their families to "dress up" for weekend activities and religious holidays. Mexican

20. For a discussion of the Mexican American barrios in El Paso and the cultural, as well as other activities the people engaged in, see Mario T. García, *Desert Immigrants: The Mexicans of El Paso, 1880–1920* (New Haven: Yale University Press, 1981), 197–232; also, see Cleofas Caballero, *Historia de la Parroquia de San Ignacio Loyola* (El Paso: American Printing, 1935), 17, 39, 69, 147; and Oscar J. Martínez, *The Chicanos of El Paso: An Assessment of Progress* (Texas: Texas Western Press, 1980). For a general assessment of border towns, see Roger Bruns, *Border Towns and Border Crossings: A History of the U.S.–Mexico Divide* (Westport, CT: Greenwood, 2019). Internal community building was an important part of establishing Mexican American barrios throughout the Southwest.

immigrants, though often destitute, sought to find ways to make life bearable. Community building, even in its most basic and often haphazard ways, became a priority, and El Paso, like many other communities in the southwestern part of the United States, became a cultural haven for those who continued to flee the revolution, or who simply came to find jobs. In these spaces they sought to create a little version of the places they left behind.[21]

These new Mexican spaces, while focused on recreating "little Mexicos," differed significantly from the homeland in that they forced the immigrants to be "more Mexican" than they were before. They now had to hold on to an identity and a way of life disdained by the larger society. Being "Mexican" came to describe not only their nationality but their place in the American social, cultural, racial, and economic pecking order. Some would become defiant, others accommodating, and still others simply let things come as they did. To many white Americans, the Mexicans' character became synonymous with laziness and a *mañana*-orientation, dirtiness, smelliness, lice-infestation, violence, and betrayal. The Mexican immigrant became an unwanted yet necessary worker who performed the manual labor, picked the crops, collected the trash, and did whatever other dirty, hard labor needed done.[22] By the early twentieth century, most white Americans had begun fleeing such jobs when they could, and especially when they could get a person of color to do them.

El Paso had a larger industrial base than most border towns. The American Smelting and Refining Company had a subsidiary there. The Santa Fe Railroad had a railroad yard, and so did the G.H. & S.A. and the Southern Pacific railroad companies. The railroad connections to both Mexico and the rest of the United States made it, as historian Mario T. García characterized it, "a perfect site to receive ores, particularly copper from surrounding areas" like the

21. See footnote 20.

22. For a discussion of how white Americans saw Mexicans in Texas in the nineteenth and twentieth centuries, see Arnold De Leon, *They Called Them Greasers: Anglo Attitudes Toward Mexicans in Texas, 1821–1900* (Austin: University of Texas Press, 1983); also, Aaron E. Sanchez, *Homeland, Ethnic Mexican Belonging Since 1900* (Norman: University of Oklahoma Press, 2021); and Richard A. García, *Rise of the Mexican American Middle Class, San Antonio, 1929–1941* (College Station: Texas A&M University Press, 1991), particularly chapter 1.

mines in Arizona and New Mexico.[23] The smelter hired hundreds of workers. Though it is unclear how many Mexicans they hired when the Balderas family arrived, by the start of World War I it employed nearly three thousand people, and most were Mexican American or Mexican immigrants.[24] The railroad lines also hired hundreds of Mexican workers to service their tracks throughout much of the West and Midwest. The railroads attracted, next to farm labor, the largest number of workers from Mexico and the Mexican American barrios of the Southwest, helping to create the numerous communities of Mexican-origin families throughout the southwest region. With the Mexican Central Railroad connecting Mexico to the United States through El Paso by 1910 came the growth of trade between the two countries. This included El Paso becoming a cattle town as both nations found the international railroad connection a way to send their animals both north and south.[25] While these industries eventually became high paying, the initial years were ones of backbreaking work, low pay, and rampant discrimination—in the north from whites and in the south from Mexican elites.[26]

Of course, major industry jobs were not the only ones hiring. Thousands of jobs were available to Mexican immigrants, from construction to retail to transportation and manufacturing as well as other service jobs. García points to the dominance of Mexican women in "domestic work and laundering," in the city's "early garment factories," and as retail clerks in both "American- and Mexican-owned stores."[27] The segregation of the Mexican immigrant, García argues, also led to the creation of numerous small businesses—restaurants, grocery stores, herbal stores, carpentry, tailor shops, cantinas, and

23. Garcia, *Desert Immigrants*, 2–3.

24. See García, *Desert Immigrants*, 2–3; also, John Burnett, "A Toxic Century: Mining Giant Must Clean Up Mess," Feb. 4, 2010, npr.org.

25. For an in-depth discussion of Mexican workers and the railroads, see Jeffrey Marco Garcilazo's *Traqueros: Mexican Railroad Workers in the United States, 1870–1930* (Denton, TX: University of North Texas Press, 2012); also see García, *Desert Immigrants*, 3.

26. See the Hector Galán's film, *Los Mineros* (Austin: Galán Productions, 1991) for a picture of the American experience, discrimination, and low pay in the Arizona mines, a situation that mirrored that of most Mexicans in the Southwest.

27. García, *Desert Immigrants*, 4.

barber shops, among others—that catered to this population and helped develop a small business and professional middle class.[28]

Apolinar eventually became one of those small businesspeople, thus escaping much of the hard labor and mistreatment by white bosses, first by working as an independent barber and then by hiring others to help him service his people in the barrio. Eduardo had no recollection of his father doing anything other than barbering, except for a short period after World War I when he bought some land in Las Cruces, New Mexico, and tried to raise cotton. But even then, barbering came first. Eventually, Apolinar found some success, at least enough to open another shop, and had other men begin barbering with him. That allowed him to move his family to a "better side of town" inhabited by mostly English-speaking people.[29]

When people like Apolinar and María came north from Mexico, they not only brought their food, music, and culture but also a desire to have their children taught the Spanish language and the history of Mexico. They wanted them to learn English too, but most Mexican children were not allowed into English-language schools, and when they were, they were often segregated in predominantly Mexican and Mexican American-serving schools. Alongside those segregated schools, "Mexican schools"—these with Spanish language instruction—popped up throughout the Southwest as Mexican parents were anxious to have their children educated. Most of these were founded by educators that had also left the violence behind, or by journalists, writers, or simply more educated individuals who saw the need to school their compatriots' children and to make some money doing something besides manual labor.[30]

Eduardo remembers his first schooling coming at the hands of a Spanish professor who had also fled the Revolution. "From him I

28. García.

29. Balderas, Oral History, 2, 4.

30. For a discussion of schools, or *escuelitas*, founded by Mexican immigrants to educate their children when they were not allowed into or were harshly discriminated against in the public schools, see García, *Desert Immigrants*, 110–26; Philis Barragán Goetz, *Reading, Writing, and Revolution: Escuelitas and the Emergence of a Mexican American Identity in Texas* (Austin: University of Texas Press, 2022); see also Laura K. Muñoz, *Desert Dreams: Mexican Arizona and the Politics of Educational Equality* (Philadelphia: University of Pennsylvania Press, 2013).

learned how to read and write ... mostly in Spanish," he said.[31] Guillermo, Eduardo's brother, recalls a "Don Jacinto" who taught them in Spanish to be proud of their heritage, to commemorate Mexican Independence Day, and to sing the Mexican national anthem, which stayed "in [his] mind."[32] Guillermo remembered him as a kind and caring man who often played the part of a third parent to children whose parents worked long hours to feed them.[33] It is interesting that both Eduardo and Guillermo remembered being instructed in Spanish, since all the official or school-board approved "Mexican" schools were set up to teach the immigrant children English, and in fact, Spanish was prohibited in those schools. Ironically, Spanish was promoted in English-language schools to prepare young white men and women to succeed in the transnational world that was El Paso. This meant that in the official "Mexican schools,"—those set up by the school district—Mexican children were forced to only speak English but were not taught the language well and thus became bilingually deficient, not speaking either language well.

Eventually, both Eduardo and Guillermo moved to one of the segregated schools on the Mexican side of town. These schools taught mostly vocational courses and English, though they did it with few resources, as the school district provided much less money to them than to those in the white part of town. The common stereotype was that Mexican children were good with their hands but were mentally inferior to white students when it came to a more intellectually stimulating curriculum.[34] Too many educators back then, no matter their sensitivities or even their love for their Mexican students, saw the home and the culture of these students as "deficient," some so deficient that they were only capable of getting a rudimentary education and learning to use their hands.

Up until the 1960s, most Mexican and Mexican American children in the southwestern United States were provided only enough education to labor in the most menial of jobs. Young girls were prepared for domestic work, and young boys for work in the fields,

31. Balderas, Oral History, 4.
32. Guillermo Balderas, "Historia," 1.
33. Balderas.
34. García, *Desert Immigrants*, 112–14.

factories, smeltery, and railroad yards. Just as important to note is that they were taught enough civics to underscore the superiority of "American ways." These segregated schools had the contradictory job of assimilating students into American society while keeping them in the peripheries of that same society. In essence, they were being "de-Mexicanized" while not fully Americanized. Too many educators saw Mexican families as morally deficient and often judged the children to be obsessed with their sexual impulses. They were also considered dirty, lacking any knowledge of hygiene and carrying all kinds of diseases, and so they were subjected to what one educator called the "two powerful agencies of American civilization [for immigrants], soap and water."[35]

Complicating the educational odyssey for Mexican school children like Eduardo, most schools for them offered learning only up to the sixth or sometimes the eighth grade. While the students could transfer to El Paso High School, most children dropped out before reaching the transferring stage to help their families with the finances or were too unprepared to continue their education. Some simply did not feel comfortable in the white educational spaces of El Paso, where they might be segregated within the school and even within the classrooms. Racism, heavy-handed discipline, and teacher insensitivity made school a difficult space to navigate for many Mexican school children. And too often, their parents could be of little help—given their own lack of education—except to encourage them to learn so as to escape the grind of hard labor. Unfortunately—and this also played a part for some in deciding whether to continue their schooling—some who finished high school ended up working alongside those who dropped out. There simply existed few expectations for most Mexican immigrants and Mexican Americans of getting a decent job in the American economy.

Guillermo remembers learning the English language quickly—and it's possible that Eduardo did too—because he found an "amicable and loving teacher."[36] Guillermo's remembrance, which seems free of any harsh memories, and Eduardo's later recollection that "never, as far as I can recall, was I conscious of any general

35. García, *Desert Immigrants*, 118.
36. Balderas, "Historia," 2.

discrimination,"[37] reflects the experience of some immigrants who came to this country. The boys put their heads down, worked hard, appreciated what they now had, and contextualized their lives within a sphere of meritocracy—it would later serve them well in the Mormon world—while ignoring much of what swirled around them. At least, that is how they later came to see their early lives. The fact that both came from a stable, nuclear family that managed the harshness of border town life, and that both came to achieve some semblance of successful lives, no doubt helped them romanticize their early years.

But those recollections do not hide the fact that neither of the Balderas boys benefitted much from their schooling: Eduardo dropped out after the tenth grade and Guillermo after the seventh, after which they found themselves in menial jobs for years—the result of a deficient education and employment discrimination.[38] Here, we can pause for a reality check of the "no-discrimination" remembrance of both Balderas brothers by looking at an interview Guillermo gave to historian Oscar Martínez of the University of Texas, El Paso.[39] This sharing of memories contradicts much of what both Guillermo and Eduardo would say publicly about their experiences as children growing up in El Paso. In substance, the interview underscores the reality that the Balderas family was an immigrant family in a town where Mexicans, for the most part, were seen as second-class citizens.

Guillermo remembers that when his family moved to an all-white neighborhood and he went to an all-white school, he was blamed for everything that was lost, referred to as "greaser," never chosen to play games, and made to feel inferior. Apolinar must have had an inclination that his son would face discrimination because he changed Guillermo's name to "William," which likely made things worse—a brown kid, with accented English, named William.[40] This caused further problems when the family again moved back to a Mexican

37. Balderas, Oral History, 3.

38. For a note on his educational attainment, see Utah State Department of Health, death certificate, file no. 18–109, Eduardo Balderas (Jan. 13, 1989). Copy in possession of author.

39. See Interview with Guillermo Balderas by Oscar J. Martínez, 1974, interview no. 148, Institute of Oral History, University of Texas El Paso.

40. Interview with Balderas, 1–3.

barrio. We don't know whether Apolinar confronted the same racial problems living in a white neighborhood or if his economic stability declined, but soon he had his children in a mostly Mexican school.[41]

The Mexican kids now took their turn ridiculing a brown kid with the name "William." That he had no accent and dressed more formally than the other students also caused him to be mocked. Here was the dilemma of families who sought to accommodate their kids to the English-speaking world—they often became unacceptable to both communities. Changing names, whether performed by parents who were afraid that their kids would be singled out or by teachers who chose not to learn the "Mexican names," caused confusion for the children. For Guillermo, it meant that he worked to lose his accent to be accepted in the white school, only to learn to talk with an accent so he could fit into his new one, and this caused him, he told the interviewer, to speak with an accent for the rest of his life.[42]

While the Balderas boys' educational experience was common among Mexican immigrants of their generation, it is important to note that Mexican American activists that came of age with Eduardo also received their first instruction in Spanish. More importantly, they learned to value their people and their culture and to see American society through different lenses. These lenses, ironically, helped them both retain their language and culture but also accelerated their assimilation into American society by providing them cultural and social stability, something that many other immigrant children did not acquire because their parents could not help them maintain any proficiency in their language beyond its most practical uses, or they taught them little about their people's history.[43] This cultural and linguistic retention, however, did not come only or mainly from the early "Spanish" schooling that the Balderas brothers received but from their parents.

Like renowned Mexican American activist Hector P. García, Eduardo remembers his parents emphasizing the Spanish language at home. His mother, who never became fluent in the English language,

41. Interview with Balderas, 2.

42. Interview with Balderas, 3.

43. See Ignacio García's *Hector P. García: In Relentless Pursuit of Justice* (Houston: Arte Público Press, 2002).

insisted on Spanish at home. Eduardo says, "When my brother and I would come in from outside speaking English, she would stop us and say, 'Now you speak Spanish to me. When you talk among yourselves or talk to me, I want to know what you are talking about.'"[44] This emphasis became particularly important when the family found a new home in the El Paso business district and both Eduardo and Guillermo began attending school with mostly white classmates. Eduardo remembers being nine years old when they moved to a "different section of town, which was mostly 'English-speaking.'"[45]

After the move, the boys never did go to a school with many other Mexican children. Nevertheless, Eduardo recalled that his family maintained the Mexican culture—the cooking, behavior patterns, respect for elders, and courtesy toward others. "All those things were from Mexico," he later told an interviewer.[46] Ironically, the two Balderas boys' ability to speak Spanish fluently at home allowed them to feel more confident in learning English at school and to use it at the playground and among their white neighbors. This would be the case with many Mexican American leaders of that generation who first learned language fluency in Spanish and came to school with the ability to communicate and express ideas in one language as they learned another. The bilingual necessity—speaking English in school and among the neighborhood boys, and speaking Spanish (good Spanish, as Apolinar and María expected nothing less) at home—helped them learn to code switch and to learn the name and meaning of things in two languages. This came in handy to both Balderas boys—Eduardo in his translation and Guillermo in his navigation of the white Latter-day Saint world of church leadership.

Another important factor in the lives of the Balderas boys and other Mexican youth was learning to work alongside the family and take responsibility from an early age. When most immigrant children were dropping out of school, they were doing so to go work alongside their parents and siblings to put food on the table. Ironically, in El Paso as well as in many other communities with large

44. Balderas, Oral History, 4. See also, John E. Carr, "Eduardo Balderas: Translating Faith into Service," *Ensign*, June 1985, 6.

45. Balderas, Oral History, 5.

46. Balderas, 13.

Mexican and Mexican American populations, parents saw schooling as an important though sometimes unachievable reality. Yet, the work ethic involved in working with the family allowed a poor community to survive the harshest of realities and not simply succumb to becoming an underclass, something that most Mexican immigrants did not become. For the Balderas family, the work ethic started at the family shop.

Guillermo remembers the example of his father in trying to make things work the best he could. Apolinar sealed the living room from the rest of the house, bought some chairs and equipment, put up a sign, and began cutting people's hair. While most of the business probably came from people in the neighborhood and passersby, eventually he began advertising in the local newspaper and possibly put out flyers as well. Apolinar's barbershop became a full-service business, and this allowed his children to earn some money while learning the value of work. He bought a shoeshine chair, and soon enough both boys became good at *el shine*. He then taught his boys how to dust off the clients' hats and coats, which brought grateful tips of a dollar or two. In the process, Eduardo and Guillermo became part of the home economy as they handed their money off to their mother, who used it to augment the family finances.[47]

It is not difficult to imagine two young boys fighting over who took the first client or counting the number of "clients" they served and winning bragging rights for that day. Eduardo had a shy demeanor, but nonetheless proved tenacious and unafraid of the public eye, as later in life he sang in public, acted in plays, and gave sermons on the radio. Guillermo, in words and in his pictures, comes across as meticulous, forceful, and confident. While neither of them surpassed their father's extroverted, forceful, and flamboyant personality, they learned enough from him to do well in public settings. Much of this learning, no doubt, took place while they watched their father cut hair, engage his clients in conversation, and direct his children to do a good shine and meticulously dust off his clients' hats and coats. Guillermo later recalled how the experience taught him to "[savor] the joy of making money through honest work."[48]

47. Balderas, "Historia," 2.
48. Balderas, "Historia," 2.

Work, however, did not fully occupy the Balderas brothers' time. Like other immigrant children, they also played out in the streets and the empty spaces scattered throughout the Mexican barrios of El Paso. Lacking equipment and organized sports in the barrio, they invented games and activities, which often grew out of things happening around them. When Eduardo was eleven and Guillermo eight, they were thrust into the world of the home front during World War I, and they witnessed troop movements, most of them coming in and out of Fort Bliss, an army base established shortly after the U.S.–Mexican War in 1848. Like many other border towns, El Paso saw World War I service personnel roaming the streets of the city. Others guarded the border region from Mexican revolutionaries and *sediciosos*—Mexican rebels on the United States side of the border who struck back at white ranches and communities in response to the violence perpetrated against them by vigilantes and law enforcement officials, such as sheriffs and Texas Rangers.[49]

The Balderas boys were too young to understand much or even be aware of this violent story, but surely Apolinar heard and probably discussed with his clients the conflicts that caused a rise in discriminatory and racist acts against Mexicans throughout the border region. It surely reenforced the idea to him and his Mexican clients that they continued to be seen as suspect by many whites. To the Balderas boys, however, the concepts of violence and war were reduced to games. Bombarded in public and in school with anti-German propaganda during the war, they and numerous other barrio kids painted a picture of the Kaiser on every wall they could—with his pointed imperial hat and an immense moustache—and then threw mud chips at the paintings. In school, they happily sang songs that came out of that time period: "Smile the While,"

49. Violence in the border region intensified from 1900 to about 1925 as white vigilantes and law enforcement engaged in the repression of the Mexican population in the region. See Benjamin Heber Johnson, *Revolution in Texas: How a Forgotten Rebellion and Its Bloody Suppression Turned Mexicans into Americans* (New Haven: Yale University Press, 2003); James A. Sandos, *Rebellion in the Borderlands: Anarchism and the Plan of San Diego, 1904–1923* (Norman: Oklahoma University Press, reissue edition, 2022); and for a more militant interpretation, see Rodolfo Acuña, *Occupied America: A History of Chicanos*, 5th ed. (New York: Pearson Longman, 2004), 60–78.

"You Kiss Me Sad Adieu," "Keep the Home Fires Burning," and "It's a Long Way to Tipperary."[50]

There are only two more things that we know about Eduardo's childhood. One is that he did not excel in school and in his youth showed little sign of the inquisitive nature that later led to his accomplishments. He took a casual approach to school and one time he almost flunked an easy Spanish course that a friend had encouraged him to take. He later recalled, "I couldn't see any sense to studying. If I could speak it, read it, and write it, why study the grammar?"[51] His lackadaisical approach earned him a failing grade, but the teacher, embarrassed that someone would question her abilities to teach Spanish if she could not teach a Spanish speaker his own language, gave him a passing grade. His lack of grammar skills came back to haunt him when he later became a translator.[52]

The other thing we know about Eduardo's early years is that he entered the labor market at around fifteen years old (most likely 1922), when hired at a "motion picture house."[53] It is likely—though we don't know for sure—that he went to work at the Palace Theater, a Moorish-style, grand theater that served as a place for movies, plays, and other communal events in El Paso.[54] The 1920s saw an American public head to the theaters in large numbers as they enjoyed an uneven prosperity, and many immigrants were pushed toward assimilation, while others saw the benefits—economically and socially—of being more "American." The dark theater spaces became places where Americans came to dream, to find fashion tips, to aspire to travel, or to become masculine men or beautiful women. This was particularly true for immigrant young men and women who were seeing life outside the immigrant enclaves for the

---

50. Balderas, "Historia," 2. For a discussion of Mexican American participation in World War I, both in the front lines and on the home front, see José A. Ramírez, *To the Line of Fire: Mexican Texans and World War I* (College Station: Texas A&M Press, 2009); and Emilio Zamora, *The World War I Diary of José de la Cruz Sáenz* (College Station: Texas A&M Press, 2014).

51. Carr, "Eduardo Balderas" *Ensign*, June 1985, 43.

52. Carr.

53. See *El Paso Morning Times,* Nov. 6, 1920, 14. This newspaper ad publicizes the reopening and renaming of what once was the Alhambra Theater but was now the Palace Theater.

54. *El Paso Morning Times.*

first time. This cultural assimilation served as an emotional and even intellectual escape from their poor neighborhoods, dead-end jobs, uninspiring schools, and their foreignness.[55]

Eduardo, no doubt, got caught up as many other Americans did with the film craze, and working in a fancy movie house struck him as good luck. His job revolved around cleaning the trash left over from the evening showings and then preparing the movie house for the matinee in the early afternoon. For that he received seven dollars a week, and remembered, "I thought to myself, 'seven dollars a week, plus watching movies every day—I think that's great.'" Educated at home to be respectful to clients and the boss and to do things right, Eduardo soon got an opportunity that further prepared him for his future translating career. Two years into his job, the manager noticed his language abilities in both English and Spanish, possibly seeing him converse with the Mexican American clientele, delivery men, or other individuals in Spanish while understanding the English instructions given him. One day he called Eduardo into his office and said, "I understand you speak English ... I've been thinking that perhaps we should change your duties. I'd like to start translating the English titles (and sound) into Spanish [so] we can show them on the screen."[56]

It is interesting that the manager implied that he had just learned of Eduardo's English skills almost two years into his employment. It is more likely that it took him that long to see this "invisible" Mexican boy. When he did take the time, he saw Eduardo's work ethic, his ability to navigate a white world—even if in a limited situation—and his loyalty. Once sure that this Mexican boy could be trusted to do more than menial work, he asked him to translate the movie titles and the onscreen conversations. This required two projectors, one to show the movie and the other the Spanish-language captions. Ironically, he later remembered that it was going to watch

55. For a discussion of the Mexican American and Mexican immigrant efforts to acculturate, see Vickie Ruiz, "Starstruck: Acculturation, Adolescence, and Mexican American Women, 1920–1960," in *Building with Our Hands: New Directions in Chicana Studies*, eds. Aida de la Torre and Beatriz M. Pesquera (Berkeley: University of California Press, 1993), 109–29.

56. Balderas, Oral History, 12.

Spanish-language movies that helped him figure out the technique, though he did not explain how.

At the age of sixteen or possibly seventeen and now a school dropout—having failed to finish the eleventh grade, which at the time was the senior year—he was being asked to do a job for which there was little training. "I can imagine now what my translations must have been like, but nobody seemed to object," he later recalled.[57] Eduardo, however, proved a tremendous asset to the theater, so much so that they made him work "almost every day" for about three to three and a half years. Over time, however, the overwhelming schedule took its toll. As a young man, he wanted his Sundays off as well as other times to enjoy what other young men enjoyed and also to attend the new church his parents had chosen.[58] So he quit. He then went to work for the El Paso Sash and Door Company, assembling parts for small cabinets and occasionally a front door for homes. There he stayed for about five years.[59]

57. Balderas, Oral History, 12.
58. Balderas.
59. Balderas, 13.

2

LOS MORMONES ARRIVE

FINDING A NEW FAITH

From the corner of his eye, Apolinar saw the book sitting on the barber chair next to him, and as soon as he finished cutting his client's hair, he walked over and started leafing through the book. It was the Book of Mormon, and all Apolinar knew about the Mormons was that they had many wives. The white young man who brought it told him he should read it, but after flipping through the index to find anything about multiple wives—or "polygamy," as Latter-day Saints called it—Apolinar lost interest because the stories of Nephites, Lamanites, Alma, crossing the oceans, angels, and so on did not attract his attention "in the minimum."[1] The young man who brought the book must have noticed Apolinar's disinterest but nevertheless left him the book with the promise to return with one in Spanish, which he did. But again, Apolinar found nothing that attracted his interest, and he remembers losing it, or maybe his boys took it to play with.[2]

A few days later, another young man, this one a Mexican, came to get the full treatment: haircut, shampoo, lotion, and so on. Apolinar remembered him as one of his best customers, meaning he spent the most. After several visits, Apolinar asked him where he worked, to which he responded, "in a church." Must be at the newly constructed Catholic Church nearby, thought Apolinar, and given the young man's spending habits, he must be one of those "deacons" who probably stole from the donation pot. One day, however, as his regular young white customer left the barber shop, the Mexican young

1. Guillermo Balderas, "Historia," Balderas Family, Balderas Family Scrapbooks, 1910–1911, 3, Oral History Program, CHL.

2. Balderas.

man met him at the door, offered him his hand, and said, "Hola, Hermano," to which the other responded, "Hello, Brother," and they then conversed for a few minutes until the white young man left.[3]

"A Mormon with a Catholic deacon," Apolinar said to himself. After getting over his shock, he asked the Mexican young man if he knew the white young man, to which he responded, "We both work for the same church." He then told him his name, Abel Paez, and the other young man's name, Trenial Pauly, and said that they were both missionaries. He offered to tell Apolinar about the church, to which Apolinar answered that he had a practice of drawing a line between his religion and that of others, and he had no desire to talk religion with anyone. Paez respected his wishes, and the conversation turned to other topics.[4] Yet, the young man continued to come for a haircut and brought other young men like him along, which was of great benefit to Apolinar.

In time, Apolinar sold his barber shop and bought another one downtown, but he soon found that his new, mostly white neighbors were not as anxious to have their hair cut by a Mexican barber, and with three other barbers to pay, he became concerned about the feasibility of the situation. After a few days, frustrated and alarmed by the lack of customers, he stepped out to get some air, and to his surprise, he saw Paez, who told him "they"—there were ten others with him—were looking for a new barber, no doubt to replace the one that had taken to cutting their hair when Apolinar moved. They then entered and put all the barbers to work, and this attracted passersby who saw all the activity—or the fact that ten to twelve white young men were getting their haircuts in this new shop, which made it "safe" for them to get their own cuts in the new shop. That night, the barbers worked late, and they continued to do well during the weeks that followed as the missionaries and the customers they attracted continued to come back.[5]

For a time, Apolinar got the best part of the deal, but one day Paez reminded him that while they continued to be supportive, he had yet to accept their invitation to come to church with them. While

3. Balderas.
4. Balderas.
5. Balderas, 4.

the missionary effort could come across as a gimmick to get him to come to church, it is more likely that they found Apolinar a good barber and a "golden prospect"—a Latter-day Saint missionary term for economically stable, smart, articulate, and respectful potential converts. The young missionaries needed a barber, and why not Apolinar? Still, they were missionaries, and their duty centered around bringing new converts to their small congregations, so they kept inviting him. After a few more invitations, Apolinar decided that it might be in his interest to keep them happy. Plus, it could mean more Mormon clients. He told the other barbers the situation, and remembering how slow business had been before the "missionary invasion," they all made plans to attend church the following Sunday.[6]

While Apolinar had an emotional religious history from his father's desire to see him as a Catholic priest and from his own experience in the seminary, his first priority was providing for his family. It is possible that seeing the young missionaries give two or more years of their lives to do God's work brought mixed feelings about his own spiritual life. After leaving the seminary, his life had revolved around finding economic stability and a niche in this new land. Religious commitments seemed only to bring complications in achieving those two goals, though he later learned that for immigrants, finding a religious home proved a way to assimilate into this new land without taking away from their own identity as Mexicans—something very dear to him, and eventually his children.

When Apolinar arrived at the address the young Mexican missionary gave him, he found a private home, not a church. With slight trepidation, he rang the doorbell, and soon a middle-aged, "distinguished-looking" fellow opened the door.[7] In his limited English, Apolinar asked for Elder Paez, to which the man responded that the young missionary had not yet arrived but would be there soon. He asked him to come in. As Apolinar stepped in, he asked if the man "speaks Spanish," to which the man responded in perfect Spanish that he did, then told him his name: Rey L. Pratt, president of the Mexican Mission of the Church of Jesus Christ of Latter-day

6. Balderas.
7. Balderas.

Saints.[8] Pratt, in time, became known among the Mexican converts as the man who most spread the Latter-day Saint gospel on both sides of the border.

Pratt was one of the first mission presidents when the church proselyted in Mexico before the Mexican Revolution. After missionary efforts stopped in 1913, he proselyted among Mexican Americans in New Mexico, California, Arizona, and Texas and established his "own" missionary headquarters in Manassas, Colorado. There was already a mission in the West, and so his work was extra-official and focused on the Mexican population of the Southwest. Then, in 1918, the Mexican Mission was opened again, and Pratt moved to El Paso as its president.[9]

In most ways, Pratt represented the best example of the early white Latter-day Saint missionary leader: committed, tenacious, loving, paternalistic, and protective of his authority. On a mission from God, missionaries like Pratt saw themselves as engaged in saving God's children while recognizing that they were not yet "equal" partners in the faith. Their mission was to take a gospel given to whites to the natives, and most of them were sincerely committed to their work, even willing to give their lives—and some did—to accomplish their religious duty to take the gospel to those who lacked it. Some were pious, some were assertive, some performed their work and went home, and others, like Pratt, committed themselves to die with their flock.

By all accounts, Pratt was beloved of the Mexican saints. He brought so many to the church, nurtured them as they learned, called many of them to lead their small congregations, and learned to love their culture and language. For most Mexican saints, that is what they saw. They also noticed his enthusiasm for spreading a Latter-day Saint gospel that resonated with those of indigenous ancestry and delivering it through one individual moment at a time. Apolinar saw this immediately, and he and Pratt became friends and developed a mentor–mentored relationship that lasted for over fifteen years. Apolinar, however, had not come looking for a friend

8. Balderas.

9. Jessie L. Embry, *In His Own Language: Mormon Spanish Speaking Congregations in the United States* (Provo: Charles Redd Center for Western Studies, 1997), 14–16.

but for more people whose hair he could cut. To his dismay, instead of middle-class people who needed to look presentable, those who soon arrived were very "humble people" with all "the markings" of extreme poverty and the language of the uncultured.[10]

Apolinar's first thought was that the Mormons took advantage of these people's ignorance to confuse them and make them change their religion. Around thirty people, all sharing similar effects of poverty and a hard life, arrived to the church service. Shortly after, so did his companion barbers. Upon seeing the people, they too realized that these were not going to be the future steady customers they first imagined. Their disappointment abated somewhat upon the arrival of Hermana Thompson and Hermana Romney, whom Apolinar described as two "very attractive" lady missionaries who soon had the coquettish attention of his coworkers.[11] It was simply not common in the Mexican society of the time to see two young, unaccompanied women, arriving by themselves and mingling with the kind of freedom usually reserved for male religionists. Their whiteness, no doubt, allowed them even more freedom to mingle among the Mexican saints than it did in white congregations, and while they could not assume more than teaching duties within the branch, their call to instruct was much more expansive among the Spanish speaking—again, because they were "supposed" to know more, which, of course, often they did.

This knowledge came from their secular education which was much more than that of the attendees who had little opportunity in segregated El Paso to go to school, and the fact that many sister missionaries came from a multigenerational familial experience in the Latter-day Saint gospel also provided them a special status. Women missionaries, in the author's many years of experience in Mormonism, have been successful teaching and converting the Spanish speaking. In part, it is because female missionaries often connect with the mother or wife and children, who see them as similar to their schoolteachers. For the adult women, it was no doubt impressive to see young women independent and out and about doing the Lord's work, confident in the way they conducted themselves in

10. Guillermo Balderas, "Historia," 4.

11. Balderas.

public. White LDS women might have had limitations within their own communities, but out in the mission field they largely depended on their own ingenuity and smarts to survive and even prosper in the work of proselyting.[12]

These young sister missionaries had not yet been beaten down by domestic chores or the hard life of the factories or the fields as were many Mexican women. They were also different (safe) from the kind of women that some husbands might have on the side. For the men, these sister missionaries might initially have been intimidating, but they soon found them to be *hermanas*—sisters in the gospel who brought the "good news" to their families. Some might have seen them as role models for their own daughters, who might also one day live a life that was less exhaustive and overburdened. Religious conversion, after all, is about imagining a better future, and in American society, *better* usually correlated with economic stability, respectability, and independence.

Apolinar, uncomfortable with his coworkers' flirting, was glad when the service began, with Pratt conducting. Almost immediately, the congregation sang the classic and emotionally laden Latter-day Saint hymn "Oh My Father"—the LDS song that first popularized the notion of a heavenly mother, a doctrine which ironically seemed easier for Mexican saints to accept because of their Catholic background and their belief in the Virgin of Guadalupe, Jesus's mother. Upon hearing the hymn, Apolinar remembers feeling "a transformation within him ... deep in his soul," as he just knew he had heard that hymn before, but where?[13] Such was the effect that he began singing along with a such a thunderous voice that people turned to look at him. But they did so, he remembers, with "sympathy and understanding,"[14] no doubt influenced by the desire of those converts—many of them new themselves—to grow their numbers and prove to the critics in their communities that they were not strange anomalies.

After the singing, Apolinar felt his cheeks wet from the tears "torn from him" by a hymn that spoke of heavenly parents and

12. For an in-depth discussion of sister missionaries, past and present, see Robert L. Lively Jr.'s *The Mormon Missionary: Who IS That Knocking on My Door* (Baltimore: CreateSpace Independent Publishing Platform, 2015).

13. Guillermo Balderas, "Historia," 5.

14. Balderas.

the sublime love of them to people like him.[15] His emotions again heightened as President Pratt spoke of the restored gospel in what Apolinar later described as an "apostolic spirit."[16] At that moment, he forgot about his companions, his desire for more customers, his Catholicism, and everything else, because his spirit "was no more in this world" but had been transported to some other sphere.[17] Apolinar had joined the fellowship even before he became an official member, which took some time.

Here, we find the power of the white preachers and teachers. It was not just skin color, dominant presence, or knowledge that privileged these men and women in the eyes of the Mexican saints and potential converts—it was all that they stood for. They represented knowledge, privilege, yet genuine sacrifice in delivering the word of God so far from home, a humility above normal humility—after all they gave up so much, or so it seemed, to preach the gospel—and a willingness to walk among them, express their care for them as loved children, and do so in such powerful language and with such concern. As father figures, and in the case of the sister missionaries, older siblings or mother figures, the white missionaries and leaders represented a pecking order for which most of these Mexican converts had been conditioned by their poverty, their lack of social standing, their limited schooling, and often by the racial pecking order prevalent in their own country. For many saints raised in this situation, it became easier to be seen as an obedient flock, one that was loved even if that love was complicated by race, class, and religious privilege. We know little about the Mexican missionaries, though we know Abel Paez was the leader of a dissident group that left the church for a ten-year period. More will be said about this later.

By the end of the service, Apolinar felt himself in brotherhood with the rest of the congregants. Something had changed. And as the members of the house-church lingered after the services, as most worshippers do when they feel a sense of community and find the sacred space of church an oasis in a cruel world, Apolinar joined them and now called them *hermanos.* "An invisible bond united

15. Balderas.
16. Balderas.
17. Balderas.

[them]," Guillermo would write of his father's feelings.[18] President Pratt then spoke with him for some time, and afterwards Apolinar rushed home, anxious to tell his wife of what he had witnessed and the joy he now felt, possibly one he had not felt since he left the Catholic seminary.

Apolinar found María in no mood to hear about his spiritual experiences. Sunday was their day of rest from the affairs of the world, and a time to go eat, seek out one of the amusement arcades, or find a good movie to watch. This was the day when most Mexican families spent the afternoons recreating and resting from their heavy work week—a day of cultural activities unavailable most of the week, and a day when many Sabbath-keeping Protestant whites did not attend the parks or arcades, thus allowing them to become Mexican spaces for a few hours. It was, for María anyway, a time to have some moments alone with her always-busy husband. María must have often felt left alone—even though Apolinar worked in the living room of their home—so every Sunday not spent with him or family was squandered. Apolinar tried to talk about his visit to the Mormon church—he likely didn't tell her where he was going when he left that morning—but that upset her even more.

She accused him of being interested in *los mormones* because they had many wives—the one common accusation all people seemed to make of Latter-day Saints then, and sometimes even today.[19] Had she seen the "attractive" sisters mingling with the men, she might well have felt justified in believing the rumors about the Mormons and their sexual habits. Proper young women did not live alone away from home and associate so casually with men. Apolinar assured her that having a harem was the furthest thing from the minds of the humble worshippers he met. It would take time, but nonetheless, he somehow convinced her to go with him the following Sunday, where she too felt the spirit among the poor parishioners, and soon she and Apolinar began receiving the missionary lessons.[20]

Oddly, even though Eduardo and Guillermo attended church with their parents and participated in a class taught by the sister

18. Balderas.
19. Balderas.
20. Balderas.

missionaries, they were not included in the missionary lessons in their home. "We children just didn't come in" to the room where the parents were taught, remembers Eduardo.[21] Children, in Mexican culture back then, were to follow their parents' example, so Apolinar's decision as it pertained to changing or not changing religious affiliation was the only one that mattered. María, despite her spiritual feelings did not always sit in on the lessons either. Apolinar's interest did not mean a quick baptism or conversion, partly because back then members were expected to "live the gospel" before baptism—that is attend church, fellowship with the members and participate in church activities—but also because he knew his commitment to the Mormon church meant sacrifices and a radical change in his life.[22]

Eduardo later remembered his father telling him of lost friends, and of people trying to dissuade him from "worshipping with the Mormons."[23] Converts, but particularly those of color, faced mockery and scathing criticism and were sometimes ostracized by friends and family members who saw changing religions as a betrayal to their community. This was particularly true for conversion to the LDS Church whose members were seen as particularly strange by both Catholics and Protestants. For Apolinar, conversion also meant giving up Sunday recreational activities and personal time with María and the children.

Though not one to spend much time outside the home, Apolinar nonetheless understood—or at least thought of—the change to come. Not all Mexicans attended Catholic services, and Apolinar seemed to be one of those, but similar to most other Mexicans in El Paso, his language, the culture he practiced, and the beliefs he deeply held reflected Catholicism and provided him an identity and a bond important to those of his community. For the Mexicans of El Paso, who faced discrimination, sometimes isolation, and often exploitation and marginalization, the sense of community allowed them a

21. Eduardo Balderas, Oral History, interviews by Gordon Irving, 1973, typescript, 5, Oral History Program, CHL.

22. Today, potential converts, while expected to begin "living the gospel" before they are baptized, are often moved through the process faster, and some find themselves baptized before they really know anyone at church, and sometimes without attending more than once.

23. Balderas, Oral History, 6.

reprieve from being strangers in the land—a land that reflected so much of their homeland.

While it is certainly not explicit, it is nonetheless implied that María might not have been too anxious at first to join the church. As the matriarch of the home, she best understood the changes to come with a new religion, especially an "American" one and one so deeply disparaged by some in her community and possibly even her circle of friends. We don't know how many other women she associated with, given that they did not attend the Catholic masses and she did not work outside the home, but those she did associate with probably frowned on the idea of changing religions. From what Apolinar shared with her of his friends' attitudes, María could easily surmise that changes to their lives were to be significant. Her hesitation to join right away, as we'll see later, might well have been responsible for the family staying in the church through all their lives. No doubt Pratt tried to alleviate their fears as he saw the value of a family like the Balderas for his congregation. It is natural, then, to assume that he spent much time talking to them, and that numerous pairs of missionaries and other members of the small congregation visited their home. It is also likely that both Apolinar and María were volunteering and working with their fellow churchgoers even before they were baptized, as it was more common then for "investigators" to participate in religious communities before they decided to formally join.

While the spiritual joy Apolinar and María felt no doubt cemented them to their fellow worshippers, it took Apolinar a year of fellowshipping to join the church, and María longer. Eduardo remembers the family not always attending church before baptism.[24] There were probably Sundays when the barber shop opened and other times when the need for spousal and familial relaxation and recreation pulled harder than the need for spiritual feasting. Having once committed to a faith wholeheartedly as Apolinar did to his Catholic faith as a youth, and then having been disappointed enough to leave, possibly made him think long and hard about such a momentous decision to join a church whose teachings and practices so deviated from all that he had known before.

---

24. Balderas.

It is also a surety that for María and her mother, who had by then come to live with them, the Catholic tradition was strong. Eduardo remembered his mother and grandmother teaching them "that there was a God, that we should pray and some ... basic teachings of ... Catholicism," but he also recalled that he rarely went to mass, never learned the catechism, and did not have his first communion, though he was baptized and confirmed at around the age of nine in the Catholic Church.[25] The Balderas's Catholicism, like that of many Mexican immigrants in El Paso, was more cultural than spiritual, though nonetheless important as an institution that kept them connected to their homeland. Most cultural events and festivities in the barrios of El Paso revolved around some Catholic tradition or teaching. And the Catholic Church served as a safe space from white America, though ironically, most of those churches had European priests who rarely spoke Spanish. Still, Mexican immigrants found ways to make it their space as much as it was possible, and over time, in the Southwest as in Mexico, their vernacular Catholicism became synonymous with being Mexican. It was so ingrained, this connection between being Mexican and being Catholic, that people lived "religious lives" even as they did secular things and believed no more.[26]

Notwithstanding the coming break with his community's traditions or the criticism from his friends, Apolinar made the choice to be baptized. Seeking to explain his conversion to his son Guillermo, Apolinar recounted the biblical story of the blind man healed by Christ. When told by the pharisees that the man who healed him was a sinner, he responded, "Whether he be a sinner or [not], I know not: one thing I know, that, whereas I was blind, now I see" (John 9: 24–25).[27] Eduardo remembered years later his father telling him, "That's exactly how I feel. Whether the church is evil, or whether the church is what my friends say, I know not. One thing I know that

25. Balderas, 3.

26. For a discussion of Catholic cultural influence even among non-practitioners, see Mario T. García, *Desert Immigrants: The Mexicans of El Paso, 1880–1920* (New Haven: Yale University Press, 1981), 212–20. During the 1960s, it was common among Chicano activists to say to their dismay that Mexican Americans were born "Catholic and Democrat," and though they were influenced greatly by those two ideologies, they knew very little of them.

27. Latter-day Saints use the King James Version of the Bible.

whereas I was blind, now I see."[28] He saw, and for the rest of his life, he chose to share that vision with those who would listen.

Eduardo remembers the relationship between his father and mother changing. They stopped quarreling, cemented their love through their work in the church, and found a purpose that brought them together. For the first two years after baptism, the missionaries dropped by often, and this helped the family make the social transition out of the Catholic barrio to the Mormon spaces that often consume most LDS converts. Apolinar caught the "missionary spirit," revealing a repressed hunger for the spiritual that once took him to the Catholic seminary, and he started going out with the missionaries. "They loved to have him," said Eduardo, "because he knew the language and … could express the concepts better than they could."[29] This skill allowed him to revisit areas that the missionaries had given up on in finding converts and helped them open new areas anywhere that people were willing to listen. Apolinar also began to talk even to his customers about the Mormon gospel.[30]

Eduardo—and Guillermo—did not take to the spiritual side of Mormonism right away. As noted before, the brothers were not invited to the missionary discussions, and except for the Sunday classes, there were no programs or activities for children or youth. The cultural programs that later became a feature of Mexican wards and branches came when more Mexicans and Mexican Americans—some better educated or at least more skilled, and thus more economically stable—joined these congregations and became leaders within them. But at the time, it was too much to expect that young white missionaries know about Mexican culture, and in spite of their love for the people, they were, like most Protestant and Catholic missionaries of the era, imbued with the notion that the "Lord's work" required assimilation, or at least some form of allegiance to the American system and not Mexican cultural activities.[31]

28. Balderas, Oral History, 6.

29. Balderas, 8.

30. Balderas.

31. This notion was particularly true for Latter-day Saints, who by the turn of the century had cast their lot with American society and in the process became hyper patriotic. They had also bought into the notion of "whiteness" as a category of racial purity. As historian W. Paul Reeve argues, by the turn of the century and through those first

Conversion for Eduardo may well be described as anti-climactic, or uneventful. He faintly remembers going to the branch on Sundays. Nothing stood out to him, and though he would become a stalwart of the faith, he had few early spiritual experiences. He simply obeyed his father and went to church when the family went and was probably happier when they didn't. The only memory of his baptism—at least that we have record of—was the morning when his father told him to stay home from school. Later that morning a car arrived, he and his father got in, and they were driven to the Rio Grande River, then known as the Rio Bravo by most Mexicans, which was quite familiar to the Balderas family who had crossed it nearly a decade before. "Before I knew it, I was under water," recounted Eduardo more than fifty years later.[32] President Pratt, who had befriended the family and become a mentor to Apolinar, baptized them both. Two months later, María, her mother, and Guillermo went into the waters of baptism. Eventually, Apolinar and María's ten children became part of the faith.[33]

Eduardo's lack of interest in the church continued after baptism. Like most immigrant children, he felt there were more important things to contemplate: a job, dating, and what to do about the future. It is obvious that Eduardo did not shine as a student, and only a few years after his conversion, at around the age of sixteen, he dropped out of school. His brother Guillermo followed suit. Whether it was the long hours at the barber shop, the time spent doing missionary work—and later, leadership assignments in the Mexican congregation— or simply the experience of having grown up by himself, Apolinar was a hands-off parent, at least when it came to their education and later their vocation.

Latter-day Saint parents then had less connection to their children than what church leaders would acknowledge today in what can only be described as a family and children-focused religion. Fathers

decades of the 1900s, "Mormon leaders were attempting to orchestrate a new image of the faith and to make the transition from a polygamous and racially suspect past toward a monogamist and racially pure future." Reeve, *Religion of a Different Color: Race and the Mormon Struggle for Whiteness*, (New York: Oxford University Press, 2015), 1.

32. John E. Carr, "Eduardo Balderas: Translating Faith into Service," *Ensign*, June 1985, 6.

33. Balderas, Oral History, 6.

taught their children about work, responsibilities, and the role of men in the family and society (mothers taught the girls) by example. Young boys and young girls were supposed to see what their parents did and then emulate them until they found their own way of doing much the same thing. It is a custom that remains today among many Latina/o Saints, and while antithetical to today's indulging parenthood, it has its value in that it allows sons and daughters to actually find their own identity sooner, given that they interpret their parents' actions without the burden of accompanying explanations. Of course, this only works if the youth are paying attention and learning to work and make decisions.

Guillermo remembered staying home on Sundays to man the public baths in the barber shop for months at a time while his father tried his hand at ranching or farming in New Mexico, where he had a plot of land. The young boy found himself working among very profane men who spoke vulgarities, told dirty jokes, drank, and often chided him for his "innocence." Eduardo, never having shown an inclination toward barbering, escaped that environment, though Guillermo wrote later that things were not any better when he went to work with Eduardo at "El Paso Sash & Door," where the vulgarity was only surpassed by the physical violence that the older men employed against the younger workers.[34] It is reasonable to believe that Eduardo also missed church a lot when his family did not attend, and as mentioned earlier, his job at the theater kept him busy on Sundays.

That Eduardo did not find much to interest him in the church seems logical given his early introduction to the Latter-day Saint gospel and institution that promoted it. His first exposure to the missionaries had little spiritual or even religious significance, given their efforts to woo Apolinar and their lack of interest in teaching the family, if Eduardo's minimalist recollection is accurate. He had no chance to think about conversion because he knew almost nothing about the religion when he got baptized. His Sunday classes, taught by sister missionaries, were not enough to fill the void of religious instruction or practice at home. There were no midweek

34. Balderas, "Historia," 8.

meetings, no youth programs, no cultural activities, no home teachers that visited him, and likely little discussion of the gospel with his parents, as almost no church literature beyond the scriptures in Spanish existed to assist them in teaching their children.[35] The children were expected to absorb the gospel by "spiritual osmosis" and to find their connection through their parents' intense commitment to the work of salvation.

Apolinar's full embrace of the Latter-day Saint gospel eventually proved important to his children, but initially it might have been an obstacle for them. He became immersed in missionary work and in the Sunday activities of the little congregation, and within two years of his conversion, he became a branch president (congregational leader), which meant that his efforts to visit his congregation members individually and help them navigate their religious journeys was an added responsibility to his going out with the missionaries, a pursuit he had no intention of leaving completely behind. In both Eduardo's and Guillermo's recollections, their father did not play a prominent role in their first growing up years. Like many fathers of that generation—both Mexican and white Latter-day Saints—Apolinar saw home as a starting-off place, and his children were to learn to navigate life through their own efforts when formal instruction was not available. While not explicitly expressed, it seems clear that Apolinar was hard on his children, not necessarily by word or physical punishment but by what he had his children do: working at the barber shop even on Sundays, leaving them in charge of unruly adults while quite young, and having them work on the family ranch in extreme conditions with no water, no heat, little furniture, and isolation from the neighbors.[36]

Eduardo did not write or talk about this period of time, but what he does say about his childhood only scarcely touches on the religious or the spiritual. Once he dropped out of school, his life seemed consumed by his jobs, and there were no religious activities that competed for his time or attention. The branch continued to have only about thirty-five or forty members for the first couple

35. Balderas, Oral History, 9.

36. See Guillermo's description of the difficult and lonely time he spent on the ranch in New Mexico in Balderas, "Historia," 8–11.

of years, and most were adults. The usual reasons for young people staying close to the church—other youth, weekday activities, service projects, missionary outings—were mostly missing back then. There was one midweek activity, but in Eduardo's recollection, "It was just a preaching service. That's all it was."[37]

Eduardo, in his interviews, did not speak of any connection to his fellow branch members, or saints—at least not until he served a mission. Going to church was a chore for him, as it has been for generations of young people who follow their parents into a new religion. Even after his father became the branch president—two years into their membership—neither Eduardo nor Guillermo have much recollection of any significant event in their religious lives. They both received the church's lay priesthood as young men, but neither one wrote or talked about it, except when Guillermo remembered never being asked to administer the sacrament or to baptize anyone as older young men would in later years. Eduardo nonchalantly recalled going "right through the various callings in the priesthood, deacon, teacher, priest" but shared no experiences about their impact on him.[38] From Eduardo's recollection, he and his brother Guillermo simply went to church and did as they should. Years later, when both were quite involved and prominent in the church, neither found any moment in their youth that could be reinterpreted or romanticized as a "beginning" of the spiritual odyssey.

Eduardo's conversion, as mentioned earlier, did not come from some spiritual epiphany but rather as an accumulative response to both his needs and the example of his father's passion for the Latter-day Saint gospel. While inactive for nearly three years because of his job at the theater, he remembers not being "opposed to the church" because his father "would insist that we stay together."[39] Once able to attend, Eduardo found only minimal interest in what he was learning in the classes and the sacrament meetings. Then one day, he later told an interviewer, "There was a sort of buzzing in my ears, then they popped, and all of a sudden I found myself understanding quite

37. Balderas, Oral History, 9.
38. See Balderas, "Historia," 6; Balderas, Oral History, 11.
39. Balderas, Oral History, 13.

plainly the principles that were being discussed in class. From then on my understanding of the gospel gradually came to me."[40]

Maybe, then, it is incorrect to say that he did not receive a "spiritual conversion." While he had no "on the road to Damascus" experience and did not hear divine voices or see something beyond this world, the cumulative effect of what he heard touched something within him. Throughout his life, expressions of faith and devotion rarely came with any kind of "spiritual epiphany" that could later be recalled. His spiritual maturity came from his "theology of action"—that is, the service that he gave to the church—and by the talks and the scriptures he translated. He was meticulous in learning and his testimony of the restored gospel came "line upon line, precept upon precept" (2 Nephi 28:30), no doubt at first from his father's preaching, later the missionary lessons and companionships, and much later from the spiritual giants for whom he translated.

In his youth, however, while his gospel learning was limited, he did not lack spiritual experiences, given his father's tenacity in living the gospel. Within two years after baptism, Apolinar took his family to the LDS temple in Salt Lake City, Utah, where they engaged in rites and ceremonies seen as crucial to the Latter-day Saint spiritual life. Eduardo remembers finding himself on Temple Square, the iconic place most Americans associate with the "Mormons," and a place he came to know quite well. There is no recollection available of the trip by any of the Balderas family members, and it is hard to know why they took a side trip to Los Angeles and then headed to Utah.[41] It might have been a vacation, or possibly a pilgrimage, before the important Latter-day Saint ritual of "sealing the family" for time and all eternity.[42] The Balderas family vacillated between economic stability and a tight budget for most of their early years in El Paso, and Apolinar never fully escaped that boom and bust so common to small ethnic entrepreneurs. By the time the family took the trip, Apolinar and María had seven children.[43]

---

40. Balderas.

41. Balderas, 10–11

42. Latter-day Saints believe in "sealing"—creating eternal bonds between themselves and their families. This is done in temples, which are considered sacred places.

43. See FamilySearch, "Guillermo Balderas Sr (1910–1991)," familysearch.org, accessed July 12, 2023.

Traveling in a car with such a large group only complicated the challenge of "traveling while Mexican." In the early to mid-twentieth century, traveling across the Southwest could be an unpleasant and sometimes dangerous trip, though mainly it was a lonely journey, as numerous restaurants and eateries did not serve Mexicans, while others did so with a suspicion that they might steal something or bring germs into their establishment. The early twenties was not a good time for Mexicans in American society, particularly in the Southwest where many white Americans were divided over the influx of immigrants from across the southern border. While seen as necessary by those who owned the agricultural fields, canneries, mines, and other places of labor, many white residents near those industries were repulsed by having to share parks, businesses, and other public spaces with them and having their children learn in the same classrooms.

We know nothing more about the Balderas family trip and their sealing in the Salt Lake Temple. It is quite possible, however, that two future "giants" in Mexican and Latina/o Latter-day Saint history might have crossed paths in the holy temple. Margarito Bautista, the first major Mormon intellectual of Mexican descent, and a man who would give the church numerous headaches in Mexico, and of which more will be said later, volunteered in the Salt Lake Temple from 1914 to 1922, never missing a day and eventually becoming involved in sealing ceremonies even though he, himself, never became a sealer. Nonetheless, it is quite possible that he served as an interpreter for those who did not speak English, but we cannot say if he met the Balderas family on their trip to the Salt Lake Temple.

Margarito Bautista was by then in his early forties and was considered a prominent figure among the small but growing Latina/o—mostly Mexican—Latter-day Saint congregation in the state, and possibly among those who came from as far away as Arizona, and in the case of the Balderas family, from Texas. It was rare if not literally impossible to see a person of Mexican descent in the temples and one that carried himself with such dignity and sophistication. At the time, Bautista served as a congregation leader (branch president) and had been heading the work of proselytizing and the work in the temple for those deceased. Bautista's church callings, his Sunday School lessons, and his demeanor attracted much attention within his community. Simply put, there was no other Mexican saint like him at the time.[44]

Eduardo never mentioned having known Margarito, though his father and brother did come to know and associate with him when they both served as congregation leaders in Mexico years later. Nonetheless, their lives would intertwine through the most important issue in the twentieth century for Spanish-speaking saints—church literature translated into Spanish, and leadership opportunities for Mexican, Mexican American, and Latin American saints, which could only come with Spanish-language manuals and the translation of the complete LDS scriptural canon.

Eduardo's early life revealed the complicated and often contradictory remembrances that young men like him—quite open to assimilation and having little connection to their home country—had of their youth. He remembers it fondly, and no doubt his association with white youth during his schooling years provided him a less critical view of them. Guillermo had a less positive experience, but he was never one to speak publicly or write in his memoirs about the difficulties that his members faced in the white stakes. Yet, there is an interview that he gave in 1974 in which he spoke about the challenges of growing up in an American religion.

"In the church of that time, 1924, '25, '26, we were second-class citizens," he told the interviewer (Oscar Martínez). "When we gathered in a [church] meeting or a conference, or any other gathering, they would not acknowledge us; we were never equal. And we [Mexican saints] would not dare to set foot in an American Mormon church."[45] He also told of those Mexican Saints who were traveling who might show up to the English services, who were quickly directed toward the Spanish-language branch, with phrases such as, "That is where your kind meet."[46]

Guillermo told the interviewer that he spoke with no ill feelings, he was simply talking about "episodes in [his] life as a Mexican

---

44. For more on Margarito Bautista, see Elisa Eastwood Pulido, *The Spiritual Evolution of Margarito Bautista: Mexican Mormon Evangelizer, Polygamist Dissident, and Utopian Founder, 1878–1961* (New York: Oxford University Press, 2020).

45. Interview with Guillermo Balderas by Oscar J. Martínez, 1974, interview no. 148, Institute of Oral History, University of Texas El Paso, 5.

46. Interview with Balderas, 5. Author's translation.

here."[47] He would go on to say that sometimes it was the Mexicans' fault that they did not fit in. They dressed poorly, had little education, and did not "know their place." He added that he only frequented places where people like him were welcomed. "If I could go to the country club, I would not because I would be out of my element. I know my place."[48] Eduardo never spoke about his early experiences in that way, but no doubt he understood the important of knowing "his place" in an American religious space, still predominantly white.

47. Balderas.
48. Balderas, 13–14.

3

THE SILVER TONGUE PREACHER

THE MISSION FIELD AND THE RETURN HOME

A rite of passage for many Latter-day Saint men, and now more and more women, is serving a religious mission for their church. While the duration of the mission has often vacillated between a year to as much as four years, and the minimum ages of those who serve have changed from twenty-one to eighteen (nineteen for women), the importance of missionary service has only become more significant over time. Not all church leaders have served missions, and there are a number of LDS youth who do not serve. Nonetheless, the mission experience has been a gold standard in judging youthful commitments to the gospel of the Church of Jesus Christ of Latter-day Saints. The thought is that if a person is willing to give up a part of their lives for the church and pay for it themselves (or have their family pay), they are more likely to stay active and to help fund the work of the "gospel."

It was inevitable that the Balderas young men were confronted with the possibility of serving missions when they turned of age. Eduardo, the oldest, faced that momentous decision first, but nothing in the interviews he gave and the writings he left indicates any discussion or contemplation of his decision. It is quite possible that his father made the decision for him. Daniel Balderas, Eduardo's youngest son, remembers his father taking him to their ward bishop and telling the congregational leader that his son wanted or needed—we don't know which—to go on a mission.[1] No prior discussion had taken place, though Daniel's two other brothers had

1. Daniel Balderas, interview by phone with author, December 3, 2020.

served earlier, so it was expected that he would too.[2] Daniel, like Eduardo, is a soft-spoken and a rather humble man.

Eduardo's action in this instance was reminiscent of his own experience when it came to his baptism. Apolinar simply told him not to go to school. Then they waited until President Pratt and some elders took them to the Rio Bravo and baptized them. It is not difficult to imagine that Apolinar, who was branch president at the time Eduardo turned mission age, told him that the time had come to serve the Lord. Daniel chalked up his own experience to his being a shy young man who as a child often hid behind his mother's skirts, but it is possible that made little difference: both generations of Balderas boys simply got "summoned" to do the work of the church without discussion. Daniel would find out much later—from the author of this book, in fact—that Apolinar had simply taken Eduardo to the bishop and said his son was ready to go serve the Lord. Eduardo thus became the first Spanish-speaking missionary—or at least Mexican-origin missionary—from El Paso, and surely the first from his branch. Eduardo did say in one interview that Elder Pratt interviewed him and told him he was old enough and that he should have that experience. Eduardo remembers his reaction as saying it would be a "tremendous experience," though it is hard to tell whether he felt that at the time or would come to appreciate it as such by the time he was interviewed in his seventies.[3]

To be fair, he had no role model of a Mexican missionary, except for maybe Elder Paez and some other Mexican or Mexican American missionaries he might have met during his teenage years—an unlikely possibility given their scarcity. There were also no other young men from the branch serving missions or who had served one. Having the Mexican Mission headquarters in El Paso, however, did expose him to countless "elders" (male missionaries) coming and going, and many of the activities in the branch were organized, supervised, and often attended by these young men serving their missions. At the same time, going on a mission was not something every young man did, whether because they married young, had much work in the

2. Daniel Balderas interview.

3. Eduardo Balderas, Oral History, interviews by Gordon Irving, 1973, typescript, 14, Oral History Program, CHL.

family farm or business, or simply found other activities to engage in. Only two years earlier, a young man, Howard W. Hunter, who later became president of the church and a revered prophet, embarked, along with his dance band, the Croonaders, to sea on the USS President Jackson to entertain passengers instead of going on a mission.[4]

None of the siblings interviewed ever remembered Eduardo talking about his mission or even hearing him talk about "going on a mission." This is quite surprising, given that the missionary experience is a constant topic in sacrament meeting talks, home evening lessons, and during quiet moments of parental counsel for members of the church. Those men and women who served missions do not shy away from talking about the "greatest years of their lives" to those who will listen. It is also common in numerous LDS enclaves for ward and stake leaders to ask all those who have served a proselyting mission to stand up, which, of course is often embarrassing to those who did not or could not serve one. It is a badge of courage, and it is often displayed in conversations as one missionary tries to "up" another—even if only in jest—as they discuss the obstacles and trials they faced on their missions. Today, those conversations about the mission are more prevalent, as many more young men and women now serve in faraway places not imagined possible when Eduardo served his own.[5]

Why Eduardo failed to talk about his mission experience, except in an exit interview, we don't know, and can only engage in conjecture, but in doing so we open up discussions of what the mission meant and did not mean both in Eduardo's time and today. In almost every instance when we talk about converts who are indigenous or of color and the small congregations they first attend, the missionaries are an important part of that story. Missionaries often play a larger-than-life role. The first reason for this is obvious: missionaries are normally—especially in earlier times when missionaries did a lot of door knocking and street preaching—the first people to talk

4. Howard W. Hunter, *The Teachings of Howard W. Hunter*, ed. Clyde J. Williams (Salt Lake City: Deseret Book, 2002), viii.

5. For a discussion of the Mormon missionary experience before, during, and after a young man or woman is called to serve, see Robert L. Lively Jr.'s *The Mormon Missionary: Who IS That Knocking on My Door* (Baltimore: CreateSpace Independent Publishing Platform, 2015). For international missions, see pages 269–306.

about the "Mormon gospel." If the people they speak to are interested, a pair or multiple pairs of missionaries guide the individuals or families into the church. They are constant visitors to the home, or initially, as in Apolinar's case, the space in which the family or individual most inhabits. Again, in the case of Apolinar and the young Balderas children, that meant both the home and the barber shop, and this was not one couple of missionaries but a multitude of them who came to cut their hair.

Apolinar later became the missionaries' "de facto" companion when preaching in the Mexican side of town.[6] Gordon B. Hinckley, a church general authority and for a long time a member of the church's missionary committee, said of him, "In February 1947, he was called on a six-months mission. He is still at it. During this period, working with various companions, he has brought the church as many new members as comprised the entire church membership of the El Paso branch … a remarkable achievement." More remarkable, Hinckley continued, "There is nothing high pressure about him." He knew he was doing the "Lord's work," and he went about it in "humility and love."[7] Whether Eduardo thought much about the mission or not, his father's example of commitment to missionary service was always there.

The Balderas family was surrounded by missionaries from the time that Apolinar first met them. Beyond cutting their hair and then accompanying them in their proselyting efforts, Apolinar befriended President Pratt, and this meant that missionary work played a big part of his family's church experience. Pratt often visited them at home and then asked ("called") Apolinar to serve as branch president—the first Mexican branch president in El Paso, and probably the first in Texas.[8] The sister missionaries taught the Balderas children for the first few years of their church membership, and Eduardo became a favorite of Pratt and actually drove the mission president to Salt Lake City for a surgery from which he never recovered.[9]

6. Balderas, Oral History, 8.

7. Gordon B. Hinckley, "The Virtues of Joseph, the Wisdom of Apollo Are His," *Deseret News*, May 23, 1948.

8. Latter-day Saints refer to being asked to serve in the church as a "calling," as in "to be called to serve."

9. Balderas, Oral History, 29.

It is hard to overstate the influence that LDS missionaries had on Mexican converts, both because of the message they brought and because these mostly white young men and women provided a different face to the American experience. Whites were usually the Mexican converts' bosses—those who made disparaging remarks to them, who segregated them, and who often disdained them in public. Mexicans learned quite early in their immigrant experience that the more you could stay away from whites, the better. To have them come to your house in humility and show an abundance of concern and even brotherly love was disarming but inviting to most Mexicans—as it was and has been to other people of color.

I remember my family's own experience with pairs of missionaries that came over numerous times to try to get the García boys baptized. My mother had been a member since her youth, having been baptized in a river in Monterrey, Mexico, but had married my father, a Catholic, and he resisted converting to the Latter-day Saint gospel to the end of his days. My brother and I found the missionaries fun to be around, and my mother always received them with hospitality and appreciated their efforts in getting us to become Latter-day Saints. Even my father, himself a religious man but with little interest in organized religion, was welcoming and had no problem with them teaching us.

My mother remembered that when she was a young convert, the missionaries came by her house to take her to weekday activities and sometimes even walked her to church. For her and her family, the missionaries were a protection from a community that did not always take well to *los Mormones*. To her, as well as to many converts, the missionaries represented authority, but also genuine concern, and knowledge, but with humility. They served as the connection to the white presiding authorities. With a few exceptions—and there were—most of these young men and women showed a great deal of comfort in associating with the Mexican members.[10]

Gina Covin, a Pākehā Māori scholar, remembers her own people's "missionary experience":

10. I tell the story of my mother's conversion in my memoir, *Chicano While Mormon: Activism, War, and Keeping the Faith* (Lanham, MD: Fairleigh Dickinson University Press, 2015), 29–32.

> The Mormon missionaries were different from the Anglican, Methodist or Catholic missionaries. They were young; they were transitory; they didn't look to purchase Māori land; they didn't have a problem with polygamy; they learned the Māori language instead of insisting that Māori learn English; and they stayed in Māori homes.... How could a young girl on the verge of womanhood not fall in love with the handsome young men who were sent into the hinterland to dance with her?[11]

One way that native leaders gained their knowledge and often their "testimonies" of the Latter-day Saint gospel was through their experience in accompanying missionaries in their proselytizing and their home visitations. This was the case for Apolinar. Many other members welcomed this opportunity because it was for them the one way to get one-to-one instruction on the doctrine and the church's protocol. It also provided many a window to how Latter-day Saints should comport. For many Mexican and Mexican American saints, and no doubt many other saints of color, the "way of Mormonism" was complicated—so different from their own personal and collective experiences that it prompted many to watch and then emulate the missionaries.

At the time of Eduardo's youth, Latter-day Saints were not held in high esteem in the larger society, even though by then the church leadership saw the church's survival and expansion dependent on its membership's ability to assimilate into American society. The need to be seen as "normal" or more American—which, at times, meant "whiter"—was a priority. We do not have much scholarship on exactly how this impacted missionary work, but we should assume it did if simply because the idea of being the "other" in American religion had caused members to shun the outside world, and that had to change.[12] We know American racism against African Americans and Native Americans impacted the way the church dealt with them,

11. Gina Colvin and Joanna Brooks, eds., *Decolonizing Mormonism: Approaching a Postcolonial Zion* (Salt Lake City: University of Utah Press, 2018), 30–31. While recognizing their attractive characteristics to the Mormon Māori, Colvin does emphasize the colonialist disadvantages they brought to the Māori.

12. See W. Paul Reeve's *A Religion of a Different Color: Race and the Mormon Struggle for Whiteness* (New York: Oxford University Press, 2015) and Thomas G. Alexander's *Mormonism in Transition: A History of the Latter-day Saints 1890–1930* (Urbana: University of Illinois Press, 1996) for a discussion of how Mormon leaders by the early twentieth century had decided that Latter-day Saints should be seen as more "American," which

but we know almost nothing on how prejudices against Mexicans and Latina/os impacted not just practice but policy.[13] There are still, as this work is being written, so many documents not yet available from the church archives for research and so many personal stories not yet told about Mexican and Latina/o saints, though the number is slowly growing.[14]

Returning to the Balderas family, we know that the boys and their younger sisters were taught Sunday School and primary lessons by sister missionaries, a common practice in the early years of Mormonism in the Southwest and in foreign lands. These sisters had the knowledge, could provide historical context, and were white, imbuing them with a sense of authority that the native leadership, when there was one, simply did not have. In the church as in the outside world, whites—including white women—led, even if these missionaries for the most part led with love and humility. Here, again, we are reminded that color mattered, and that all nonwhite converts could look forward to becoming "white and delightsome" someday, and thus the blessings not yet available would come to them in their fullness.[15] This idea, so often taught in one way or another to Mexican and indigenous converts, so permeated the Latter-day Saint gospel they received that even some of the most nationalistic of Mexican converts bought into the idea of a "color disadvantage."[16]

---

they interpreted as being "white"—something that had eluded earlier Latter-day Saints who were often not considered white because of polygamy.

13. For a discussion of the Latter-day Saint view of saints of color, see Armand L. Mauss, *All Abraham's Children: Changing Mormon Conceptions of Race and Lineage* (Urbana: University of Illinois Press, 2003).

14. For an example of these works, see the author's *Chicano While Mormon*; also, Jessie L. Embry, *In His Own Language: Mormon Spanish Speaking Congregations in the United States* (Provo: Charles Redd Center for Western Studies, 1997); and Elisa Eastwood Pulido's *The Spiritual Evolution of Margarito Bautista: Mexican Mormon Evangelizer, Polygamist Dissident, and Utopian Founder, 1878–1961* (New York: Oxford University Press, 2020).

15. The phrase "white and delightsome" was found in the Book of Mormon (2 Nephi 30:6) before 1983 and was then changed to "pure and delightsome" afterward. Though Mormon historians have found that the church founder, Joseph Smith, had made the correction shortly after the first printing, it was not corrected in the actual publication until the 1980s.

16. Margarito Bautista, though a strong religious Mormon nationalist, had no problem with this teaching, and while it was not a big part of his teachings, it was part of his own theology. See Pulido, *Spiritual Evolution of Margarito Bautista*.

Eduardo entered the mission field in November 1929, at the age of nineteen, but he did so during difficult financial times for the Balderas family, which later complicated his mission. President Pratt, understanding the family's economic circumstances, chose not to send Eduardo to Salt Lake City for missionary training. Rather than raise the funds, Pratt probably felt comfortable that Eduardo, with his father as branch president, and possibly him having hung around the missionaries often, and with Pratt's mentoring, could manage his mission without training the usual way.[17] He was, after all, going to a Spanish-speaking mission, and he knew the language and had shown a comfort with, if not a passion for the Latter-day Saint gospel. For leaders like Pratt, having a native Mexican Spanish speaker bode well for the missionary effort, and it went well with his own desire to see the Spanish-speaking church expand dramatically.

To this end, Pratt chose to take Eduardo under his wing to prepare him for his venturing out to teach the gospel. It is unclear whether the mission president asked Salt Lake for permission or whether he took it upon himself to prepare the young man himself, but it was not beyond the charismatic mission leader to make his own decisions, especially one that involved his "flock."[18] No other president in the history of the Mexican mission or the missionary work in Mexico or the United States Southwest ever held sway like he did. Paternalistic but loving and fully dedicated to the Mexican people, Pratt saw something special in Eduardo, something he did not see in too many of the other converts he came across. The Balderas family were what LDS missionaries came to call "golden converts," or people who quickly accepted the gospel, but just as important, they were capable of leading their people and doing so while remaining faithful to the doctrine and to the leadership.

In temperament, Eduardo differed from Margarito Bautista, a natural preacher and an organic leader who had moved first to the Mormon colonies in northern Mexico and then to Salt Lake City in the early 1920s. He became the first president of the Spanish branch in Salt Lake City and then moved back to Mexico to continue to preach the LDS gospel and to teach his people about genealogy. By

17. Balderas, Oral History, 18.
18. Balderas, Oral History.

then, however, Bautista was a different man, willing to disagree with church leaders, particularly the white mission presidents, and to interpret doctrine in ways that privileged the role of the Mexican saints. This angered Pratt, and he soon took to trying to discredit Bautista with the Mexican saints, and eventually this and other disagreements led to the formation of a dissident Mormon group known as the Third Convention and later Bautista's excommunication.[19]

What Pratt did not understand, and neither did most of his immediate predecessors, was that native organic leadership had different ideas about how to spread and even live the restored gospel. Mormonism at the time, and still to some extent at the end of the twentieth and early twenty-first centuries, continued to preach an "American" and to some extent a Eurocentric gospel. Church leaders were not then ready to appreciate that time, place, circumstances, and lived experiences create different avenues by which to live an expansive doctrine that unfortunately had too fully accommodated to American values. Mormonism was not colonialist in the same sense that other American and European Christian sects were, but it could be just as white-centric and dominating, even when it sought a global fellowship.

Pratt sought to make sure Eduardo followed a different path from Margarito, and so he instructed him on "how [he] should behave, how [he] should conduct [himself, and what was expected of him]."[20] Behavior, conduct, and expectations were important elements in the creation of a missionary force that stayed loyal but also knew how to act in all the strange—to them—lands they were sent to and with the different peoples they would interact with. The kind of missionary discipline that came to be expected in the latter twentieth century was missing then, but it was the beginning of a uniformity that had to be self-sustaining and create self-discipline for young people so far away from home and so uninformed about the new lands where they were sent to preach and convert. In going out to do the work, all were made cognizant that many early founding leaders had been

19. Pulido, *Spiritual Evolution of Margarito Bautista*, 91. For a discussion of his differences with Pratt and for more on the Third Convention and his excommunication, see pages 159–182.

20. Balderas, Oral History, 15.

sent out without script into strange lands, with little language training, often leaving behind sick and penniless family members. But, the stories go, many came back with incredible stories of miraculous conversions, great healings—some having even raised people from the dead—and of course, the one thing most missionaries would treasure for life: the love of those they taught.

Ironically, the one thing that Eduardo did not remember receiving was instructions on how to teach, and at the time there were no manuals with specific lessons and little written literature on the church. Even if there were a few materials, almost none of them were in Spanish. Missionaries during Eduardo's time, like those iconic figures of earlier years, were truly on their own. It is quite possible that those "miraculous" moments mentioned earlier seemed to come more often in earlier times because the efforts to succeed had to be momentous, and both the missionary and the converts' faith had to be boundless.[21]

Eduardo served in the Mexican Mission, whose name was a misnomer since its missionaries did not proselytize in Mexico, having been forced out of the southern neighbor in 1913 when the Mexican Revolution became more ideological and anti-foreigner and the church worried about its nearly all white missionary group. Over the next two decades after the revolution, the Mexican government undertook a campaign to limit the power of the Catholic Church, which at one time had held a firm sway over Mexican citizens, particularly those in rural areas who depended on the church as others might have depended on the government for educating their children, getting marriage licenses, documenting their children's births, and so on. One of the government's most powerful weapons against this religious overreach was a law passed in 1926 that limited the Catholic Church—and this applied to all churches, as well—from bringing in foreign-born ministers.[22]

21. For a short discussion on the part that miracles play in a missionary's life, see Lively Jr., *Mormon Missionary*, 28, 60, 210–11, 310, 323.

22. For a discussion on the conflict between the Mexican state and the Catholic Church, which eventually affected many other churches, see Jean A. Meyer, *The Cristero Rebellion: The Mexican People Between Church and State, 1926–1929* (Cambridge: Cambridge University Press, 2008); Jim Tuck, *The Holy War in Los Altos: A Regional Analysis of the Mexico Cristero Rebellion* (Tucson: University of Arizona, 1983); and for the effects

Eduardo, at the time not yet called, remembered attending a special missionary meeting in which Elder Kenneth Haymore, who was serving as the acting mission president because President Pratt had accompanied an apostle to South America to expand missionary activities there, began reassigning all the missionaries serving in Mexico to Southwest communities. Ironically, Eduardo, born in Mexico, would have been allowed to preach in his native country, but as he recalled, he would have had to do it alone as even the white missionaries born Mexican in the Latter-day Saint colonies in Chihuahua served in the United States rather than Mexico, at least until the 1930s.[23]

President Pratt, who headed the missionary effort at the time of the first removal of the missionaries, had moved to Colorado to continue the missionary efforts among Mexicans in the southwestern states. The Mexican Mission was newly reestablished in May 1918, and this time it stretched out along the border and up into places like Colorado, Arizona, New Mexico, Texas, and California. The Mexican Mission again expanded its efforts into Mexico in 1921 but removed them again after the 1926 law and limited its efforts to Mexicans in the Southwest. The Mexican Mission, however, caused jurisdictional problems in the West for a number of other missions proselyting in the different regions of the Southwest. This caused tension among missionaries and mission leaders and led Pratt to not send missionaries to certain areas and to avoid establishing branches in others.[24]

At the time that Eduardo began his mission, Repatriation—a supposedly voluntary program to send unemployed Mexicans home—was nearing its end, although in some form or another, the idea of "encouraging" Mexicans to leave remained through much of the Depression.[25] Whether the economic woes or the rise of conversions in California prompted it, the mission headquarters moved to

of the state religious laws on Latter-day Saints, see "Mormon Schools Are Ordered Closed," *Los Angeles Times*, Feb. 28, 1926.

23. Balderas, Oral History, 16.

24. For a discussion of Pratt's efforts to expand the missionary work among Mexicans and Mexican Americans in the Southwest and the conflict it created with other mission presidents, see Embry, *In His Own Language*.

25. A Discussion of Repatriation can be found in Francisco E. Balderrama and Raymond Rodriguez, *Decade of Betrayal: Mexican Repatriation in the 1930s*, rev. ed. (Albuquerque: University of New Mexico Press, 2006).

Los Angeles during Eduardo's second year in the mission. It seems from his recollection that Eduardo first served in Mesa, Arizona.[26]

But whether in Mesa or Los Angeles, Eduardo saw the effects of the economic depression that began even before the period known as the actual Depression had garnered attention. There were few Mexicans or Mexican Americans, in his recollection, who had a comparable financial status to their white counterparts, and there were so many unemployed. Others had simply decided to go back to Mexico, either because they took the Mexican government's offer of land and jobs to those repatriated or they felt pushed out. Eduardo did not indicate whether this type of economic situation impacted missionary work, but it is difficult to imagine that it didn't in some form or another. Working long hours, barely surviving, living in dilapidated dwellings, and facing harsh discrimination hardly made it attractive to spend time listening to missionaries talk about golden plates, heavenly beings visiting the earth, pioneer stories, or Salt Lake City as a Zion city in the mountain top. Yet, ironically, those people were often the type of people who did listen and convert.

What we know of Eduardo's mission comes mostly from an interview he gave near the time of his retirement, and there we learn he showed little sophistication when it came to race relations and the impact of white supremacy on the Mexican communities of the Southwest. There were probably several reasons for this, some that had to do with being an immigrant whose family had fled violence and who saw in this new land an opportunity to do what could not be done in his native land. Apolinar and María never revealed hostility toward their homeland, and they would, in fact, live back in their home country for a number of years and might have stayed there had the economic situation been better. Still, some immigrants looked toward their new homeland as representing something better than what they left, and they had no desire to go back.

Other immigrants, however, understood that they lacked "the means and opportunities for preparing themselves."[27] Having dropped out of school and worked in menial jobs, and lacking any kind of meaningful future, Eduardo understood how these circumstances could impact

26. Balderas, Oral History, 17.
27. Balderas, Oral History.

a fellow Mexican's life. No doubt having been brought up with both the Latter-day Saint notion of self-reliance and the American concept of a racial pecking order, he could find no explanation other than to blame his people—which there is no record that he did—or accept the situation as just a reality. Whichever it was, he would later tell the interviewer, "I don't believe it was because they were held down."[28]

It took a kind of bootstrap approach to succeed in American society, as individual uplift is acceptable but a collective one is dreaded because it challenges the idea of meritocracy—a much admired trait of American society—which by its nature exacerbates class differences and separates people into "winners and losers." In no way, at least not consciously, were Eduardo and Guillermo being selfish or disdainful of their people, as both showed by their actions an incredible commitment to their people's well-being. However, they knew no other way of defining the problems their people faced except by what they had seen and experienced in their own lives. While Mexican American reformers of their generation made efforts to change both the circumstances and attitudes of their people, individuals like Eduardo and Guillermo sought to teach their people how to simply navigate American society.

Because he came from a border community like El Paso, where a small shopkeeping and professional sector had developed, he saw his community as self-contained, fully responsible for its own fortunes or misfortunes. He shared:

> You take a good-sized population where they have their own shops, where they can be taken care [of] in their own language, and you find that they would much rather be where they don't have to bother about learning English and trying to communicate their needs in that language. Neither in El Paso nor in Los Angeles, where I spent a good part of the time, did I ever see any indication or any sign that said "You're not welcome. Why don't you go to your own people?"[29]

It is, of course, quite possible that Eduardo did not see those types of signs or confront blatant discrimination because he proselytized in the Mexican side of town. If they existed, it would be in those parts of town where the Mexican and white populations met, or in the small communities outside of the larger cities where

28. Balderas, Oral History.
29. Balderas, Oral History, 17.

the social boundaries were kept rigid against Mexican immigrants and even longtime Mexican Americans. Twenty years after Eduardo served his mission, signs like "No Mexicans ... Served" were still seen in some parts of Texas.[30]

Ironically, Eduardo felt proud of those who maintained their identity and found pride in their ancestry. "A person is never ashamed of being called Mexican ... they could see no point in saying, 'No, I'm not a Mexican. I'm Spanish-American or I'm Mexican American,'" he told his interviewer.[31] He, no doubt, thought of immigrants like his father and possibly himself, but there was, however, a social and political movement among Mexican Americans, particularly among the middle class and the military veteran sector, that called themselves Mexican Americans, and an earlier generation described itself as Spanish Americans and even Tejano Americans, or simply Tejanos, to distinguish themselves from the more recent immigrants.[32]

This need felt by some to differentiate themselves from the immigrants grew as a result of the racism and discrimination that came with the rise of nativism in the 1920s and 1930s, which caused some American-born Mexicans to believe that separating themselves from the immigrants would somehow protect them from white hostility. These feelings turned the border, for some, from a geographical boundary into an ideological and social one, thus creating a separation between the two communities that lasted until the 1960s when activists from both came together to fight for their rights.[33] Again, Mexican immigrants and Mexican Americans were following a script perfected by the first third of the twentieth century that argued that to be truly American one severed their ties to the old country and accepted discrimination and contempt of their ancestry as the price to pay for the rights of American citizenship.

30. See Cynthia Orozco, *No Mexicans, Women, or Dogs Allowed: The Rise of the Mexican American Civil Rights Movement* (Austin: University of Texas Press, 2009); and Ignacio M. García, *White But Not Equal: Mexican Americans, Jury Discrimination, and the Supreme Court* (Tucson: University of Arizona Press, 2009).

31. Balderas, Oral History, 17.

32. See Mario T. García, *Mexican Americans: Leadership, Ideology & Identity, 1930–1960* (New Haven: Yale University Press, 1989); also, Aaron E. Sánchez, *Homeland: Ethnic Mexican Belonging Since 1900*, vol. 2 of *New Directions in Tejano History* (Norman, OK: University of Oklahoma Press, 2021); and Ignacio M. García's *Hector P. García: In Relentless Pursuit of Justice* (Houston: Arte Publico Press, 2002).

33. Sánchez, *Homeland.*

Eduardo, however, seemed oblivious or chose to consciously avoid entangling himself in his community's identity conflicts, but he was more attuned to another divide within the Mexican community in which he proselytized: a religious one. The Mexican communities that he went to preach to in both Mesa, Arizona, and Los Angeles, California, were predominantly Catholic, religiously and culturally. He remembered many of the people saying to him, "It [the gospel message] sounds interesting, but my mother is Catholic, my father is a Catholic, my grandparents were Catholics, and I can't see any reason for changing."[34] To Eduardo, whose family had moved away from at least a cultural Catholicism and who did not grow up in that faith, it seemed almost unbelievable that people could find value in his message but still refuse to convert.[35]

If the Catholic Mexicans resisted conversion, the Protestant Mexicans provided the fiercest opposition. Protestant ministers, remembered Eduardo, "would ... really go out of their way to hold meetings and instruct their people, 'Don't pay any attention to what they say.'"[36] Some Protestant preachers and their congregants followed the missionaries around and removed the tracts (leaflets) they left on the doors and warned the people that they would "burn in hell" if they listened to these predominantly white missionaries.[37] At the time of Eduardo's mission, Protestant missionary efforts were intense. Protestantism became the major competitor for Mexican Catholic souls, and both groups found the going tough, though the Latter-day Saint missionaries often carried an extra burden: most of them were white and culturally clung to their American cultural baggage in ways that Mexican Protestants did not. The Mexican Protestants had decided, unlike the Mormons, that they were not there to make their converts into Americans, notwithstanding that some of their white leaders did believe in Americanism.[38]

The concept of making converts American may have also been the

34. Balderas, Oral History, 18.

35. Balderas, Oral History, 19.

36. Balderas, Oral History, 18.

37. Balderas, Oral History.

38. For a discussion of Mexican Protestantism, see Juan Francisco Martínez, *Sea La Luz: The Making of Mexican Protestantism in the American Southwest, 1829–1900* (Denton: University of North Texas Press, 2006).

reason why Mexican Protestants were so fiercely against Latter-day Saint proselytizing. The Mexican Protestants also confronted their own challenges navigating a white Protestant religious world, but they had already started pushing back against it and had even begun establishing their own congregations and conventions—loose federations of small Mexican congregations. They also developed leaders willing to be critical of their white Protestant brothers and sisters who discriminated or who did not allow the Mexican Protestants equal standing. Mexican Latter-day Saints in Mexico, too, engaged in their own pushback, but that was still a couple of years away.

Interestingly, while cultural "Mexicanness" played a part in both the Protestant and Latter-day Saint proselytizing efforts, Eduardo seemed oblivious to its role. When asked years later whether his Mexican ancestry made any difference in his ability to communicate with those Mexican individuals he taught, he admitted to never having thought about it, which meant, at least in his mind, that it might have made little difference. He believed that his companions, especially the more senior ones, handled the language well, even though at the time most missionaries did not go through a language training center.[39] Here, one has to wonder how much Eduardo reflected on what went on around him. He seemed, throughout his life, to focus on the immediate chore and often saw the work of the church through rose-colored glasses, which meant that if the gospel they preached was true, then God had prepared his missionaries well, or at least not placed them in situations in which they could not accomplish the task.

Eduardo talked little about particular individuals or families that he met or taught on his mission. This silence also extended to any special moment in his time as a missionary. Certainly, he had spiritual experiences, as is the case with most who fondly remember their missions, but there is no recorded account of any of them, and neither his writings nor his children's recollections speak to any of them. His quiet and humble demeanor did not prompt him to talk much about himself, and his lack of writings prevent us from knowing his feelings about the mission. It is, however, quite possible that

39. Balderas, Oral History, 19.

he simply took his missionary life one day at a time, and many things were lost within the confines of the memories he chose to remember but not share.

What he did later share said much about what was happening with the youth in the Mexican homes of the Southwest. "I think that many of them were brought up the same way I was, with perhaps one exception, that there was less restrictions in their homes about speaking English."[40] Here, he spoke about the homes' cultural practices and the effort by Mexican families to keep their children from losing their native tongue. In one of the few times that he revealed any disagreement with the way his parents raised him, he pointed to the advantages that speaking more English in the home gave these youth in their interactions with the world at large but also emphasized that some of these young people lost, somewhat, their ability to fully understand Spanish—and we may add, more critically, their ability to speak it. This loss made many of them bilingually handicapped since they had limited command of either language.

For the parents of those Mexican children allowed into white schools, there arose a deep concern that their children would lose both the language and the culture of their community and distance themselves from their families. By the time that Eduardo entered the mission field, a quiet—and sometimes not-so-quiet—debate raged in the barrios of the Southwest over how much Americanism to allow into their homes, and language acquisition played a big part in that debate.[41] Retaining their children's ability to speak Spanish was important to the immigrant community, many who believed they would one day go back home. For some Mexican Americans, particularly to an emerging new generation of civil rights reformers, assimilation offered the only way to prosper and to be accepted by the larger white community. This belief came not only by the

40. Balderas, Oral History.

41. As a community activist in some Mexican barrios of South Texas, I saw this parental concern, and witnessed firsthand the distancing of some youth from their parents because of the language barrier. But the loss of language impacted the communities in other ways because, at the time, Chicano and other activists of color were seeking to redefine and recreate both the Spanish and English languages into ones that provided them a way to articulate their concerns and their own views of how to resolve the issues that impacted them.

realities they saw on the ground—educational and economic challenges they faced—but also from the massive repatriation campaigns that had just occurred and the constant pressure they received from social reformers, educators, and politicians to become assimilated into American society, even while many were excluded from full participation.

This debate within the Mexican and Mexican American communities created an ideological divide that fueled harsh stereotypes that each community—and sometimes groups within each community—had of the other. This animosity, it's important to note, did not much alter the standing of Mexicans and Mexican Americans in society because both suffered from discrimination and marginalization from those who made no distinction between a native-born, a naturalized citizen, or a recent immigrant.[42] The generation of Mexican American reformers of the 1930s to 1960s was a bilingual one, and that allowed them to understand—when they chose—their people's concerns about speaking their language, maintaining their culture and finding their own identity in the United States.

Eduardo might have been oblivious, to this raging debate, but it nonetheless impacted his future family and home environment. None of his children would learn Spanish, and the only true Mexican thing in their home was the cuisine. By their own admission (or lack of admission) they appreciated only a small part—the food and the festive atmosphere—of the Mexican branches they attended in their early childhood. They made the decision on their own to go to church with their white friends, and Eduardo eventually acquiesced. Their appreciation of the language and the culture came much later, once they embraced their father's legacy within the Spanish-speaking Latter-day Saint world. To be fair to Eduardo, he was as much a victim of the marginalization of the Mexican in American society, and he chose like many others to "survive" rather than to fight against a forced assimilation. Suffice it to say that many would be shocked to know this about one truly iconic figure in Latina/o Mormonism.

All of this notwithstanding, Eduardo focused on doing the work he was called to do. As mentioned earlier, he served in Mesa, Arizona,

42. See Sánchez's *Homeland*, especially the first two chapters, for a discussion about the way the two communities distanced themselves from each other.

and Los Angeles. In the former, his first few months were spent in construction work helping build the first chapel for Mexican saints. While the church by then had their chapels erected by construction companies, many smaller LDS communities, especially those for Saints of color, still constructed their own chapels.[43] Most of the members there were too poor to contribute more than 10 percent of the cost of the chapel, and many were too busy in their jobs to help much in the work. Eduardo was part of a group of seven missionaries called by President Pratt to construct the Mesa chapel. He warmly remembered, "I had my turn at making adobes for the chapel, laying the foundation, etc."[44] He left, however, before they finished the windows and missed an opportunity to use the carpentry skills he had learned at the lumber yard he worked in before he left El Paso.

While in Mesa, he got a chance to see Mexican leadership in the church. His father had been the first and only Mexican he knew that led a Latter-day Saint congregation. The experiences of seeing his father lead a congregation, and also of seeing local leaders in Mesa, left such an impression on him that it made him a strong advocate for native leadership. He believed that missionaries called to lead small congregations tended to lean toward the side of proselytizing, while a native leader tended to look more after the flock. Just as important, the local leader could understand the concerns of the members of his congregation better than a young missionary in his twenties still learning the language and the culture of the people he taught. Though he believed that the members had no more devotion for a local leader than they did for a young missionary "because we're taught to respect our leaders, regardless of who they are," he understood the need for local leadership.[45]

As would be expected in proselytizing among Mexican immigrants, the missionaries emphasized the Book of Mormon and the promises to the Lamanites that the book contained. That is what

43. The first chapel I attended in the United States was built by construction missionaries with the help of local members. I still remember that we took food to them as they worked. The chapel showed signs of the limited construction knowledge of the workers, but it was a warm and inviting place, and it was ours. For my own experiences in that chapel, see my memoir, *Chicano While Mormon*.

44. Balderas, Oral History, 19–20.

45. Balderas, Oral History, 20.

Eduardo had grown up with, and he found the message resonated with those he taught in both Mesa and Los Angeles. Unfortunately, he left no record of any particular discussions he gave, nor did he expound on what those promises meant to him or what role they played in the conversion of his people. Again, we are left with only bits and pieces of his thoughts and feelings, but we do know that later, as he translated the church's literature and worked with its leaders, he strongly promoted the belief in the promises from Mormon canon that the Mexican and indigenous saints would "blossom as a rose" (Doctrine and Covenants 49:24), and part of that blossoming meant they would play an important role in the leadership of the church.

These teachings, and we know little about the details or their essence, came out of the missionaries' perception of what they were supposed to teach. Whether by President Pratt's design, or his conforming to the tradition of sending out missionaries without script, Eduardo remembers the missionaries being basically on their own. They met with Pratt periodically, mostly when, as mission president, he took visiting general authorities on a tour of the mission, and they submitted reports and occasionally he wrote back to commend them for their work, to suggest a change in strategy, or to remind them to be "true representatives of ... heavenly father," but not much else.[46]

Pratt's letters of commendation meant a lot to Eduardo and the other missionaries, who often experienced little success in their proselytizing, spending long hours "tracting" (what LDS missionaries called going house to house to teach, preaching in the streets, and handing out church pamphlets). In Los Angeles, Eduardo shared that duty with five other missionaries, of which one served as the supervising elder, whose job it was to make the reports and to keep them honoring their commitments. The commitment to doing their work as missionaries, notwithstanding the supervising elder, resulted, in Eduardo's words, from "personal devotion and dedication to the work."[47] Hard work was not a problem for him, as he had been working—sometimes seven long days a week—since he was a young teenager, and that work could at times be followed by work at the barber shop.

It would be appropriate to consider what the mostly unsupervised

46. Balderas, Oral History, 22.

47. Balderas, Oral History.

missionary workday entailed. It began by getting up early and studying the scriptures and planning out the day—to the extent that it could be planned, given that they rarely had appointments and had no way of contacting people ahead of time. It meant knocking on doors for hours and finding "very little interest" among those who chose to open.[48] In between knocking doors, the missionaries might take time to preach to passersby or to hand out pamphlets to those who did not stop and see many of those pamphlets thrown on the street only a few steps later. The missionaries found shade under a tree to eat their lunch, if they had one, and spent many a time in plazas or other public spaces where they would talk about their day or assess what the afternoon might bring. It is quite likely their feet hurt most days and that they were hot and sticky and often thirsty and hungry. And the weeks and months were often repetitive, as they canvassed neighborhoods in an assigned district and then waited a couple of weeks and went back and did the same thing.[49]

If people accepted their pamphlets at individual houses the first time, the missionaries came back to see how much further they could get with the individuals or families. Eduardo remembers people being up-front about their religious affiliation, believing that if they let the missionaries in, it meant no particular animosity to non-Catholic missionaries and also that they had no priest or minister warning them of "going to hell" if they spoke to the Mormons. Once inside, the missionaries had to use the spirit to figure out what to teach at that moment. Of course, there were subjects the companionships selected before they went out, and most of those came from experiencing numerous and varied reactions to prior teachings. Eduardo remembers focusing on God to provide the investigators a clear sense of what Latter-day Saints believed about deity and then moving on to the apostasy—for a long time one of the key elements of Mormon teaching was that the Christian world had fallen away from the teachings of Jesus Christ, and a restoration of his teachings was necessary. That would lead not only to the need for repentance and baptism but also to the right church. Somewhere in there, the story of Joseph Smith and the Book of Mormon took center stage.[50]

48. Balderas, Oral History, 23.
49. Balderas, Oral History.
50. Balderas, Oral History.

If a family showed interest in the message, the missionaries then asked them if they could have a "cottage meeting" in their homes and have them invite friends to hear the Mormon message. Once a group of individuals or families gathered, the elders began with a hymn and a prayer, and then one or both missionaries spoke. They used the Bible and the Book of Mormon to emphasize their point, and they rarely confronted arguments because most of the people knew little of the scriptures and simply accepted or rejected the message based on their ability to live according to the concepts taught or after an assessment of how the message might change their lives. There were, however, times when the investigators "set a trap" for them. They accepted a cottage meeting and invited some friends and neighbors but then asked their minister to be present. This often led to discussions, then debates, and, if the missionaries allowed themselves to be drawn in, to arguments. Most of those confrontations usually revolved around scriptural references particular to the minister.[51]

Disadvantaged, the missionaries sought to convert—in those instances and others where there were unanswerable questions—with "testimonies" or by showing their converts an abundance of love.[52] These methods worked only if the missionary had the spirit or if they actually loved those they taught, something that differed from missionary to missionary. Eduardo left no record of his encounters, but years after his mission some would remember him as a very good preacher. Since his father was known as a silver-tongue, it is possible that Eduardo had already learned the value of a good set of rhetorical skills. Seeing him speak so well must have surprised many a missionary companion, as it would many others with whom he associated in his church work, because during personal interactions, he spoke softly, rarely referred to himself, his callings, or his spiritual experiences, and came across as a listener.[53]

Teaching the Mormon gospel forced Eduardo to confront questions that he normally did not think about, having been a child when

51. Balderas, Oral History, 24.

52. Testimonies are heartfelt declarations by Latter-day Saints of their belief in the truthfulness of their gospel.

53. This information comes from how some people described him, from the answers to his interviews, and from conversations with his children and daughter-in-law. Nothing in my research contradicted this perception.

his father chose his faith for him. If his father had particular questions, Eduardo never mentioned them. In his own experience teaching, he confronted questions about church protocol, such as, "Why do you do this?" or "Why is it done this way?" Mormonism was truly different than the Catholicism and Protestantism that most people had experienced. There were also, however, questions about baptism for those who had already been baptized as children or when they first joined a Protestant church.[54] To respond to the question of baptism meant questioning the authority of other religious leaders and of other churches. The Latter-day Saint gospel offered a restoration of the primitive church after what had been a "great apostasy" from true Christianity. This meant that all others' priesthood authority was not valid, that prophets now roamed the earth as in ancient times, and that there was only "one true church."

Another discussion usually had among the Catholic individuals the missionaries taught revolved around the idea of saints and the Virgin Mary. Most of the homes which Eduardo entered surely had images and artwork that depicted saints and the mother of Christ, and when he and his companion taught them the "wrongness" of their ways, many simply stopped accepting them in their homes. Eduardo remembers that most people kept things to themselves: "I don't recall anyone ever having said, 'I'm not going to take my saints down'... but in the majority of cases, after we told them that this was what the Lord wanted them to do, they would be gone [not home] the next time."[55]

This type of reaction forced Eduardo and his companions to proceed at what he described as a "snail's pace," trying not to offend, to be "discreet," and to take whatever time it took to get them to accept the gospel they were offering.[56] Like his own family, these individuals and families were being asked to not only leave a religion behind but also to construct a communal religious family in a city that had few Latter-day Saints and even fewer that were Mexican or Latina/o. The communal family is fundamental to the Christian gospel and key to member retention. Without it, most converts find

54. Balderas, Oral History, 25.
55. Balderas, Oral History, 25.
56. Balderas, Oral History, 26.

themselves swimming by themselves in a demanding religion that takes years to fully understand. Latter-day Saints are also expected to fellowship others going through the same process, and in this the Los Angeles saints fell short, in Eduardo's view.[57] He shared, "Few went out of their way to accomplish this [fellowship]. They would be happy to see the converts in church, of course, and would be friendly and polite to them in church, but I don't think anyone ever made a special effort to go see a neighbor around the block."[58]

Eduardo's expectations might have been unfair, given that most of the members in Los Angeles were still trying to create their own space within Mormonism. The formality of fellowshipping that became a cornerstone of Latter-day Saint practice continued to plague the Latina/o and Mexican members for years. They were willing, as Eduardo wrote, to be welcoming, to visit those who were sick, and to provide a helping hand, but they struggled with the formality of fellowshipping that over time became a requirement for good standing through the church's home teaching and visiting teaching programs, which codified the idea of visiting your neighbor as a duty.

The way Mexican families accepted the missionaries had not changed since Eduardo's own family received the elders in their home. Apolinar and María listened to the lessons, but the children were not required or even invited to attend those sessions. "The parents couldn't see why the children should be present," remembers Eduardo.[59] They simply went along if their parents were baptized, as had been the case with Eduardo. It was also common to have the wife and children in a family become members but not the father. The men, most often those who rarely went to mass or any church service, saw the religion as requiring too much, especially when it came to not working on Sundays, paying 10 percent of their income to the church as tithing, and assuming lay leadership in a congregation.

To deal with the multiple challenges that they faced with their new converts, and to get them to establish the kind of community

57. *Fellowship* is the term Latter-day Saints use to describe the process of getting to know new members, becoming their friends, visiting them, and being there as they make the transition from converts to established members.

58. Balderas, Oral History, 26.

59. Balderas, Oral History, 27.

most of them were leaving behind, the missionaries, remembering their own communal Mormonism, sought to create activities that went beyond the strictly religious. Eduardo must have remembered his own youthful experience when Sunday church was the only thing he knew. To this end, he translated "two or three" plays that he knew from his Mutual Improvement Association (MIA) years.[60] (The MIA was the church's youth program, and from it grew many of the more formal activities that LDS youth would grow up with.) The missionaries then recruited some members and put on their production for the rest of the congregation. "We met with a good deal of success, I might add," Eduardo recalled.[61]

The missionaries, and possibly other white members from English-language congregations, also sponsored evening activities when young people came together to create friendships, play games, and even learn activities that came out of the LDS repertoire. Plays, sing-alongs, motivating lectures, and sports activities all played a part in getting the members to feel confident with each other, their leaders, and the missionaries. These activities also played a part—whether the missionaries were fully conscious of it or not—in assimilating these Mexican members into the American religious bubble. In many cases, this proved successful simply because it competed with little that the Mexican saints experienced on the outside. Most activities in the Mexican community at the time were adult-focused, and children simply found their own niches within the peripheries. Once converted, most found some of these traditional Mexican activities "too worldly" for them and their families.

In the last year of his mission, Eduardo drove President Pratt to Salt Lake City for a hernia operation, at which time during convalescence they expected to work on the translation of the work *Latter-day Revelation*, which Pratt had already started. Eduardo did not remember how he got the news that Pratt died, but he served as a pallbearer and then later drove Pratt's wife and two children back to Los Angeles. For two months, the mission had no president and the missionary secretary—more like an administrative assistant with

60. Balderas, Oral History.
61. Balderas, Oral History.

ecclesiastical authority—took the reins of the work and the missionaries until Antoine R. Ivins became the new president.[62]

Eduardo left no record of his feelings at the passing of his leader, mentor, and friend. Rey L. Pratt had been a presence in his life since Apolinar first went to church seeking new clients and ended up being a missionary seeking new converts and then a leader of his own congregation. Throughout that time, Pratt loomed large in the Balderas household. It seems he struck a close relationship with Eduardo, and when the young man entered the mission field, he used him to help in the translation of literature for the young elders. While Eduardo helped in making the words more accessible to the Mexican public, Pratt taught him much about religious translation and about the language of Mormonism. Eduardo learned about church history and leadership from a man whose Mormon roots stretched all the way back to the founding of the church and who had few qualms about calling Mexican men to lead their own people.

Pratt's comfort with Mexican saints taking an ecclesiastical role in their congregations allowed Eduardo to experience native leadership not only back home in El Paso but also in Mesa, Arizona, and in Los Angeles, cementing him to the idea that Mexican saints could run their wards and branches. Though he did not, some missionaries did occasionally serve as presiding officers in those units. It was, Eduardo remembered, the responsibility of the mission president to provide leadership training, but because of the distance, most training was limited. Nonetheless, he felt the branches in those places he served compared well with the one in El Paso, being his only point of reference. Seeing native leadership during his mission and experiencing his own father's ministry is one reason why he rarely ever critiqued—even when given a chance to speak on the topic—his own people's ability to minister to their own.

These men, and the women who assisted them as auxiliary leaders, choristers, note takers, and so on, did their work with so few resources, and most initially had to conduct sacrament—and all other meetings—in rental halls. They came early, sometimes accompanied by the missionaries, to sweep all the cigarette butts from the dance

62. Balderas, Oral History, 29.

or activity the night before. Without doubt, the smell of beer and food lingered in the air even as the church talks spoke of heavenly things. It may also have been humorous to talk in that setting about the church's Word of Wisdom, which prohibited drinking alcohol and smoking tobacco. But after experiencing the dance hall scene, Eduardo got to see the small congregation in Los Angeles move to the Knights of Pythias hall, which had a stage and was kept cleaner.[63]

Eduardo's time in the mission field provided him—as it would to many other young men and those women who served—with experiences that changed his life and gave him, unbeknownst to him then, a direction in life. His mission must also have underscored in his mind the need for Spanish-language materials for the new converts to read and for the missionaries to learn how to preach the gospel in the people's native language. Just as important, the Spanish-language gospel provided the congregation leaders the ability to govern their flocks within a culturally sensitive environment.

63. Balderas, Oral History, 29.

4

FINDING THE ETERNAL PARTNER

"Definitely," responded Eduardo when asked whether his mission "was a period of spiritual growth and spiritual development."[1] When asked whether the mission had affected "[his] later life in other ways," he responded that it had "as far as the church activities are concerned ... yes, very much."[2]

This response reflected Eduardo's understanding of the place of the church in the Mexican members' religious worldview and that of many of those who came from nonwhite worlds. The church represented a safe space, a place of growth, a protection from the world, and a community that replaced the one left behind. It shielded them from two worlds; the Mexican immigrant world with all its social, cultural, and secular challenges, and the white world that often saw them lacking as citizens and as people. Even in places like El Paso, where city fathers promoted the "bicultural" nature of their city, discrimination and bigotry were rampant.[3]

Those internal communities—as inviting as they were with all their activities and spaces in which Mexican immigrants could speak their language, eat their food, listen and dance to their music, and hang out with others like themselves—were nonetheless problematic for the new and old converts who could not drink alcohol, speak some of the feisty language of the barrio, celebrate on the Sabbath, or

1. Eduardo Balderas, Oral History, interviews by Gordon Irving, 1973, typescript, 30, Oral History Program, CHL.

2. Balderas, Oral History.

3. Historian Mario T. García described El Paso as a place where "total racial sepae ration" existed in certain sectors of the city. Garcia, *Desert Immigrants: The Mexicans of El Paso, 1880–1920* (New Haven: Yale University Press, 1981), 127.

revel in the often Catholic celebrations, notwithstanding how much these had been secularized. Their church now wanted them to be "in the world but not of it," whatever that might mean to the Mexican saint who never lived or heard of the sequestered life of the Utah pioneers, a life that now became operational in the LDS kingdom in the West and everywhere else that saints found themselves a minority.

Eduardo, whether he fully understood it or not, set out to build such a sanctuary—beyond Sunday services back home. He shared:

> I was able to go back home and organize an MIA. I asked my father's permission to do so, he being the branch president. He wasn't too favorable [*sic*] impressed. He thought that meetings should be strictly sacred activities. But I think he counseled with the mission president who told him to go ahead, and so I was able to start an MIA meeting. I was able to obtain some of the things that I had heard about from my missionary companions and translated them into Spanish. We'd have a class from the Book of Mormon or the Bible, and then afterwards we'd have social games for about half an hour or so. And it really helped the young people. It strengthened them spiritually and were [*sic*] able to also bring in quite a few friends who liked this social activity.[4]

It is possible that this flurry of activities felt like an extension of his mission, something he needed after having come back from his service four months early. His father had written him that in the midst of a depression he could no longer support him on his mission. His parents found themselves struggling financially, and in two years became victims of the Depression.[5] It is quite possible that his early return impacted the way he saw his mission and most likely the reason we have no record of him talking about it much.

When Eduardo returned, he faced the dilemma he feared: few jobs were available during these difficult economic times. Though neither Eduardo nor Guillermo talked much about their relationship, it is likely that they were close. The returned missionary soon joined his brother at the ranch—more like a farm—in New Mexico, hoping to help his brother make a go of the cotton enterprise the family had invested in, but it soon dawned on Eduardo how difficult the ranch

4. Balderas, Oral History, 30.
5. Balderas, Oral History, 31.

or farm life could be. The fact that Eduardo discovered on his mission that he liked to be around people and engage in all kinds of church and social activities made the lonely rural life too much to handle, and within two weeks he left for El Paso, and Guillermo followed a few months later when the cotton market fell through the floor.[6]

On his return to the border city, Eduardo was fortunate to resume his job at the Sash and Door Factory, but within a month it closed—another victim of the Depression. Luckily for him, Arwell L. Pierce, bishop of the English-speaking ward in El Paso, offered him a job working in his lumber yard across the border in Juarez. Pierce furnished Eduardo a car to go all around the Mexican border town to collect accounts due. In this job, he spoke Spanish ten hours a day, which "helped [him in] expanding [his] vocabulary and knowledge of the Spanish language." Talking to people, some well-educated and others not so much, helped acquaint him with "idiomatic phrases" unknown to him at the time. In his view, the position took the place of going back to school in the effect it had on his future endeavor as a translator. He worked with Bishop Pierce from 1932 to 1939, his last job before he moved to Salt Lake City to translate for the church.[7]

His first calling back home was that of mutual president, a position he kept for several years. While he directed the MIA, the branch youth and those adults who participated in helping, or just "hung around," became involved in sports activities—several times competing in different events against the Rama Mexicana in Mesa, Arizona. They also developed a choir, staged plays, and held speech festivals. All these activities, as was the case among secular mutual aid groups, were meant to assimilate and integrate the youth into American society, but they also played a dual role in helping to create a sense of community and strengthen their own culture, in essence creating a Mormon Mexican culture to replace the one they left behind or the one they experienced when not in church.

As one high school principal would say at the time, these kids had to become more Mexican before they became more American.[8] Not

6. Guillermo Balderas, "Historia," Balderas Family, Balderas Family Scrapbooks, 1910–1911, 192, Oral History Program, CHL.

7. Balderas, Oral History, 32.

8. See Ignacio M. García, *When Mexicans Could Play Ball: Basketball, Race, and Identity in San Antonio, 1928–1945* (Austin: University of Texas Press, 2013), 98–103.

all social reformers or religious leaders thought that way, but some did. They wanted the immigrants to feel safe within their own spaces as they moved toward assimilation. The view promulgated the idea that education, employment opportunities, language acquisition, and a knowledge of American society facilitated an immigrant's journey to becoming American. Given the difficult straits in which the barrios of the Southwest found themselves, the lure of America proved strong, and yet this effort to assimilate could not hide the reality of the youth's experience outside the church space. They still had little education and few job prospects beyond those that paid low wages, and they faced rampant racism from many of their white neighbors and coworkers and confronted discrimination in stores, restaurants, parks, and government offices. Thus, rather than becoming factories of assimilation, the MIA activities became "safe spaces" in which Mexican saints could practice their religion, possibly find a spouse, make friends, and for some, develop leadership traits.

For Eduardo, the MIA might have been the most enjoyable calling he ever received in the church. He loved to sing, so he created a singing group that sung across the city in church activities, festivals, and wherever he could find an audience that paid or provided them publicity. He also loved performing in plays and would translate a number of Mormon favorites into Spanish and writing or adapting some of his own. He had a good voice and he loved to dress up for those singing engagements. Eduardo lived in an era—still with us in some parts of the Mexican and Latina/o Latter-day Saint space—in which saints from small Mexican branches put on festivals, sang, and fed their white counterparts. They wanted to make sure that the white brothers and sisters knew that they were good people and good saints.

This performance for acceptance and recognition followed a well-beaten path among immigrants and even colonized people. You smile, make those outside your community comfortable, and show that you are safe, or at least harmless. While there might have been a lot of sincerity in the actions of white leaders and fellow members, they often established an asymmetric relationship between themselves and saints of color. Latter-day Saint missionaries and their leaders did not follow the conquering armies, and for the most part did not engage in economic domination, but they did at times carry the "white man's burden" view of the people they taught. Their duty, in the case of missionary work outside of Europe, Canada, and the United States, was to carry the gospel message to those willing to listen among the colored masses, and to "whiten" them in the process. Skin color and racial genealogy to many members, and a number of leaders, reflected obedience and fidelity—or lack of it—in the pre-earth life, and the earthly existence was a time to overcome the bad beginning.[9]

Eduardo found his groove in American–Mexican spaces, and while he might not have noticed, many Mexican American reformers of his era also searched for a space or a niche in which their people could prosper to the extent possible in a segregated society. LDS theology did not necessarily limit blessings that members of various groups could acquire—except for those of African ancestry, who could not receive the blessings of the priesthood and the temple ordinances. It did, however, minimize the abilities of some members to lead beyond their own congregations because they developed into very different people of Mexican descent. Mexican American reformers helped create these American–Mexican spaces, but they were meant to be more transitional—at least initially—than those Eduardo envisioned, because while these reformers fought against discrimination and segregated schools, law enforcement violence, and a lack of employment opportunities, they also sought to Americanize their own people, pushing them to learn English, become acquainted with American history, join the military, and even fix their homes. While strong advocates for their people, these reformers were not beyond seeing them as not meeting their obligations as American citizens. There is no record, however, of Eduardo ever talking disparagingly of other Mexicans, or implying that they did not meet their obligations to the church.

Eduardo's life, in these American-Mexican spaces took a big leap forward when two sister missionaries, Rhea Ross and Alicia Dives, arrived in El Paso. Sister Ross, in particular, came interested in meeting Elder Balderas, whom congregants in Los Angeles where

9. Armand L. Mauss, *All Abraham's Children: Changing Mormon Conceptions of Race and Lineage* (Urbana: University of Illinois Press, 2003).

she had served raved about him.[10] Whether by inspiration, curiosity, or a desire to simply meet a good man, Rhea quickly connected with Eduardo, and in something quite unacceptable with today's missionary rules, she befriended him. There was nothing in their relationship that we know of that indicated any more than a mutual attraction kept within bounds—at least in the beginning.

Missionary rules would tighten over the years to make sure that missionaries concentrated on their work, did not become infatuated with their converts or other missionaries, and avoided appearances that hindered their proselyting efforts. In the 1930s, LDS missionaries faced scrutiny from other ministers and priests and also from conservative communities that sought to protect their daughters from the young men who served. Of course, there was also the fear of young men being sought out as good catches by those Mexican families seeking benefits from connecting to a white family, a not completely uncommon desire among some who sought not only religious but also social benefits from such a relationship. Often in a sincere effort to find a good mate for their children, they reflected the asymmetric relationship between whites and Mexicans inside and outside of the church.

Rhea, along with her companion, came to help run the branch's primary program as well as to proselytize. She and Eduardo also likely saw each other in the church headquarters, which by then had gone back to El Paso, where he translated missionary materials or served as an interpreter, and when her assignment required meeting with her mission leaders. Their common hallway chats about missionary work or families being taught soon evolved into longer conversations. Guillermo remembers Eduardo urging him to accompany him to visit the sister missionaries and to engage Rhea's companion in long conversations. Guillermo remembers becoming quite close to her, but only as friend, sometimes talking about his own challenges with the woman he was dating at the time. Sometimes Eduardo, as the MIA president, took the boys along for the visit, trying to always keep things appropriate, which in terms of intimacy, they were.[11] The visits, according to Guillermo, were "no

10. Balderas, "Historia," 193.
11. Balderas, "Historia," 193.

clandestine affairs," since they mostly spent time conversing in the living room or the garden.

In talking with the lady missionaries, both Eduardo and Guillermo were no doubt looking to find young women within the church with whom to have a relationship. By now, both seemed ready to dedicate their lives to the Latter-day Saint gospel, and that required a believing spouse. In this arena, white sister missionaries were no doubt particularly impressive because they came across as independent, more versed in LDS teachings, and surely committed to the church given their sacrifices to teach miles away from home. Neither Eduardo nor Guillermo mentioned the names of any Mexican women in their congregation—there were probably very few—though at the time of the visit to the sister missionaries' apartment, both seemed to have been dating Mexican women. We are not, however, certain they were Latter-day Saints.

Constructing Eduardo and Sister (Rhea) Ross's relationship in detail is difficult since neither left a journal nor shared their relationship with their children, and Eduardo said almost nothing about it in his interviews. What we can piece together comes from a series of letters that are available from the two years before their marriage and a couple letters exchanged after their marriage. The first impression they give is of an Eduardo totally in love and a Rhea whose love seems to grow over time, though it did begin with a strong attraction and a feeling that Eduardo was a man she could spend the rest of her life with. They also reflected the difficulties and often messiness of interracial relationships at a time when Latter-day Saints were affirming their move toward assimilating into an ever-whitening American society, and American society itself was creating ever stronger demarcations between races. We will see this in examining when Rhea and Eduardo's relationship turned serious.

In his letter of April 1934, which has no specific day, Eduardo wrote to her from Salt Lake City while on church business, probably accompanying Harold Wilcken Pratt, the third mission president with whom he served, in one of those frequent trips to church headquarters. He tells her about meeting her parents, mentioning that her mom is "grand," her father, "nice" and her baby sister, "cute." No doubt the descriptors were meant to endear him to her. He danced all night, he continued, and though he does not mention the Mexican branch, it was probably the Mexican saints who sponsored the dance, and in attendance were several returned missionaries. He planned to go to dinner with her parents, he wrote, accompanied by Roberto, a person that popped up in their letters frequently, and who it seems was someone he met back home—possibly a returned missionary that served either in El Paso or in the Mexican Mission, which meant that he met Eduardo in conjunction with missionary efforts. Unfortunately, there is no way to figure out who Roberto was, though it is possible that it was Roberto Thurgood who served in the Mesa Mission at around the same time as Eduardo.[12]

At the end of his letter, he tells her that he is going to Los Angeles, most likely also on mission duties.[13] Harold Pratt (Rey L. Pratt's half brother) had by then begun having Eduardo accompany him on mission business. Pratt had no need for a translator as he spoke Spanish well-enough, but it is likely that he found it easier to have Eduardo accompany him to deal with any translation issues and to have him edit or look over documents, pamphlets, and the like that missionaries were translating. It is most probable that Pratt liked the company and saw Eduardo as the kind of Mexican saint he wanted to help develop into a leader. His experience—like that of Rey L. Pratt—with the now-evolving intellectual Margarito Bautista had been bittersweet, as the Mexican young man who seemed full of the spirit in his early years as a convert had begun preaching in a style that upset Pratt. Another reason Eduardo might have volunteered to accompany Pratt was that Rhea, it seems, might have returned to Los Angeles. There is little doubt that if the two were having conversations daily, someone may have noticed and had her sent to Los Angeles for the sake of both.

Eduardo's cheery description of his meeting with Rhea's parents only told his side of the story. While her mom seemed less opposed to her daughter's friendship—which at the time was within appropriate boundaries—she was not beyond telling her daughter to wait

12. This letter, along with those to be discussed in this chapter, unless otherwise noted, comes from a private collection of letters held by Eduardo's daughter Ana, copies of which are in the author's possession. The possibility of Roberto being Elder Thurgood comes from scholar Sujey Vega who has done significant work on Mesa Latter-day Saints.

13. Eduardo to Rhea, Apr. 1934.

and think hard about any relationship with Eduardo. Her father seemed opposed from the beginning and acted cordial but not enthusiastic, assuming—and it is hard not to assume—that he had an inkling of Eduardo's intent in meeting them and talking much about Rhea. Eduardo tended to be quite transparent in his interactions.

No doubt her parents, or at least her mother, saw it as nice that she had friends from her mission, or at least one who associated with the mission headquarters, and they were more than willing to host someone who could speak about her, but it still might have seemed strange that a young man would take the time to visit the home of a sister missionary and seek to spend that much time with her family. The thought must have crossed their mind, as it would for many missionary parents over the years, about the desire of converts of color to connect with American families, whether true or not.[14]

In a letter dated May 1934 after she finished her mission and sent from Los Angeles, Rhea asks Eduardo, "Are you standing straight and are you smiling? Always do that for me." While it is not unusual for a woman—and it is usually the woman—to advise her boyfriend on etiquettes or about other things that have to do with behavior, it is less common for a "missionary friend" to give such advice. Yet we see from the letters that over the course of their relationship, she did so frequently. One explanation is that Eduardo, a humble person from his early youth, might have hunched over a bit and been rather tight lipped when meeting other people, though that does not seem to be the Eduardo that comes out in pictures. He loved to sing and to act in plays, and she had heard of him being a silver-tongue like his father. Still, around her, he might have been shy.[15]

At the same time, as we will see, Rhea also told him to keep his teeth clean. Her words do not come across as condescending, but they do seem to reflect a way for Rhea to bridge Eduardo to her white world. Beyond wanting a man who stood straight and smiled,

14. In my own experience, this was a topic of conversation in both white and Mexican families. Racial intermarriage has long been a practice among Latter-day Saints with the advent of international missions, and that practice seems to be increasing even more today. Unfortunately, no statistics are available, but see Deborah Bulkeley, "Mixed Marriages on Rise," *Deseret News*, Apr. 13, 2007, deseret.com, for a discussion of the challenges inherent in the courtship of such marriages.

15. Rhea to Eduardo, May 1934.

she did not want her family seeing a slouched Mexican with a grim face and less than sparkling teeth—though real white teeth were not common in that era. She had already taken the step of seeing Eduardo's qualities, above all his attentiveness toward her and his commitment to the church, which were two valuable characteristics to a young Mormon woman who sought to create a family much like that of her church-devoted parents and what was preached about in Latter-day Saint society.

The idealism of a potential relationship, however, played itself out in their religion's bubble, where as a woman of God she served her fellow man with her teaching and converting, and he, as a young man who loved the same God, moved the work along with his translating. He was fun to be around, and while their relationship had been slightly unusual—she being a missionary and he a single young man—their actions had been appropriate and open. And were there not some male missionaries bringing home women from their missions—not common then, but still happening? Yet, upon returning to her family and the overwhelming conservative white society of Salt Lake City, Rhea could not help but become overtly conscious of his "Mexicanness," though ironically, neither ever used the term *Mexican* in their letters, though they did talk about living in Mexico.

The word *Mexican* had become a derogatory term quite early in the interactions between whites and those who came from Mexico. It became a particularly difficult descriptor to those who were thus described.[16] Being called a "Mexicano"—that is, describing nationality in Spanish—was not a problem, but in English it was demeaning, and so Mexican Americans developed multiple names to describe themselves that either avoided or "softened" the word: Mexican American, Spanish American, American of Mexican descent, Texan-Mexican, Latin American, and so on. For Mexican Latter-day Saints, it was *the Spanish-speaking* or *Lamanitas*, the term that came out of the Book of Mormon, and one that Eduardo used frequently.

16. See Diana Rojo-García, "'Mexican' is Not a Bad Word," *Free Press*, Mar. 8, 2020, joplinglobe.com, for a light-hearted discussion of the term "Mexican." When I was growing up, and still today, the word *Mexican* as pronounced by a white person seemed to always have a double meaning, one of which was derogatory.

From the earliest letters after her mission, Rhea expressed her love for him. Like any other potential suitor, she sought to improve some aspects of her companion, but in this case, they were each other's advocates to their communities. For Eduardo, the task seemed much easier. She was an ex-missionary in a faith community that depended on the sisters to teach their children and fulfill those duties available for women in the branch. Rhea, as a white LDS woman, was special to a saint community awed by those who brought them the gospel and for the most part still administered their religious life. She was from Salt Lake City, the religion's mecca, from where Mormonism exuded out to the world. But it was not her race or color, per se, but rather her willingness to be there with them when she did not have to, her expression of love and concern for them when many whites did not feel that way, and her desire to live among them as she would for most of her life that endeared her to Eduardo's community.

For Rhea, their relationship posed a different challenge—one that unfolded in each letter, as we see in the letter of June 23, 1934, when the topic of their unusual relationship arose. After asking her whether she loved him, because she had delayed in writing to him for days or possibly weeks, Eduardo inquired, "I wonder if what I said to you isn't coming true." He does not explain what he told her, but it seems obvious, especially when he followed up by expressing concern that "many people" might be telling her "what a mistake it would be if she married" him. Was she caving in to the pressure? He sounded depressed.[17]

By now, he recognized that their relationship pushed against Mormonism's "white grain." While concern with racial mixing had begun many years earlier, it became codified around the time they began dating. The second president of the church, Brigham Young, had at first promoted the saints' intermarriage with people of indigenous background as a way to both assimilate them into the faith and to fulfill the church's obligation to bring the gospel to the Lamanites.[18] Eventually he changed his mind as Mormonism rushed toward

17. Eduardo to Rhea, June 23, 1934.

18. For a view of the LDS Church's ambivalence toward the Lamanites, see Mauss, *All Abraham's Children,* 50–71.

whiteness and acceptability in United States society. Ironically, when the church moved to ban Black saints from the priesthood and temple ordinances, it also intensified its outreach to other, particularly foreign, people of color, but it did so with a clear pecking order.[19]

These saints of color were to remain within their own communities, even as the gospel message was to expand throughout the world. "Separate but equal only over time" became the unofficial but codified strategy after years of practice by church leaders and bureaucrats, a strategy that has come to haunt the church ever since. This, in essence, is what Eduardo and Rhea confronted—and yet their experience, and that of other young missionaries who found love "in all the wrong places," (still rare in their time), had begun punching holes in this racial and ethnic separating wall. Missionaries fell in love with the families they taught across the world and sometimes with their sons and daughters, and as in the case of Eduardo and Rhea, they chose to follow their hearts. Yet, this eventual victory over the forces that sought to limit, if not outright prohibit, racial intermarriage in the church was not certain at the time that Rhea and Eduardo were falling in love, and so the topic continued to intrude in their letters, even if at times mostly in cryptic terms.[20]

This counsel against racial mixing would be explained as a legitimate concern over a couple's ability to overcome the social, cultural, and familial barriers that might arise by marrying a person of a different racial or ethnic group, and sometimes that concern also manifested itself in marrying across class lines. In today's views, however, most of the concerns sound like a justification for keeping the races apart, and maybe more important, for keeping white Latter-day Saints white. Forty-plus years after Rhea and Eduardo were contemplating a life together, one general authority said this about intermarriage:

19. For a discussion of the Mormon effort to be seen as a white community, see W. Paul Reeve, *Religion of a Different Color: Race and the Mormon Struggle for Whiteness* (New York: Oxford University Press, 2015).

20. For the church's views on intermarriage, see Boyd K. Packer, "Follow the Rule," *BYU Speeches*, Jan. 14, 1977, speeches.byu.edu. For a glimpse of the church's racial views, see Mark E. Petersen, "Race Problems—As They Affect the Church," address given at Brigham Young University, Aug. 27, 1954, archiveswest.orbiscacade.org. Also, see Ezra Taft Benson, *Civil Rights, Tool of Communist Deception* (Salt Lake City: Deseret Book Company, 1969), for a look at how some church leaders viewed the fight for equal rights.

> We've always counseled in the church for our Mexican members to marry Mexicans, our Japanese members to marry Japanese, our Caucasians to marry Caucasians, our Polynesian members to marry Polynesians. The counsel has been wise.... You ... might say, "I can show you local leaders or perhaps general leaders who have married out of their race." I say yes—exceptions. Then, I would remind you of that Relief Society woman's near-scriptural statement, "We'd like to follow the rule first and then we'll take care of the exceptions."[21]

This counsel pushed against Rhea and Eduardo's courtship again and again, as we will see.

The couple's letters also dealt with other concerns. More than once Eduardo wondered out loud if he should write to her in Spanish because sometimes his English reflections were "just a jumble of thoughts," and more than once he asked her to forgive his mistakes and ideas.[22] No doubt that worrying or at least thinking about their difference in language, especially as he thought beyond their romantic bubble, made him aware of the other things that made them different from each other. While his letters reveal his command of the English language, his daily hours speaking Spanish for the lumber company in Mexico, his talks, the lessons he gave, and his socializing in the branch all forced him to articulate his thoughts in his native language, and his translating made him think harder about his Spanish and study it more. It must have dawned on him that the Spanish language of translation still left much to be constructed, notwithstanding the translations done before. For years, Eduardo would spend his time editing and at times rewriting what had been translated before.

His letter from June 29, 1934, again revealed that his relationship with Rhea had been unusual for a sister missionary and a person of the opposite sex—not that it revealed anything intimate between them at the time of her mission, but it did hint that their feelings had grown to the point that, a couple of months after her mission, they were speaking about an emotional intimacy. He wished that he could put his head on her lap and wondered "if I will ever get the

21. Packer, "Follow the Rule."
22. Eduardo to Rhea, June 24, 1934.

thrill of feeling your *deditos* (fingers) on my forehead."[23] He could fill, he wrote, two to four pages with "I love you and miss you." It was getting harder, he emphasized, to bear their separation, and he admitted that he constantly felt the "blues" being away from her. Still, he was trying to do what she asked of him, such as straightening his back, and he happily told her that after a dance his mother had said that he was "much straighter" than he was before.[24]

The same letter confirms that one of the things that united them was their commitment to the youth of the church. In the letter, he told her about a youth conference in which he "elected to arrange all the details," where the youth in the branch were to "compete in drama, dancing, singing, public speaking, and basketball." He was "thrilled," he wrote, "plain crazy with joy," and he asked her to meet him "there" with "there" being Mesa, Arizona, a place that became a gathering ground for Mexican Mormon youth activities.[25] No doubt these youth conferences took their cue from the larger "road shows," sporting events, and other cultural activities that became part of the larger Latter-day Saint community's communal gatherings, often meant to get young people together so as to have them eventually pair up to create eternal families.

Rhea, who became a big part of Eduardo's mutual activities in his branch, wrote on July 1, 1934, that she had bought him some books that he needed for MIA. These would be part of the material that she sent him throughout their time apart that he used in creating activities for the young people of the branch.[26] She sent him music sheets and operettas, and often suggested plays he could translate and put on during those youth activities. Here again was the mixing and matching of American material with Mexican cultural traits. While translation itself did not make these songs, operettas, and other materials Mexican, the way they were adapted to the youth's abilities and to Eduardo's direction—and he had little training or experience in American social activities—allowed these "American" works to become Mexicanized in the minds of the youth who

23. Eduardo to Rhea.
24. Eduardo to Rhea.
25. Eduardo to Rhea.
26. Rhea to Eduardo, July 1, 1934.

took part as well as the audiences that watched and listened, many of them immigrants themselves also trying to find their niche in American society.

The concern for the Mexican youth of the church became a common theme during the couple's correspondence. No doubt that Rhea helped him fulfill his assignments as MIA president because of her love for him, but she also seemed to enjoy the arts in church and cared about the Mexican youth. We see this when, shortly after returning to Salt Lake City, she began attending services in the Mexican branch and even taught one of the unit's youth classes.

Eduardo's letter five days after Rhea wrote him about the books underscored how his translation efforts for the mission took more and more of his time, and no doubt his passion.[27] "I've been helping Pres. [Harold] Pratt all day translating some new tracts [missionary lessons], and I'm so tired, I can hardly keep my eyes open," he wrote, adding that he worked through Sunday School and almost gave in to the temptation to miss all the other Sunday meetings. "But we decided to stop till tomorrow night."[28] These translating marathons were invaluable to Eduardo, but they often came at a cost as he worked full time with the lumber company and he had his plate full of MIA activities, which he enjoyed immensely. The translation work gave him an opportunity to give back to the church he loved and a chance to work alongside a man he saw as a father figure—much like he had with Rey L. Pratt. "Bro & Sis Prat [*sic*] sure are nice to me. I could almost think they were my papa and mama if they were a bit older," he wrote.[29]

He added that his boss (Brother Pierce) was another person "that's been so swell and nice to me."[30] What he most liked about him and his coworkers, most of them white, he said, was that they did not meddle in his business, particularly in his desire to marry a white woman. "They don't try to tell me about what a mistake we're going to make by marrying, or anything like that."[31] Or at least, he added, not around him. There is no doubt that for Eduardo, talking

27. Eduardo to Rhea, July 6, 1934.
28. Eduardo to Rhea.
29. Eduardo to Rhea.
30. Eduardo to Rhea.
31. Eduardo to Rhea.

about Rhea and telling the world about her caring for him would have been a joy, and undoubtedly he told friends in his small branch about Rhea and he discussed his feelings for her with his parents. But outside that small sphere of understanding individuals, talking about their relationship brought the possibility of criticism or unwanted advice. It was still difficult in the 1930s to talk about mixed marriages, particularly among Latter-day Saints who continued to develop a more rigid opinion about race mixing.

Two days later, Eduardo received a letter from Rhea where she told him that she spoke at the Mexican branch, or as she put it, "I gave them a little diddy,"[32] by which she probably meant a short talk. She gave the talk in English to a congregation that had only a few who could speak the language. "I'm getting worse," she wrote, which presumably meant that she was losing her Spanish fluency, something that she never really acquired on her mission.[33] Years later, her son Daniel referred to her poor Spanish skills as one reason none of the Balderas children learned the language. At the same time, she spent much of her life, except for the later years, in Spanish-language branches and wards, so she must have been more than capable of holding a conversation with Spanish speakers.

Rhea was proud of herself for speaking at the branch, and she wrote that Roberto and Rositta [*sic*] had been there, and they would later report on her performance—or at least Roberto, who seems to have corresponded with Eduardo and appeared in her letters quite often. Roberto also spoke at the sacrament meeting, but he did so in Spanish and probably teased her about it.[34] She, no doubt, felt comfortable among the Mexican saints, and they welcomed her with open arms, a trait that remains today in Mexican and now Latina/o wards and branches. It is no secret that saints of color appreciate the way some white members learn the language and enjoy worshipping alongside them.

Her letter then gets serious as she speaks around a "certain subject." That subject was their marriage, though she never uses the word in the letter. She had thought a lot about it, she writes, but does not

32. Rhea to Eduardo, July 8, 1934.
33. Rhea to Eduardo.
34. Rhea to Eduardo.

want him to "dream too much" about it. "I'll always be yours," she added. She then mentions a bracelet that he gave her that someone else had taken and asks him to send her another, but then maybe not if he has no money, she adds, which he needed to buy a car. Then she writes that things were "what I thought they'd be" at home. From the letters, it is obvious that she loves her mother and father, but she expresses disappointment with them. "Honey, I guess I shouldn't have had the mother and father ..." She does not finish the sentence but instead adds, "and my dad shouldn't hold the position he does in the church." It was hard on her, she wrote, but she was not going to give up on their relationship or be miserable. "We were both meant to be happy," she wrote, but she still could not come to see him "until [she had] permission."[35]

As expected, Eduardo did not receive the news well, but his response indicates he understood how difficult their predicament was. "It gets ... harder to be away from you," he wrote in the opening line of his response. The waiting for a response to a wedding date had now become complicated as he learned of Rhea's parents' attitude toward her relationship with him. Being far away now had him simply "waiting, waiting," unable to do anything including talk to them in person, though he probably thought that if the impression he made on them when he first visited did not open their hearts to their potential son-in-law, what would? It could get worse before it became better.[36]

Eduardo, however, could not just focus on his relationship to carry him through the day. Revealing an ecumenical side that served him throughout his life, he told her about his contacts with Protestant churches in the area. Early on, Mexican immigrants and Mexican Americans still saw their ethnic solidarity much stronger than their religious ones, though that would end as the competition for souls became more intense. "We went to the big Mexican Baptist church downtown and sang for them," wrote Eduardo, and he continued, "I think we did pretty good tho [*sic*] the kids realize now just how much practice means ... they'd be better along that line from now on."[37]

35. Rhea to Eduardo, July 8.
36. Eduardo to Rhea, July 15, 1934.
37. Eduardo to Rhea.

He wrote about the MIA: "I got the music for our contest songs and, dear, you should hear them. They are arranged so beautifully and have the prettiest harmony! I'm sure glad I chose them. The [way] they are worked up, I think they'll be beautiful."[38] For Latter-day Saint members today, it is difficult to understand how important a part the MIA played in the life of the church, its youth, and particularly its ethnic youth. For white church leaders, it might have all been for the purpose of bringing them closer to the body of the church, but for individuals like Eduardo, all of these activities simply allowed them to create their own space in which they could help the youth practice their lives as Mexican Mormons. Yes, some of the activities tied them to white youth in the church, but the bond was mostly about proximity and did not assimilate them to the extent that they lost their ethnicity or cultural identity. Ironically, the efforts to assimilate them often served to develop among them a Mexican identity on this side of the border.[39]

For Eduardo, it is likely—and we have no documents to confirm or deny this view—that his work in the MIA set the standard for what he would spend the rest of his life trying to do in the church. It was about finding a niche in the Mormon world that bound his people to the rest of the church but did not eliminate their differences. Being bilingual, even bicultural, within the church was not for Eduardo a temporary stage on the road to total assimilation. While his own children would make the full transition—partly because, like many other Mexican American parents of his generation and others since, he struggled to prevent it—his work in the Mexican branches underscores that he did not believe that others had to do so to that extent.

The discussion of what others thought of Eduardo and Rhea's relationship, especially her parents, came up again in a letter from Rhea that had the same date (July 15, 1934), indicating that both were thinking the same thing and acknowledging that their relationship was being strained. Rhea responded to Eduardo's question of

38. Eduardo to Rhea.

39. I remember my own time in mutual in which all the American activities were practiced and understood within the context of us being Mexican, living in the barrio, and treated as different in the larger society.

whether there was any hope in their relationship: "I think we talked that over," she said, seemingly vexed by his insistence on knowing when she would marry him. "I love you to the bone," she wrote, and then shifted to talk about her parents. She told him that her parents thought that he "was one in a thousand."[40] They praised him. Though she did not say it, she must have realized that what they said about him was probably what many LDS families might say about a young man who joined the church, seemed particularly nice, and was devout. At the same time, he was from another racial group, and his life meant little to their own, unless he married their daughter.

"When the ring came," she wrote, probably referring to a call from him, "I told them I intended or wanted to go back to you.[41] Then, there was a 'scene.' I don't think I have to go into detail. But when it came down right to it, the only reason they could give was the one you spoke of, and they are ever changing their opinion there, and finances."[42] "Finances" probably meant they did not think Eduardo could provide their daughter the life she was accustomed to. Her mother also brought up the point about Eduardo "living in Mexico."[43] "I don't care," she continued, "what the rest of the world thinks ... but mother and father will always be mother and father. If I couldn't come home when I wanted and feel at home ... we [will] just have to wait a while longer and I know how that makes you feel."[44]

For the first time in their correspondence, Rhea revealed an exasperation with their situation and her inability to give Eduardo a straight answer to his questions about marriage. She told him, "If you want to quit and have found somebody you love, I ... can't stop you." But she added that she did not want him to marry "for spite" and reiterated her love for him.[45] At the moment, there seemed to be no way forward for them given that her parents were going to take time to come around, or they might not, and she did not want to marry without their consent. Though she would imply, in prior

40. Rhea to Eduardo, July 15, 1934.

41. It is also possible that she meant a ring that she would mention later as having been lost or taken and not returned by an acquaintance.

42. Rhea to Eduardo, July 15, 1934.

43. Rhea to Eduardo.

44. Rhea to Eduardo.

45. Rhea to Eduardo.

letters, her willingness to marry without their permission, she knew it would be extremely difficult to do so. Also, losing the familial ties and not being a part of an extended LDS family was something no good Mormon woman wanted.

She then added a line that is hard to decipher. "Sometime, if you want to tell Pres & Sister Pratt that it isn't ok I don't care, because they will find it out sooner or later, and you never told me what Anderson said?" Not having explained what "it" was, it is hard to know what thought she was transitioning to. It might have been that Eduardo could tell the Pratts that their relationship was over, or that they were in love no matter what the president and his wife thought —we do not know. The question about Anderson (another of Eduardo's bosses) was surely about what he thought of their relationship, as Eduardo had likely told him about it since he worked with him.[46]

But the letter was not all bad news for Eduardo. "I think I told you about them asking me to work in the mutual of the branch. Mother is sure glad, she says, and she also said she'd like to go with me sometime."[47] Rhea assumed by then that Eduardo wanted to attend a Spanish branch when and if they got married. He was at the branch because his father was branch president and he was working in the MIA. At the same time, notwithstanding his comfort in working with white Latter-day Saints, he probably felt that his chances of receiving callings (church assignments) were less likely in white wards and branches. Or, most likely, he simply felt more comfortable among his own people. Having Rhea attending and assisting in the Salt Lake City Mexican branch must have had him thinking of when one day they would both be serving in a Spanish branch or ward.

The topic of what others thought about their relationship did not stop coming up because others did not stop bringing it up. In a letter dated August 5, 1934, Rhea wrote, "I wish you were here honey where I could talk things over and get them off my chest." She had preceded that line by saying that she was "sure mad at somebody." It seems that in a gathering of friends, several individuals brought up Eduardo's name and what they said upset Rhea, though she never spells it out for him. "Even little quiet Elaine Hulse," she wrote, "told

46. Rhea to Eduardo.

47. Rhea to Eduardo.

me ... many things I wish she'd kept to herself." Then she added that they talked about the "trouble he had at one time," though she did not specify what that was, but she was upset that "all know about it." It is most likely that it was about one of his former girlfriends, one named Elena.

Nothing more is said about Elena or what other diamond ring besides Rhea's Eduardo had given out. He might well have proposed to someone else before he met Rhea. Most offensive to her, it seems, is that her friends brought up the question of whether he was hoping to marry her because she was "an American girl especially an L. M. [lady missionary]." She had once asked Eduardo that herself. His response, according to her letter, was that he was, and was "even [willing to] give up a Mexican girl." "I never ... realized until Sunday how much you desire to [wed a white woman]," she wrote.[48]

Unfortunately, we have no letters available from Eduardo responding to her questions and concerns. In fact, we have no letters from Eduardo until more than two months later, in October. How did he respond? Did he try to clarify or justify his supposed answer to her about marrying a white woman? Was he simply trying to impress her by saying he was willing to give or give up anything for her? Was that a conversation between two lovers that could only be understood within the context of their relationship? Lastly, would it make any difference if he had a preference for a particular kind of woman?

Rhea must have understood that her letter upset him because one week later she apologized: "I'm so sorry I wrote last week's letter the way I did. I often wonder ... just where I'm going to land."[49] This latter phrase no doubt revealed her anxiety over the standstill of their relations. It dawned on her that their love remained complicated in the eyes of her family and some of her friends. She recounted a dream she had. She was on a swing and as she swung, she kept saying, "I don't know, I don't know," to which she added, "Honey, I don't either."[50]

Rhea also wrote about the stake president and a member of the women's mutual organization who came to her house to ask her to

48. Rhea to Eduardo, Aug. 5, 1934.
49. Rhea to Eduardo, Aug. 12, 1934.
50. Rhea to Eduardo.

serve on the mutual stake board, to which she responded, "I already had a job [calling]. I was going to work at the branch." She then mentions having a "scene" and the stake president telling her she was needed more in the stake board than in the branch and gave her a few days to respond to the call. The stake president also told her that she would not be released from her current calling in the ward Sunday School. "So what am I going to do?" she asks Eduardo. She wanted to work at the branch even if "everyone says no." Eventually, Rhea worked it out to where she could work in both callings, twice a month on each, mostly taking care of activities.[51]

On August 29, she mentions a letter from Eduardo that might have been an answer to her letter on August 5. "I guess I had it coming to me," she wrote, and added, "I've read and reread it for just one sweet word like you usually write but it wasn't there." Whatever he told her, she thought it was "uncalled for" but then she asked, "Forgive me?"[52] She went on to write about trying to get him some music sheets and a drama book for his mutual activities. Through their correspondence, it was clear that she supported him in his work in MIA and tried to get him the latest plays and music sheets and even had others looking for good musical pieces to send him. It is also likely that she became involved not only in teaching in the branch's MIA but participating in its activities.

As we see in his letter of October 28, 1934, not everyone in Eduardo's family supported his efforts to get the youth in the branch involved in all kinds of activities. Apolinar, still the branch president, did not like him taking the "kids for activities," and threatened to go to President Pratt and resign. He added, "He wants them for local missionary work."[53] This disagreement between Eduardo and his father over the role of youth in the church had been going on for more than a year, and Eduardo believed this difference had hampered his work with the youth. He wrote Rhea that he felt tired and disappointed and said, "If I had my way … I'd just drop everything and let somebody else do the worrying for a while."[54]

51. Rhea to Eduardo, Sep. 9, 1934.
52. Rhea to Eduardo, Aug. 29, 1934.
53. Eduardo to Rhea, Oct. 28, 1934.
54. Eduardo to Rhea.

One week later, Eduardo felt much better, and a good reason for this was his translating for Elder John Widtsoe, a member of the Quorum of the Twelve, who toured the mission. Eduardo wrote, "I translated his talk in the morning, his wife's … in the afternoon, and his talk again at night."[55] He felt pleased for being in the spotlight as much as the visiting authority. Little did Eduardo know that this was a practice run for all the in-person translating that he would do for church authorities over the years. This kind of translating—standing next to the speaker without notes and without much time to think of the corresponding word or phrase—was, he told an interviewer years later, initially his favorite way of doing the work of translation. No other experience forced him to study, ponder and prepare as did the instant translation. Just as important, it made him feel a part of spiritual teaching moments that he would not be privy to without translating, given his lack of leadership opportunities.

In a letter on November 8, 1934, Eduardo informed Rhea that he'd taken a step up in his job at the lumber company and would now be supervising two individuals, allowing him more flexibility in his scheduling, which he hoped to use in visiting her in the spring. By the following month, he had a job offer that paid him as much, but it was in Mexico. Hs father had recently returned to El Paso from Mexico City, where he had spent some time looking at the possibility of moving down there.[56] Like many other Mexican immigrants, he did not know what to expect in the United States as the Depression grew more widespread, and many Mexicans were being deported while the Mexican government of Lazaro Cardenas offered returning Mexicans jobs and lands. According to Eduardo, Apolinar liked what he saw in Mexico City, and soon enough he had his whole family ready to go, with the exception of Eduardo, who still clung to the hope of marrying Rhea in 1935.

President Pratt had found Eduardo a job in Mexico and wanted him to assume leadership of all the mutual work in the country. "You have no idea how bad he wants me to go down there," he wrote. "If you are coming with me, you'll sure have your hands full of mutual

55. Eduardo to Rhea, Nov. 4, 1934.
56. Eduardo to Rhea, Dec. 2, 1934.

work, would you care?"[57] In the letter, Eduardo reveals his desire to serve the church in Mexico, especially with Rhea by his side. "It just thrills me to think of working down there," he added. While no countrywide mutual leadership calling existed in the Mexican church, President Pratt would create one if he could get Eduardo down there. Pratt understood that Mexico needed native leadership, and he had confidence that Eduardo had been trained well enough to provide that leadership. Just as important, he had seen what Eduardo had done with the youth in El Paso.

Beyond keeping the youth busy and out of the streets, Eduardo had created a program that taught the youth to prepare, to stand up before an audience, to memorize lines, and to be fully engaged in activities that often took months to plan and execute. The Mexican church needed that kind of training and experience for young men and women who would one day serve missions and then return and provide leadership to their own congregations. Eduardo had exhibited an ability to take a calling with little instruction and few resources and make it function in ways not usual outside of Salt Lake City. It would be a brief preview of what he would do in the work of translation in the future, also with little instruction and few resources.

In his letter of December 30, he told Rhea that President Pratt wished him the best of luck in his relationship with a "wonderful girl." By now a small but growing group of people knew of his relationship, and in his earlier letters it is obvious that even those individuals close to him had their doubts about their relationship.[58] This uncertainty about their "happiness" frustrated Rhea, and she told him that they might have been born with the "wrong families," though she writes that her mother was satisfied that she would be happy. She makes no mention of her father.[59] In the same correspondence, she tells Eduardo that she is enclosing a letter from Elder Widtsoe and writes, "He must think lots of you." She showed it to her parents, she wrote, and they thought, "it was grand."

We have no copy of the letter from Elder Widtsoe, but the fact that he wrote to Rhea indicates that he got to know Eduardo well

57. Eduardo to Rhea.
58. Eduardo to Rhea.
59. Rhea to Eduardo, Dec. 31, 1934.

enough to learn about his relationship with her. Since she described his letter as "nice," it is reasonable to assume that it revealed no qualms about her relationship with Eduardo. While Widtsoe did not spend more than a few days with Eduardo, he recognized that the young man was the type of person that the church wanted to develop among its nonwhite members. He was impressive in his abilities to translate but also knew how to comport himself among church leaders, a trait that took some saints many years to foster, and some never did. Protocol is important to Latter-day Saints because it is a way to develop a sophistication that other churches transmit through their seminaries and divinity schools.

In her letter of February 10, 1935, she noted that Pratt came to Salt Lake City but had not come to see her. Whether this meant that he had visited her before during his trips to church headquarters, we do not know, but if he did, or if he communicated with her before, it was obvious why he did not at this time—he wasn't going to change anyone's mind. "I would like to have talked with him. He can't change my mind now I don't believe but I would like to have seen him anyway."[60] We can only assume that in spite of the nice words he had said about them earlier, there was still the feeling, at least for Rhea, that he was not fully convinced their marriage was the right thing. Those qualms might well have been about protecting them from the backlash of a mixed marriage, or simply his belief, shared by many church leaders, that their interracial marriage went against church preaching.

On the same day she was writing her letter, Eduardo was addressing one to her. In it, he mentioned that Pratt was going to ask the presiding bishopric to employ someone to translate the "lessons"—most likely the missionary lessons or possibly the lessons taught in Sunday School or in priesthood meetings. Pratt probably told him that if the position came about, he would be hired, and he was already contemplating doing the work in the evening after his present job. He and Pratt had started working on a translation of the Doctrine and Covenants, or better said, a brief selection of it. He envisioned having the work printed by May, and "then after …

60. Rhea to Eduardo, Feb. 10, 1935.

there's the Articles of Faith. Your boy is trying to keep pretty busy."[61] Those two works were the LDS Church's scriptural contributions to the Christian world, and, at the time, the two most responsible for deeper doctrine and church organizational structure.

In a subsequent letter, he wrote about "spending all night" with Pratt on an outline in Spanish of the "work and organization" of the church. "We discovered ... that neither of us knows the Spanish language. It ... made us laugh to discover that some of the things that we have said all of the time were wrong." He then added, "If I could do every day what I did today, I sure would learn a lot about the Spanish language."[62] It was on-the-job training, and little did Eduardo know that would be his technique and approach years later as he undertook the translation of the church's literature without training and without a university degree. In this, he would follow the path that many church leaders, extending as far back as Joseph Smith, would take in writing about and in leading the church for nearly the first hundred years.

There are other letters between Rhea and Eduardo, including a couple from after they were married, but most of them are about their seeing each other soon—a "soon" that kept being pushed back—about his work in mutual, about their friends, his translation efforts, and his father's health, as well as Pratt's insistence on him moving to Mexico City and taking over as branch president. What is clear from the letters is that Rhea and Eduardo were deeply in love and that love would last a lifetime. They battled prejudices, separation, and some insecurities, but they never wavered in their love for each other.

61. Eduardo to Rhea, Feb. 10, 1935.
62. Eduardo to Rhea, Mar. 24, 1935.

5

CALLED TO SERVE IN ZION

THE CHURCH OFFERS A JOB, BUT EDUARDO ACCEPTS A CALLING

We have seen from their letters that both Rhea and Eduardo confronted skepticism that their marriage would work, or that it was even appropriate. Where they did not initially expect resistance to their eternal union was from the leaders they served. Mexican Mission president Harold W. Pratt, who succeeded Rey L. Pratt and worked closely with Eduardo on numerous translations, "told me he had some misgivings," remembered Eduardo years later.[1] Rhea confided to Eduardo that when Antoine R. Ivins, her former mission president, now a resident of Salt Lake City, heard about their engagement, he tried to discourage her from marrying him.[2] While not directly speaking to those efforts, Eduardo later categorized resistance to interracial marriages as "ignorance" [by] those "not acquainted with people from other countries."[3] Of course, this rationalization could not have applied to either Pratt, who was born in the Mexican Mormon colonies, or Ivins, who studied law in Mexico City and ran the church's sugar plantations in Laie, Hawaii, from 1921 to 1931 before taking over the mission presidency in 1931.[4]

Notwithstanding those and possibly other efforts to keep them apart, Eduardo and Rhea were sealed on October 10, 1935, in the Mesa Arizona Temple, a surprising occurrence given that her parents

1. Eduardo Balderas, Oral History, interviews by Gordon Irving, 1973, typescript, 36, Oral History Program, CHL.

2. Balderas, Oral History.

3. Balderas, Oral History, 37.

4. Antoine R. Ivins, Introductory notes, 1931, box 1, fds. 1–4, ACCN 1541, Antoine R. Ivins Papers, J. Willard Marriott Library Special Collections, University of Utah.

were in Salt Lake City and his own family had been sealed there.[5] The Arizona temple, however, was closer, and Eduardo knew the city better, having participated there in a number of youth activities. Mesa also had the next largest Mexican Mormon population and had one of the newest temples, and one dedicated to the work to be done among the Lamanite people. Whether Eduardo fully understood that the church leaders had actually meant the Native American saints, we do not know, but we do know that over time, the Mesa Temple became the temple for saints from Mexico, Central America, and the Spanish speaking of the southwestern part of the United States.[6]

Three years after their marriage, Eduardo took over as president of the South El Paso Branch, which, shortly after, was closed and he became president of La Rama de El Paso de la Misión Hispano Americana, and Rhea became a counselor in the branch's Relief Society. We have little record of his time as branch president, which lasted a little over a year, but his brother Guillermo remembers Eduardo starting a landscaping project to beautify the grounds of a new chapel built for the branch members that numbered around seventy-five to one hundred individuals. He also organized the branch's home teaching program, which assigned priesthood holders to visit members at their homes to provide them a lesson or assist them in whatever spiritual challenges they might have.[7]

Eduardo felt proud of the new chapel, which gave them a home for a more enhanced youth program and for sporting events, two things that he loved to be part of. He believed that the building of the new chapel was "a big event in the lives of the members of the branch, to have their own building."[8] He also believed that the missionary effort improved as the missionaries did not need to apologize to those they taught as they had before when they brought

5. See, Maricopa County, Arizona, marriage certificate no. 532 (1935), Balderas–Ross, Clerk of Superior Court, Phoenix. Being "sealed" is the Latter-day Saint term for marriage—for time and all eternity—performed in one of their temples.

6. Richard O. Cowan, "The Historic Arizona Temple," *Journal of Mormon History* 31, no. 1 (Spring 2005): 99–118. See also Henry A. Smith, "200 Lamanites Gather in History-Making Conference, Temple Sessions," *Church News*, Nov. 10, 1945.

7. See Balderas, Oral History, 33; and Guillermo Balderas, "Historia," Balderas Family, Balderas Family Scrapbooks, 1910–1911, 303–7, Oral History Program, CHL.

8. Balderas, Oral History, 33.

them to rented halls, which often smelled of alcohol or cigarettes. Now they would come to a small but clean chapel with classrooms and grass and flowers.[9]

Eduardo got a glimpse of the value of his future work of translating church material when he learned that no manual of instruction existed for branch presidents. Leaders outside of Utah, like Eduardo, often did what they saw their own leaders do or what they heard from the pulpit in the numerous conferences and meetings they attended. The Latter-day Saint bubble had its own ways of leadership, but those congregations outside of the region, and even those in other countries, were supposed to be administered, led, and directed by the young missionaries from the homeland, mission presidents like Pratt, or, if led by local leaders, be supervised by visiting authorities. Latter-day Saint leadership, except in the most extreme cases or in lands far away, remained in white hands, and this was made possible by a lack of written material governing church units, which then meant these units had to depend on experience and already acquired knowledge.

In Eduardo's case, he learned his Mormonism under the watchful eye of three mission presidents: Rey Lucero Pratt, then Antoine Ridgway Ivins, and finally Harold W. Pratt. Still, given the amount of work and travel these presidents did, little formal instruction was ever given. This often meant that the leaders of congregations outside of Utah, both white and other, had to figure out the needs of their members and then teach them what they themselves knew. For Latina/o or Mexican congregations, it also meant that leaders looked around to see what other congregations were doing and also quietly mimicked what they saw in Catholic parishes or in the few Mexican Protestant congregations that existed at the time. Already, we've seen in his letters to Rhea that Eduardo had made contact with other Protestant churches and even had his MIA boys sing at their services. While many of these Protestant groups were often hostile to Mormons there were some who probably found a closer affinity to their fellow Mexican and Mexican American Latter-day Saints than they did to their white congregations, given the discrimination they encountered both inside and outside the church.

9. Balderas, Oral History.

While many of these Protestant congregations were led by mostly non-degreed individuals, these ministers and pastors were more likely to have some kind of ministerial training, could often dedicate full time or at least more time to their congregations, and had more autonomy. The looser hierarchical structure allowed them an opportunity to grow by trial and error. Mexican Protestants, quite early, began to develop their "Hispanic Ministry," which allowed them to see themselves not as attachments to their white counterparts but as their own community of worshippers. This did not mean that their ministries were devoid of conflict or interference from their white leaders, especially if they were affiliated with one of the larger Protestant groups, but it did give them more elbow room than existed in the Latter-day Saint Mexican congregations, especially those that belonged to a mission.[10]

Eduardo seemed content to perform his duties in whichever capacity he was needed. Of course, it might have been quite obvious to him that the Latter-day Saint pecking order was difficult for anyone not connected to Salt Lake City church elites or who did not have a distinguishing feature, be it religious, economic, or familial. By every indication, Eduardo was a humble man, ever willing to be serviceable and seemly content, though not complacent, with what life brought him. This may be one reason that President Pratt took a strong liking to him. Unlike the other disciple that Pratt knew well, Margarito Bautista, Eduardo did not challenge Pratt's view of how Mexican converts were to act.[11]

Bautista, a much more charismatic and forceful proponent of the LDS gospel than Eduardo, and which was noted earlier, converted in Mexico but lived in the United States for a number of years and believed that the Lamanites—Spanish-speaking converts—were

10. See Juan Francisco Martínez, *Sea La Luz: The Making of Mexican Protestantism in the American Southwest, 1829–1900* (Denton: University of North Texas Press, 2006) for a discussion of Mexican Protestantism in the early years. Also, see Michael O. Emerson and Christian Smith, *Divided By Faith: Evangelical Religion and the Problem of Race in America* (New York: Oxford University Press, 2000) and Arlene M. Sánchez Walsh, *Latino Pentecostal Identity: Evangelical Faith, Self, and Society* (New York: Columbia University Press, 2003).

11. See Elisa Eastwood Pulido, *The Spiritual Evolution of Margarito Bautista: Mexican Mormon Evangelizer, Polygamist Dissident, and Utopian Founder, 1878–1961* (New York: Oxford University Press, 2020), 93–95, 108.

now ready to lead themselves and that white church members needed to step aside. In his view, white missionaries were preaching about the blossoming of the Lamanites and yet did not allow them to lead themselves. Bautista believed Pratt suffered from the same misconception that many foreign missionaries did: converts were to be nurtured and led until sometime in the future when they could govern themselves. This paternalistic view, often couched in love—and many times sincerely—had nothing to offer men like Bautista (and one might say even Balderas), who were particularly bright, committed wholeheartedly to the Latter-day Saint gospel, and ready to lead their people.

While Eduardo always seemed intent on fulfilling his duties as defined by his leaders, he proved innovative in his work and understood the importance of providing church literature to his people. We know little about his translation work in the church before he went on a mission, but we do know that once on his mission, he began translating church content. At first, he began with proselyting materials—probably pamphlets and tracts, to the extent that there were any—and some commonly used scripture citations. Eventually, he helped President (Rey L.) Pratt translate material that the latter wrote. According to an article in the *Deseret News*, Eduardo helped Pratt revise the first edition of the Book of Mormon translation in 1931.[12] Unfortunately, we do not know much else about this effort nor about Eduardo's actual part in the translation, but Pratt must have seen his abilities even then. When Rey L. Pratt died in 1931, he and Eduardo were working on translating the Doctrine and Covenants.[13] Later, President Ivins finished the partial translation, and it was published shortly after as selections from the Doctrine and Covenants. Eduardo continued to do work on translating with Harold W. Pratt, though we know little of that work.

Coming to Salt Lake City, the mecca, or Zion as Mormons called it, offered Eduardo a new experience, one that no doubt greatly influenced the way he translated. It was in Utah, among the church hierarchy, that Eduardo saw the magnitude of the work, and probably

12. See Trent Toone, "Book of Mormon Translation in Spanish: Help from Above to Make It Right," *Deseret News*, Feb. 23, 2012.

13. See Balderas, Oral History, 43–44.

even more than his leaders, how his work had the potential to impact the religious lives of the Spanish-speaking people. He understood, from his missionary experience and that of his own family and the small congregation to which he belonged both as a young convert and a branch president, how a good translation of the gospel message could enhance the church's work. More importantly, he knew how that message, translated into their own language, could enhance the growth and maturity of his Mexican saint community.

Rhea, as a counselor in the Relief Society, proved a significant help to Eduardo. She knew how the church functioned in Salt Lake City and had experienced life in a more established Mexican branch there, where she was active in teaching the youth and participating in mutual activities. Eduardo leaned on her knowledge and experience as well as his own ideas about how the church functioned, which he developed while working closely with three mission presidents. The women in the branch, no doubt spurred by Rhea's leadership, proved particularly valuable to the branch's function. They visited families, provided nourishment to those ill, taught classes, and at times even served as branch clerks, helping to count the tithing money, keep membership records, and serve in whatever capacity they were assigned.[14]

Eduardo and Rhea's life changed dramatically, however, when in a letter dated July 3, 1939, Antoine R. Ivins informed Eduardo that the First Presidency of the church had approved the creation of a "bureau or office" to "do … translating," and he had been suggested as "a suitable person" to do the work under his [Ivin's] supervision.[15] Ivins offered him the job but told him it would pay one hundred dollars a month "without much chance of increase" and be authorized for only one year, with a possibility of extension but also of termination "for any of several reasons."[16] Ivins does not mention who suggested Edu-

14. We will see this in the discussion of the Rama Mexicana in Salt Lake City, and I have experienced this in my life-long attendance in Mexican and Latina/o units. My own wife proved to be particularly helpful when I served as bishop twice. She connected with women who were less likely to come to their bishop, and she mobilized them to help in all the ward's activities and service projects. She learned this in her own ward as an adult convert and from more experienced women who had been doing these things most of their lives. See Balderas, "Historia," 297, for an example of women serving as clerks.

15. Antoine R. Ivins to Eduardo, July 3, 1939, from private collection in possession of Eduardo's daughter Ana.

16. Ivins to Eduardo, July 3.

ardo, but it is possible that it was Ivins himself, as he had worked with Eduardo on translating some mission literature. It is also possible that they asked Harold W. Pratt, who at the time was also working with Eduardo on translating mission material. It could also have been any one of the church authorities who visited the mission and were impressed with Eduardo's translation of their talks.

On July 8, Eduardo responded in the affirmative, saying he felt grateful for being "considered worthy to fill the position offered me."[17] While others, including church officials, saw this as a job, Eduardo saw it as a call to serve in the spiritual work of the church and would feel that way throughout his time as a translator. Back then (and often still today) many Latter-day Saints saw working for the church as a calling to serve the kingdom of God. For Eduardo, it was a culmination of his years translating for the mission and for visiting authorities. He often spent numerous hours translating during the week and sometimes a full weekend to get material ready at a moment's notice. The idea of working full time as translator and the opportunity to rub elbows with the church's leading authorities was a dream come true, whether he had ever thought about it or not. It is, however, likely that he did as he once mentioned to Rhea that Rey L. Pratt had also talked to him about assuming a translator's role for the church, though nothing came of the idea then.

At the time the job was offered, Rhea and Eduardo had just had their first child, Marta Nancy, and would be unable to travel for at least six weeks. However, given that Rhea's sister was visiting until the latter part of August, and Eduardo's employer (Brother Pierce) had consented to him leaving "any time you [Ivins] may call him," Eduardo announced himself ready to assume his duties. He only asked for an idea, *mas o menos*, of when the job might become available. Later, he would tell an interviewer that Rhea was all for going home.[18] Already, in a letter to her folks, Rhea had expressed a desire to be near them, feeling frustrated with the work of being a wife and mother with a husband gone for stretches of time doing unpaid translating work and having no one in her family to spend time with.

17. Eduardo to Ivins, July 8, 1939, from private collection in possession of Eduardo's daughter Ana.

18. Balderas, Oral History, 38.

Rhea never expressed any misgivings about living on the border and associating mostly with Mexicans and Mexican Americans, but no doubt she missed her own people.[19]

By 1939, when he arrived in Salt Lake City, the Spanish-speaking church found itself in crisis in Mexico and to some extent in Utah's Spanish-speaking Latter-day Saint world. A third of the church in Mexico had broken away from the LDS Church nearly four years earlier. The break had come over the issue of native leadership in the church in Mexico, but probably just as significant, it had to do with the role of the Lamanite in the church. This "revolutionary moment," which lasted until 1945, impacted Mexican saints profoundly and accentuated the Book of Mormon stories in ways that white leaders could not imagine.

Intellectuals like Bautista and other Third Convention leaders saw in the Mexican revolution and its indigenous underpinnings the dawning of the promises that the indigenous people of Mexico—especially those who were converted, and thus Lamanites—would blossom as a rose and fulfill their existence as a people. One part of this fulfillment meant native leadership in Mexico, and this was seen as not only necessary because there were now Mexican LDS leaders but also because Mexican law forbade foreign ecclesiastical leadership. The church got around the law by calling Harold W. Pratt from the Mormon colonies in northern Mexico as a leader, who though white was technically a Mexican citizen. When Pratt left Mexico because of the dangers it posed to Americans and other foreigners, the Mexican saints fended for themselves for about three years, not only developing their own leaders but Mexicanizing part of the worship services as best they could without manuals and fully translated scriptures.[20]

---

19. Rhea to her parents, Feb. 9, 1936, from private collection in possession of Eduardo's daughter Ana. Rhea writes about how tough it is to keep the house clean and that she misses them. She reiterates her love for Eduardo and, in fact, lets him write some things at the end of the letter.

20. See Pulido, *Spiritual Evolution of Margarito Bautista*, 157–67, 170–79; also see Aidan Caplan and Tristan Caplan, "Expulsion and Reconciliation with the Mexican Saints: The Third Convention, 1936–1946," *Journal of Mormon History* 47, no. 2 (Apr. 2021): 75–100; and for a more friendly article to the church, see F. Lamond Tullis, "A Shepherd to Mexico's Saints: Arwell L. Pierce and the Third Convention," *BYU Studies* 37, no. 1 (1997): 127–57.

The disagreement over leadership lasted ten years and revealed the church's effort to not only retain administrative control but to set the timetable as to the "blossoming," a timetable that yet remained ambiguous and in the church's control. By 1935, however, Bautista and others were claiming that the "blossoming" had arrived, and white saints needed to let go of the reins. Eventually the church, while providing some accommodations, won the battle of leadership, convincing the Third Convention leaders that their demands would be fulfilled as more resources flowed southward, but native leadership at the regional level did not come for another twenty-plus years.

The Rama Mexicana that Eduardo attended for almost twenty years also had its leadership crisis, though in the case of the branch, the Mexican saints had little choice but to accept white leadership imposed on them three years after their Spanish-language congregation was founded by one Spanish and two Mexican converts. Juan Martínez, Bautista, and Francisco Solano had all come from different directions but united their efforts to first convert other Spanish speakers and then request the creation of their own congregation in 1920. Ironically, the branch and the Mexican dissidents had one person in common: Bautista, a convert from Atluatla, Mexico, who came to the United States in 1910, united with the other two to engage in extra-official missionary work, and then petitioned with their small group for recognition. He served as the first branch president and then left on a genealogical mission to Mexico. The Spaniard, Solano, was chosen to replace him.[21] Upon his return, Bautista sought to reclaim his presidency, and this caused a split in the branch that gave church leaders an opening to replace the branch leadership with white men they trusted.[22]

That trust lasted nearly forty years and prevented many faithful and capable Mexican and Latino men from leading their fellow brothers

21. See Betty G. Ventura, *The History of the Salt Lake Mexican Branch, 1920–1960* (self-pub., 1998), 5. Also, see Pulido, *Spiritual Evolution of Margarito Bautista*, 97–98, to see how some Mexican saints in the Mexican branch felt about being led by white leaders. For a less favorable view of the desire to "have Mexicans lead Mexicans," see James Vernon Sharp, missionary journal, 1925–1990, MS 28810, J. Vernon Sharp missionary collection, 1925–1990, CHL, 106.

22. See Pulido, *Spiritual Evolution of Margarito Bautista*, 101; also, William Walser, interview by Gordon Irving, June 1, 1973, OH 38, 23, Oral History Program, CHL.

and sisters, though it allowed many future white leaders to get their experience leading a community many church leaders still believed was the future—albeit very far into the future—of the church. The Lamanites, according to the Book of Mormon, were to be gathered in order for the Second Coming to occur, and these individuals in the Rama Mexicana were, unlike those in Mexico for the time being, the experimental group.[23] Could they—and other saints of color—be trained, spiritually refined, and eventually trusted to lead their own until the day came when they would lead in the church? That was a question that caused problems in Mexico and other lands outside of the United States and remained for years a question to be answered when it came to the higher echelons of the church.

Unfortunately for the Mexican saints, white church leaders in the first part of the twentieth century seemed to reassess what this "flourishing" of the Lamanites meant in practical terms, especially as it applied to their own status both in the church and the kingdom to come. If there were discussions of what this meant, they are locked up in the archival vaults yet unavailable to the historian. There would be leaders, like future church president Spencer W. Kimball, who spoke for many years about the future of the Lamanites, and actually did much to bring this fulfillment to fruition, but the idea of the flourishing and future leadership of the Lamanites eventually faded from the pulpit and the collective mindset of the white membership, except possibly when their sons and daughters went on missions to the Spanish speaking.[24]

This debate over the Lamanite's future leadership in the church came at a prodigious time, just when Latter-day Saints recognized

---

23. See 3 Nephi 5:21–26; 2 Nephi 30:4–5; Doctrine and Covenants 3:18–20, 49:24.

24. For a rejection of Spencer W. Kimball's vision of the Lamanite importance in building what Latter-day Saints called the "New Jerusalem," see Bruce R. McConkie, *A New Witness for the Articles of Faith* (Salt Lake City: Deseret Book, 1985), 519. McConkie called it nonsense and chastised Elder George P. Lee, a member of the Quorum of the Seventy and a disciple of Kimball, for preaching it. For a short account of that controversy, see David G., "Elder George P. Lee and the New Jerusalem: A Reception History of 3 Nephi 21: 22–23," *Juvenile Instructor* (blog), Aug. 27, 2013. For an example of white Latter-day Saint rejection of the Lamanite—Mexican in this case—see Rey L. Pratt, "The Gospel to the Lamanite," *Improvement Era*, Aug. 1913, 1021–25, in which Pratt chastises white saints who do not want their children to go on a mission to Mexico and work among those people.

their ability to become acceptable to American society, and, more important, to benefit from the acceptability of their Americanism.[25] Yet, by the time that Eduardo came to Salt Lake City, the depression had devastated the Utah economy and the state had become fully dependent on federal monies, causing a major debate among Latter-day Saint church leaders and rank and file members over whether church members should be taking relief funds. Among the populous, the debate was over, as thousands of church members were on the dole. But this was not the case among some leaders. This, it seems, was a debate between those who "had" and those who did not. Church leaders, in spite of the economic depression, always had a little more, and this, for some at least, made them believe that everyone could pull themselves up by their bootstraps.

Eduardo must have considered himself quite lucky to have a job, and the fact that he had one reflected the importance that the church—itself struggling financially—saw in investing monies in translating its canonical works, manuals, and hymns for individuals who had few resources. It would be easy to question why the church chose to recruit an official translator when much of the work of translation had been the responsibility of each mission, depending on individuals like Eduardo to move the work along among non-English speakers. But here is where Eduardo's life connected with that of Margarito, whom he really never met (though his brother and father did, and actually befriended him).

The branch which Margarito helped establish and where Eduardo spent the first decades of his life in Salt Lake City well reflected the reality in which Mexican immigrants in and out of the church lived. They confronted numerous problems that came from having diverse Mexican communities coming together, belonging to a thoroughly American religion, and living in a community that had an ambivalent view of them. This situation—differences within and feeling isolated from without—often led to discord within the branch as each group sought to survive and to prosper, at least spiritually. This disharmony spilled out beyond the branch, and it led the

25. See Paul W. Reeve, *Religion of a Different Color: Race and the Mormon Struggle for Whiteness,* (New York: Oxford University Press, 2015) for further discussion on Latter-day Saint efforts to become American and white.

stake leadership to send emissaries to resolve the conflicts. Shortly after its establishment, the stake sent a brother J. Oscar Anderson as "missionary and representative of the high council" to help the members with the conflicts.[26]

The fact that the church sent someone to mediate the conflict is likely to have made little difference and might have exacerbated the problems. Having Anderson take part simply highlighted the differences between members, took the resolution of such problems away from the differing parties themselves, and put them in the hands of an outsider, someone who could only see the differences within the context of his views of the Mexican saints. We know little about Anderson, who might have sincerely tried to mediate the conflicts, but he likely saw the Mexican branch members as spiritual children, arguing over the most insignificant of things, and not having the maturity to resolve their differences, which, of course, ignored the constant conflicts that white Latter-day Saints had in their own congregations.

Shortly after Anderson's arrival, Bautista was sent on a genealogical mission to Mexico. There is no known record to confirm but it is possible that Anderson might have recommended that Bautista be sent away. Already, in his early years of membership in Mexico, Bautista had caused concern among mission officials, particularly Rey L. Pratt, who disagreed with his theological views as well as the influence he had on the Mexican saints. One missionary remembered Pratt begging church officials not to send him to Mexico.[27] One early Mexican member interpreted Pratt's dislike as coming from "jealousy" and "racial bigotry."[28] Bautista not only spoke forcefully and authoritatively but also understood how to make Mexican members feel both the gravity of their membership and the promises that the Mexican Latter-day Saints were to receive through their faithful adherence to the gospel of the Church of Jesus Christ of Latter-day Saints. Tenacious and fully committed, Bautista was initially considered the prototype saint that needed to be developed in

26. See, Ventura, *History of the Salt Lake Mexican Branch*, 4.

27. Walser, interview, 24.

28. This observation came from Guadalupe Monroy, the sister of the Mexican martyr Rafael Monroy, who befriended Margarito Bautista. See, Pulido, *Spiritual Evolution of Margarito Bautista*, 94–95.

Mexico, but soon enough, his preaching caused concern, especially his advocacy of the Book of Mormon promises to the Lamanite.

While Pratt, Ivins, missionaries, and other LDS members preached the Book of Mormon teachings as a way to attract Mexican converts, they did not fully understand how those receiving the message might come to understand it within the context of their lives. It became apparent that some were to see those promises in the context of the Mexican Revolution and its exulting of mestizo and indigenous cultural roots. While white Latter-day Saints tended to be conservative in the Intermountain West where most had settled, Mexican saints were more diverse in their leanings. When the revolution exploded in 1910, and the fighting raged in one form or another for the next two decades with political and ideological debates continuing until the mid-1940s, the Mexican saints were impacted, and some took sides.

In their excellent chapter, "The Church of Jesus Christ of Latter-day Saints in Mexico," Rex Eugene Cooper and Moroni Spencer Hernandez de Olarte describe the activities of some *Mormones* during the revolution, which often included taking up arms, with those in the South participating with Emiliano Zapata's indigenous army in its quest to free Mexico from the oligarchy that ruled for so many years and from foreign influence. Mexican saints even formed a "Mormon Zapatista Battalion," emulating the story of a group of two thousand Lamanite warriors in the Book of Mormon who fought to defend liberty as well as the Mormon Battalion that fought in the United States–Mexico War (ironic). Like Bautista, who succeeded them, they too believed that the Mexican Revolution was part of that blossoming.[29]

As mentioned earlier, in Bautista's absence, his counselor in the branch presidency, Spaniard Francisco Solano, became the branch president, and this caused contention once Bautista came back from his mission. Bautista believed that his mission to Mexico had not relieved him of his calling, but the mission leadership felt otherwise. His release and a reorganization of the presidency occurred on

29. This chapter is in *The Palgrave Handbook of Global Mormonism*, eds. R. Gordon Shepherd, A. Gary Shepherd, and Ryan T. Cragun (Switzerland: Palgrave MacMillan, 2020), 369–95.

May 15, 1923. The Misión Mexicana Local was renamed the Rama Mexicana. During the change, the stake president, Nephi L. Morris, quite transparently declared that the stake presidency's first inclination was to dissolve the branch and send everyone to their respective geographical congregations so they could learn the language, join their priesthood brethren, and pay their tithing. "We believed that was the best for you," he told the congregation but then admitted they had been unable to work it out. The stake presidency had then decided to create the new branch and have the members continue to worship in Spanish, pay their tithing, and proselytize among the *Lamanitas*.[30] In organizing the branch, the stake presidency called all the teachers and auxiliary leaders, an uncharacteristic action almost always left to the branch presidencies.

The commitment to keep the branch open, however, only lasted until September of that year, when Morris dissolved the branch during a meeting and asked the members to go worship with their white brothers and sisters. This action followed what President Solano described as "a difficult crisis," which had to do with the immigrant saints' precarious economic situation, their lack of English skills, and their difficulty in understanding the "Mormon way."[31] Interestingly, Morris again admonished the Mexican saints to pay their tithings and offerings. This repeated admonition seemed to reflect two important points. One was that the church was financially strapped, and the other the feeling that the white members were not going to subsidize—though they had to the first few years—separate services for Mexican members. The ability to "pay to pray" remained an attitude for many years, as seen by the constant admonishment to pay tithings. While maybe not among the top church leadership, this attitude among some of the local and regional leaders did not differ from the attitude that many white Americans had that Mexicans wanted to be on the dole.

No doubt that white stake leaders saw the branch as part of the church's commitment to bring the light of the gospel to the Lamanites, but they soon found the actual implementation of the prophecy to be more difficult and unpleasant than they might have assumed.

30. Ventura, *History of the Salt Lake Mexican Branch*, 5.

31. Ventura, 6.

Real-life *Lamanitas* were not the docile people that needed to be nurtured, taught, and saved. They were living people with particular challenges, and they were not as quick to make cultural or social changes in their lives or to see things the way their leaders taught. Their inability to master the language, or even become functional in it, bothered some leaders, and so did the belief among some that they were incapable of leading their own.

Branch leaders, however, did not accept the closing of their branch without a fight. Solano wrote Anthony W. Ivins, counselor in the church's First Presidency, about his concern over the closing, and branch members Cástulo D. Martínez, Manuel S. Torres, and Rafael Torres went to see him personally and pled their case. They soon found that neither Ivins, nor any other member of the First Presidency, had any knowledge of this decision by the stake president. Upon learning the facts, Ivins asked President Rey L. Pratt, Solano, and the stake president to meet, and this resulted in the reversal of the decision. In what must have been an uncomfortable moment, Morris came back to the Mexican saints and told them that the decision had been made to have the branch members continue to meet as they had and that the Spanish language would continue to be the worship language.[32]

It was particularly uncomfortable for Morris to reverse himself in front of the church president, Heber J. Grant, and Ivins, who were there in attendance. Their presence underscored the importance of the Mexican branch to the church's mission to proselytize among the Spanish speaking. Unfortunately, there are no known records of the meeting between the stake president, Solano, and possibly the full First Presidency, but there is reason to believe that the discussions touched not only on the branch's problems but also on the future of ethnic and language branches. Those discussions would continue for many years, and up until the twentieth century, church general authorities found themselves reversing stake leaders' decisions—some well-intentioned and others less so—to try to integrate Mexican and Latina/o saints without much concern for those who did not speak the language or felt uncomfortable among fellow members who did

32. Ventura, 6–7.

not understand them.[33] To their credit, some white leaders did try to provide gospel doctrine and Sunday School youth classes in Spanish and be sensitive to their new members, but that often ended after the difficulties of implementing Spanish-language classes and providing them leadership opportunities proved cumbersome. Some of this simply ended with a change of local or stake leadership.

In his reversal, Morris emphasized that Solano would continue to be the branch president and had the same authority as a bishop. "His mission is here with his people," said Morris, "and he has the responsibility for his branch, and my hope," he continued, "is that you progress, that you love one another and that there might be unity."[34] Morris was then followed by Pratt, who expressed his joy at being with the members and for the decision that had been made. He reiterated Morris's words and what the members of the First Presidency had said earlier. He then told the Mexican members, "You should be happy for this privilege you have been given, the privilege of having all the authority in your small branch, and of being instructed in your language the principles of the gospel."[35] Unfortunately, this change did not mean that the branch members' power over themselves was more than it had been before, but before we look at that situation, we need to understand the conflicts in the context of Mexican saints living in Utah.

The crisis that the branch encountered had many causes, some more serious than others. Mexican saints, for all the immigrant comradery and efforts at unity, were confronting a religious space quite different from any they had experienced before. If they were religious individuals before conversion, they were likely to have been Catholic, and the Latter-day Saint religion did not have many practical similarities that made the transition easy. Their new church required more active participation, had dietary restrictions, demanded 10

33. The main reasons given for dissolving Mexican and later Latina/o branches and wards—and this is also true for other ethnic wards—were that there was no capable leadership, there were too many internal conflicts, or, more often, that the Spanish-speaking saints were better off integrating into "regular" wards and learning English. See Jessie L. Embry, *In His Own Language: Mormon Spanish Speaking Congregations in the United States* (Salt Lake City: Signature Books, 1892), 85–128, for a short history of this disagreement among leaders—local and general—over the role of ethnic branches.

34. Ventura, *History of the Salt Lake Mexican Branch,* 6–7.

35. Ventura, 7.

percent of their income, and often promoted a middle-class dress code, all of which separated them from their working-class friends, family members, and neighbors. To be a Latter-day Saint in the barrios of Salt Lake City often created burdens that were hard to shoulder. All of this had the tendency to create a difference of interpretation and divided the congregation between those disciplined and obedient to institutional norms and those for whom religion was important but not necessarily a model—particularly a "white" model for transforming their everyday living.

By the nature of its hierarchical structure and its multiplicity of rules and social and cultural traditions, Mormonism has always created a dichotomy between the "truly faithful" and those who go to church to find a sanctuary from the challenges of the world. The former are people who believe, often respond to serve when asked, and are likely to make up the overwhelming majority of those who congregate on most Sundays. They are the "best and the brightest" within the context of the institution. They are also most likely to form the nucleus of the leadership group within each congregation, see what happens in the church as being correct, and are the least likely to challenge the leadership, particularly of the highest echelons of the church. The latter are often the majority of members who are often willing to serve and sacrifice for the church but often do not have the economic stability or institutional knowhow and they are willing to judge their leaders' actions within the context of how decisions affect their lives.

The asymmetric relationship between the Mexican saints and the white members only compounded the conflict as one group chose to follow while the other resisted what they saw as unfair interference by white leadership. Mexican men and women chosen to lead the branch and its auxiliaries were expected to convince their white leaders that they understood and followed a protocol developed culturally over years. That protocol, by the late 1920s, had a strong middle-class, Victorian orientation and sought to refine the membership—first the poor whites and later the ethnic members—and make them not only good followers but also "acceptable" American citizens. Over time, this kind of pressure on ethnic branch and ward leadership created leaders that at times were strict and insensitive to their members' cultural quirks that offended white saints, and these concerns made them feel the need to look over their shoulders to see if their white leaders were looking. Mexican saints could not totally escape the realities of their asymmetric lives in American society because white members did not leave their Americanism at the doorsteps of the chapel.

It would be naive, however, to assume that all the conflicts came from the members' relationship to their white brothers and sisters. The reality is that migration from their country to a new land complicated their own Mexican identity. While the Mexican Revolution began to create a sense of national identity for the nation to the south, not all regions consolidated into the new revolutionary fold at the same time. Mexican society had been regional in nature, and so while Salt Lake City Mexicans all came from the same nation, they did not all come from the same Mexico. Regional differences no doubt played out in the branch, and so did class differences—although for the most part they all were working class. But even the working class has its pecking order, with some being skilled workers, others working in factories and mines, and still others working in restaurants, construction, or other jobs available to them.

The rate of assimilation also caused divisions between members. This assimilation did not limit itself to cultural issues but also to the relationship with white leaders. Some Mexican saints came to believe that not only did white leaders know the gospel better but they were also, in some circumstances, more "Mexican" when they came to lead than many of their fellow members.[36] Some white leaders came with experience of serving missions in Mexico, and some had received academic training in the language, history, and culture. Still others had grown up in the Mexican Mormon colonies. Those who saw white leaders as much more "Mexican" were often those who were moving toward cultural assimilation, were deeply impressed by

36. These perceptions come from my years of attending ethnic branches and from conversations with Latina/o saints across the country. White "overseeing," especially when it misunderstands ethnic or racial saints' peculiarities, tends to create congregations divided by those who see white members as the arbiters of how to live the religion and those who want a more organic practice, or who simply do not want white influence, already suffocatingly present in their daily lives, to follow them into their sacred space.

the religious life of white Latter-day Saints, and who had little confidence in their compatriots' ability to live the gospel.[37]

While the Latter-day Saint gospel is a universal one, by the early twentieth century, what Balderas and other Mexican saints like him found in Salt Lake City was that it had become an American-focused, middle-class-triumphant gospel, where white saints were the norm, and saints of color were stepchildren to be nurtured, led, and loved. Many Mexican saints were impressed by those men who chose to come lead them, who learned their language—or at least learned to communicate with them and appreciate their culture—and particularly those who chose to stay for most of their lives in the Rama Mexicana. Unlike Protestant missionaries in foreign countries who often influenced the economic and political—and sometimes cultural—lives of those they led, these men and their wives, as well as other women called to "labor" among the Mexican saints, mostly kept to their ecclesiastical mission to prepare Rama members to flourish and essentially govern themselves.

This was the religious world that Rhea entered when she began volunteering in the Rama Mexicana upon her returned to Salt Lake City after her mission. She never assumed any type of leadership, even when she married Eduardo and officially became a member of the branch, but women like her were crucial in helping the youth and the Mexican sisters understand and assimilate into the church fold. She represented another aspect of the white presence in the branch—an outside member who did not lead but simply helped, who loved the members and often saw them as equals. Rhea and a number of individuals and families—notwithstanding the cultural, linguistic, and social differences—related to the Mexican saints as brothers and sisters, and their non-administrative and non-leadership presence underscored both the equality of the saints of both groups as well as the ability of Mexican leaders to minister over whites (women) within certain contexts.

37. Self-doubting Mexican saints were present when I was growing up in the church and they remain present today, though their misgivings about their people have different shades. Some are happy being in Spanish-language wards and branches but feel better when white leaders are in charge. Others will not attend a Spanish-language unit except when they want to participate in the commemorating of special Mexican holidays or they are assigned by stake leaders to do so.

This notion of equality encouraged Mexican saints, especially the youth, to go on missions and come back to serve in the branch's ministry, and for those who left to other places, to become leaders in their new communities. The Rama Mexican sent out numerous young men and women to the mission field and their work, particularly in Mexico but also in other Mexican communities around the Southwest, enhanced the church's proselyting effort and its goal of taking the gospel to the "Lamanite" or *Lamanita.* No matter their relationship to their white companions, these Mexican missionaries no doubt felt they were preparing their people for a glorious time when the "blossoming" of the Lamanite people came. The fact that they brought language skills and some administrative experience—as many had already served in auxiliary, cultural, and sport activities—allowed them to see themselves as leaders among their communities.[38]

More research and analysis still needs to be done to understand the branch's influence in expanding the LDS gospel among their people—and those in other Latin American countries—providing leadership training to them, and impacting the church's ministry to the Mexican and later Latina/o membership. I remember as a young man, still new to the LDS gospel, being inspired by a young Mexican missionary from the Lucero Ward—the successor to the Rama Mexicana. He was confident, knew both languages well, easily attracted the youth, and received enormous respect from the adults in the Spanish Fourth Ward in the Mexican side of San Antonio, Texas. In a ward of mostly older leaders, he provided the first example of a young Mexican LDS leader, nurtured within the womb of the church. He was, if my recollection serves me well, one of the first missionaries with whom I went on "splits" with.

The Rama Mexicana provided a safe space for Eduardo as he sought to find his bearings as a newly hired employee of the church and as a future iconic figure among the Spanish-speaking saints

38. Over my years in the church, I have seen young men and an occasional woman missionary dedicated not only to promulgating the gospel but also to preparing their people to lead. They serve as role models to the youth, but also to the men and women who, until they saw them, could not conceive of themselves as leaders and teachers. My early years' construction of my Mormon identity came partly from seeing and associating with missionaries—both white and brown, and also Korean.

worldwide. When Eduardo came to Salt Lake City and the Rama Mexicana, he arrived at a brief moment when the Mexican branch seemed ready to move past the complete dependency on white leadership. James Vernon Graves was called as president on May 8, 1938. He was familiar with the Mexican saints, as he spent time in the branch learning Spanish, and he would make the Spanish-language unit his home for most of the rest of his life. For the first time in fifteen years, two Mexican men were called as counselors. Rafael Torres, a veteran member of the branch, became first counselor, and Eufemio Salazar replaced a white member as second counselor, with another veteran member, Manuel S. Torres, as ward secretary. Graves reorganized the branch and named many Mexican members to positions of leadership with only the Relief Society and the Young Men's organizations remaining in white hands. A returned missionary became the Young Men's leader, and Graves's wife replaced another white woman as president of the Relief Society. It would be another three years before a Mexican sister became president of the women's auxiliary.[39]

Within a short time of his arrival to Salt Lake, on September 24, 1939, Eduardo received his first calling, replacing José Zuñiga Jr. as music director, and that same year, he became director of a newly formed teacher training course.[40] No doubt the fact that he came to work for the church impressed the members and leaders of the branch, and his calm demeanor and his proximity to important leaders in the church probably did as well. At the time few Mexican saints could claim to have the ear of the Brethren (church leaders). It is likely that members of the branch might have overstated his role in church ministry, though in one sense they were right about his importance to the church, as we shall see later.

By the time Eduardo arrived in Salt Lake City, four years had elapsed since one-third of the church in Mexico—in the form of the Third Convention—had split from the main body, and it is quite likely that this split had prompted the church leaders to take more seriously the need to provide church literature to Spanish-speaking members. Before Eduardo began translating, Spanish-language literature was limited to the Book of Mormon and selections from

39. Ventura, *History of the Salt Lake Mexican Branch*, 79, 191.

40. Ventura, 23.

some of the other canonical books as well as some excerpts from church presidents. Bautista once referred to the church offerings to the Spanish speaking as a "spiritual diet of milk," whereas he promoted an "exceptionalism" that came with being part of a people for whom the Book of Mormon had provided a future blossoming that would surpass that of the white saints.[41] Ironically, according to his biographer, Elisa Eastwood Pulido, he learned this from the early missionaries to Mexico, who gave Mexican indigenous converts a "new founding narrative" that made them more exceptional than their colonizers and those elites who looked down upon them.[42]

Ironically, one of the leaders of that movement that came to be called the Third Convention was Bautista's nephew and the first missionary to proselytize the Balderas family: Abel Paez. Paez would become the head of the breakaway group after Bautista was expelled from the organization for preaching about polygamy, a practice he had learned from the years he spent in the Mormon colonies as a teacher of Spanish. The elimination of the "Principle," as many called this particular early church teaching, led many saints, including some prominent leaders, to leave the church. While this happened many years before Bautista joined the church, it was still talked about and "lived" unofficially in the colonies outside the United States. The Mormons who most befriended Bautista and saw his potential as a leader were polygamist leaders.[43]

It is difficult to know how much Eduardo learned about the Third Convention at the time or if he understood the problem it caused the church in Mexico. He must have known about it, since both his father and his brother Guillermo were in Mexico and knew both Bautista and Abel Paez. We have no letters from them to Eduardo that speak about the schism in Mexico, but there is no doubt that they probably told him about the conflicts when they spoke or corresponded. Having worked closely with Harold W. Pratt (who presided over the mission at the beginning of the break), having served as branch president in what was then the most important port for Mexicans to enter the United States, and being an immigrant

41. See Pulido, *Spiritual Evolution of Margarito Bautista,* 61, 92.

42. Pulido.

43. Pulido, 56–59.

and refugee himself, Eduardo understood better than other church leaders why some of the conflicts arose. It is also likely that some of the things that Third Conventionists were saying were things often talked about in Mexican congregations, even if not to the degree to which they were in the breakaways.

The discussions about native leadership and more resources, including more literature, were things that I heard and thought about growing up in my Mexican ward in the West Side of San Antonio. These discussions paralleled those occurring in the barrios outside the church, where people were talking about Mexican American participation in the city's politics, the need for more resources to the poor side of town, and the lack of bilingual literature for the Spanish-speaking population. While we were careful not to talk about these issues in front of our white stake leaders, it was a common discussion among ourselves, though often tempered around those Mexican saints who saw no wrong in the actions of the white leaders. Eventually, some of those discussions were elevated by those members of the congregation who believed that the church had to do more for its ethnic members. The same happened in Mesa, Arizona, and probably other places throughout the Southwest.[44]

For those who saw the church as divinely inspired, efforts were made to create a "theology on the ground" that could sustain their fellow Mexican members in the church. It is important here to note that religious devotion and commitment to any church not only requires that believers know—to the extent that their education and intellect allows—the doctrines and teachings of the religious entity but also necessitates them creating a set of beliefs, personal or collective rituals, and ways to practice them that helped them create their own sacred space. What follows are some activities—mostly cultural but some devotional—that the members of the Rama Mexicana engaged in. These examples somewhat focus on Eduardo, who seemed to be the most artistic of the branch's members and also the one that could provide a cohesion to the members participating in these activities.

The idea of constructing a safe and sacred space for themselves did not originate with the members or leaders of the Rama

44. See Ventura, *History of Salt Lake Mexican Branch*, 78.

Mexicana. Spatial development has a long history among immigrants from Europe, Asia, and Mexico, and among religious groups like the Latter-day Saints. Often times, the Latter-day Saints were known as much for their cultural characteristics as they were for their religious beliefs, as they loved to dance, sing, sponsor festivals, and produce theatrical productions. This is one aspect that alienated other Christian groups, who were much more sober in their cultural activities and who often saw these types of cultural celebrations as too Catholic or too secular in style.

We know from an earlier chapter that Eduardo needed President Pratt's support in getting his father to approve activities such as dancing, singing, athletics, and theatrical production among the youth of the branch.[45] His father, Apolinar, was of the attitude that one went to church to worship, not to have diversion. In this he took the side of church leader and one-time member of the First Presidency, J. Reuben Clark, who nearly fifteen years later lamented that "we overemphasize amusement, making it an end in itself rather than a means to an end."[46] He did not favor much of any cultural or recreational activities in the mutual program, saying that they reflected that "they were in a rut ... young people wanted religion."[47]

The reality, however, was that youth had to be attracted to church by activities that brought them together with other youth and which showed an "interesting" part of the LDS gospel. This was the case with Eduardo, who showed little enthusiasm for church attendance early in his member years. Having worked in a movie theater and proselytized in Mexican communities where recreation was important, his love of singing moved him toward activities as a fundamental part of his religious life. Through Rhea, he fell in love with operettas and became an amateur stage director, translating American plays into Spanish and having the youth present them, not only to his congregation but eventually to the wider public, by performing either in other churches or during fundraisers open to the public.

Eduardo did not invent these types of activities for the Rama

45. Balderas, Oral History, 30.

46. For J. Reuben Clark's views on these kinds of activities and his influence in their change, see D. Michael Quinn, *Elder Statesman: A Biography of J. Reuben Clark* (Salt Lake City: Signature Books, 2002), 115.

47. Quinn, *Elder Statesman.*

Mexicana, as members there had either seen or participated in the mutual aid societies already operating in Salt Lake City. The *History of the Salt Lake City Mexican Branch, 1920–1960* records dances, dinners, plays, picnics, and sporting events throughout its history, and we see Eduardo soon after his arrival in Salt Lake City not only participating in these activities but eventually being one of their strongest proponents.[48] These activities often included numerous members of the branch and had them meeting often and praying together that the performance would turn out as they wished or that the team would win their competition. If these activities were like the ones I've participated in with numerous wards and branches throughout five states, there was also always a time to talk about religion and about the gospel.

Eduardo may not have specifically set out to create a "theology" for the branch or for Latina/o Latter-day Saints in general, but he was conscious—and so were other leaders before and after him—of the need to create a religious safe space where Spanish-speaking members could put into practice what they learned from their leaders, both white and brown. Just as important for Eduardo was to see Mormonism practiced within familiar spaces by people like him to affirm their value to the church's ministry. His experience in El Paso, both as a translator and a leader with few materials to guide him in his presidency, prompted him to not only translate what was given to him, but to push for more material to be translated into Spanish, as we will see in the later chapters.

48. Throughout Ventura's *History of the Salt Lake Mexican Branch*, there are numerous pictures and references to Eduardo's participation in branch activities.

6

SWEET SOUND OF MUSIC

EDUARDO EXPANDS AND ADDS TO THE *HIMNARIO DE SIÓN*

Balderas's transformation into what would be a highly successful and influential translator began quite early, as it no doubt does for many young immigrant children who end up, willingly or not, as translators for their parents. We do not know much about Apolinar's or María's English knowledge during Eduardo's early years in school, but it was likely limited, and Eduardo and Guillermo followed the practice of many immigrant children who helped their parents navigate an English-speaking world.

From parental-focused translating, Eduardo moved on to being a custodian and translator for the theater he cleaned. What made that particular experience so meaningful had to do with the fact that he was the "expert" in that job. Translating from Spanish to English or English to Spanish when he accompanied his parents made him aware of the act of translation for transactions, but at the theater, he translated not only words but also concepts, and neither the audience nor the owner of the movie house had any way of knowing whether the translations or the concepts they transmitted were correct. This gave him confidence in his work, which came in handy when he fully took over the translating for the church, which as we will see, was not immediate.

When he became a salesperson for the Door and Sash lumber company, Eduardo continued to refine his ability to exchange languages in his conversations and to explain items and concepts that his clients might not have understood. The company had its headquarters in Mexico, but his job was mostly selling to American customers, and in that job, he admitted later, he perfected his

Spanish by learning new words that explained the product and by using the language in conversations that went beyond the mundane. It was at that company, owned by a member of the church, where Eduardo learned to be comfortable among English-speaking bosses, and over time he took over the management of the office, assigned workers to different jobs, and took care of the bookkeeping. That ease, or at least that ability to work with such bosses came in handy when he went to work in the church headquarters where the asymmetry went firmly from top to bottom.

Working with Rey L. and then Harold W. Pratt in the mission headquarters brought him fully into the work of translation. Both mission presidents, versed in Spanish as well as any white missionary could be, recognized the mission's need for someone to translate material that crossed regional boundaries which could be used by white missionaries to preach the gospel. Both Pratts (but particularly Rey L.) prided themselves on their abilities to speak Spanish and to do some translations, but their duties, especially their travels as president, limited the time they could devote to it. Just as important, they needed someone else to expand the material to be translated. Both, no doubt, saw Eduardo as a godsend.

My own sense is that he loved the "work" of Mormonism—how it encompassed a person's daily routines; required mental, emotional, and behavioral growth; and offered "importance" to a person, even if that person had little education, a menial job, and found themselves isolated from the larger society. The church gave men like Eduardo a sense of meaning, allowing them to teach, administer, and provide leadership to other men and women. From the moment that Rey L. Pratt took him under his wing, and then Harold Pratt did the same, Eduardo's importance in the eyes of his community grew, including among the occasional white elder who saw his proximity to the president(s) as significant. Mormons were—and for the most part still are—adherents to a religious life with a strong pecking order and an affinity for those on top, whether they are in the first layers of leadership in a ward or branch or in the highest presiding quorums of the church. A person's—particularly a man's—proximity to those in authority is often seen as indicative of a person's spiritual character, and to an extent it is true in some cases because Mormonism requires people with religious and spiritual devotion to manage its multiplicity of "callings," which are seen as a sign of God's trust in a person.[1]

The first Pratt's brand of religion was focused on preaching the word and seeing how that word changed the person. Because he often saw himself as a father figure, he took young and not-so-young Mexican men under his wing, at least we know that he did that with Margarito Bautista, Apolinar, Eduardo, and to some extent, Guillermo. For LDS leaders such as both Pratts, it was a fulfilment of prophecy that someday those they referred to as Lamanites would become leaders among their people and preachers of the gospel. Unfortunately, what exactly it meant for them to be leaders and preachers in the first half of the twentieth century remains unclear. While the Book of Mormon thoughts on the matter implied leadership and influence in the latter days, church leaders had not—nor have they—developed a theological transition process for this to happen. Bautista saw the fulfillment of prophecy with the Mexican Revolution as one element of it, and so he wanted white saints and leaders to simply step out of the way and let the Lamanites take their rightful place in the church and in the kingdom of God on earth.[2]

Unfortunately, white leaders were just beginning to see the fulfillment of their own blossoming as they saw the growth of the church not only in the United States but in other places around the world, and just as important, they saw the church slowly finding acceptance in American society and their members finding their place therein. By this time, though in some way it had always been the case, Mormonism had become identified by its strong promotion of whiteness. Brigham Young had begun that process with his move to bar black males from having the priesthood and prohibiting them and their wives and other black women from going to the temple where the important rituals of the faith took place. By the turn of the century,

1. Joseph Smith, the faith's founder, was—according to one of his biographers—a man who loved being with his people, doing the "work of the Lord," and establishing communities, unlike some of his contemporaries who most loved contemplating their beliefs and their relationship to the divine. See Richard Lyman Bushman, *Joseph Smith: Rough Stone Rolling; A Cultural Biography of Mormonism's Founder* (New York: Alfred A. Knopf, 2005).

2. Elisa Eastwood Pulido, *The Spiritual Evolution of Margarito Bautista: Mexican Mormon Evangelizer, Polygamist Dissident, and Utopian Founder, 1878–1961* (New York: Oxford University Press, 2020), 86–87.

black second-class citizenship in the church had been codified by quasi-religious justifications, and dark skin, regardless of ethnic or racial origin, became a symbol of the "other," yet to be fully redeemed.[3]

Eduardo, depending on the picture you see of him, was either fairly brown-skinned, though not dark—or slightly less dark than others—but what skin color meant to him, we unfortunately know nothing about. Rhea, as we learned in an earlier chapter, once asked him whether he "always" wanted to marry a white woman, though in that case she seemed to want to affirm that he loved her and not her white privilege (a term not around at the time but understood even in subtle ways).[4] She did not doubt his sincerity in expressing his love for her, but on the day she asked or shortly before, her friends had questioned his motives. Unfortunately, we don't have a subsequent letter from Eduardo addressing the issue, nor do we have any record of them discussing their interracial relationship, other than to acknowledge that there were those who did not approve of it.

While Pratt saw a bigger role for Eduardo, even confiding in him that he "would speak to the Brethren" about a job as a full translator, nothing came of it, as the church leadership at the time did not yet focus on the Spanish-speaking members. By the time Ivins left the mission presidency, though, the church had taken notice of its Spanish-speaking members because of the rumblings in Mexico. Within the first year of Harold W. Pratt's time as mission president, the Third Convention had taken one-third of the Mexican membership over the issue of native leadership. While at first the church's First Presidency might have seen this rebellion as a momentary glitch in the church's progress in Mexico, by 1937, it became clear that the Third Convention leaders were not only serious about their separation unless they got native leadership, they were also competing with the LDS church for converts as they preached the Book of Mormon and did so with the face of their movement being Mexican. It was a powerful message, though no record exists of their success.

3. For a discussion of race in the LDS Church, see Armand L. Mauss, *All Abraham's Children: Changing Mormon Conceptions of Race and Lineage* (Urbana: University of Illinois Press, 2003); also, Paul W. Reeve, "Race, the Priesthood, and Temples," in *A Reason for Faith Navigating LDS Doctrine and Church History*, ed. Laura Hales (Provo: Religious Studies Center, 2016), 159–78.

4. Rhea Ross to Eduardo Balderas, Aug. 5, 1934, from a private collection in possession of Eduardo's daughter Ana.

Margarito Bautista, as we saw earlier, had underscored the need for more literature and manuals that white church members had in Salt Lake City. He told them that they were being fed a religion of "milk" and no doubt told them about temple rituals and other activities that the Mormons in Salt Lake practiced. If the *Lamanitas* were going to take their place in the kingdom of God, they needed their own leaders, and they needed to know their theology. Church leaders were thinking the same thing, but in a slightly different, or maybe a more significant way. If Mexican saints wanted to know more, they were going to know it from the church's mouth and not from dissidents who church leaders believed knew so much less about the Latter-day Saint gospel.

By the time Ivins took over the Mexican Mission presidency, church leaders had begun to travel more widely, and a number of them came both to speak to the missionaries and to inspect the work of the mission. While Ivins knew Spanish, having gotten his legal training in Mexico City, it would have been seen as inappropriate for the mission president to be translating for a presiding authority, at least from the perspective of Ivins, a man of order and very much institutionalized into the protocols of the church. Under both Pratts' tutelage, Eduardo had become the mission's translator, and so Ivins used him and even began to expand his work within the mission, having him travel with visiting authorities.

In an interview years later, Eduardo remembered having translated for church authorities such as Richard Lyman, John A. Widtsoe, and Oscar A. Kirkman. It was one thing to translate documents and another to translate for leaders who had little experience with someone translating their words as they spoke. Some forgot that he stood next to them and went on and on until they remembered that he was there. Elder Kirkham once got so carried away telling a story, and as he finished, he remembered Eduardo, who no doubt had tried his best to make mental notes to make as coherent a translation as he could. "Oh, you are still here," said Kirkham, but instead of repeating the story, he told Eduardo to tell the audience what he could recall.[5]

5. Eduardo Balderas, Oral History, interviews by Gordon Irving, 1973, typescript, Oral History Program, Archives, Historical Department of the Church of Jesus Christ of Latter-day Saints, Salt Lake City, 37.

It must have dawned on Eduardo that these educated men, some who loved to quote literature, were going to challenge him, and so he tried to prepare, possibly asking a bit about them and trying to anticipate some of the things they might say and sources they might use. One time, Apostle John Widtsoe quoted a writer without identifying him, and in translating the quote, Eduardo said in Spanish, "By way of explanation ... this is from Shakespeare." Surprised but impressed, Widtsoe quoted another well-known writer and then turned to Eduardo and asked, "Now, who was that from?"[6] In his recollection, Eduardo does not tell us his answer, and so it's quite possible that the name escaped him either at the time of the translation or when he gave the interview. But he so impressed the visiting authorities that at least two of them, Richard Lyman and John A. Widtsoe, sent him autographed books.[7] Eduardo appreciated the gifts, as he became an avid reader after shunning the practice in his early years. It is probable that Eduardo's interest in Shakespeare and other topics came out of what he saw as an intellectual trend in the church. Pratt had a great influence on him as the mission president translated, wrote poetry, and included secular knowledge as he preached the gospel. While not as highly educated as Ivins, Pratt fit in nicely with his cohorts, who were not afraid to speak to issues not directly coming from church manuals or even scriptures.[8]

In the 1930s, intellectuals such as John Widtsoe, James E. Talmage, Henry Eyring, and others brought their secular education into their preaching and writing. While that tradition had probably started with B. H. Roberts, one of the church's first intellectuals and a member of the Quorum of the Seventy who combined science and literature with his religion when he spoke and wrote, it would not be until about the 1920s that church intellectuals made it to the top of the LDS pecking order, at a time when other religious groups were also mainstreaming ideas that earlier had been seen as heretical.[9] While mainstream Protestantism was moving toward a

6. Balderas, Oral History, 37.

7. Balderas.

8. There was an intellectual trend among some members of the church hierarchy who were former educators, scientists, businesspeople, or government officials and who saw the need for the church to adapt to the wider society.

9. See, Gary Bergera, ed., *The Autobiography of B. H. Roberts* (Salt Lake City: Signature

more liberal social gospel, Latter-day Saint intellectuals were moving toward using the truths of the world to expand the interpretation of the Mormon gospel.

Religion, in the view of many religious people, was under attack, and while many evangelical and more conservative Protestants were retrenching and moving away from their mainstream coreligionists, Latter-day Saints were trying to create a tent big enough for diversity in spiritual thought, though in the end this type of intellectual Mormonism gave way to a rise of conservative thinkers who moved the church to the right and toward conservative politics. This shift, according to some scholars, actually served as a foundation for the rise of Western-style conservatism, and it made many Latter-day Saints see morality only in terms of sexual activity, libertarian economics, and Republican Party politics.[10]

Eduardo was only privy to the intellectual battles raging in Salt Lake City from the outside, but he benefitted from listening to traveling church authorities that spanned the ideological spectrum and from church manuals that were much more friendly to science and history than those that came later. Whatever the philosophical debates going on in the halls of the church's headquarters, however, there seemed to be a consensus that the church had to develop a better system of translating its literature and getting it to its members. In Mexico and parts of Latin America, the only Spanish material that existed were, as previously mentioned, "selections" of church doctrines that Pratt had translated and the Spanish-language Book of Mormon. Church literature was important for the development of leaders, and the Third Convention had demonstrated that leaders would arise with or without church literature.

Books, 2018); also, see Thomas G. Alexander's *Mormonism in Transition: A History of the Latter-day Saints 1890–1930* (Urbana: University of Illinois Press, 1996), 134–35, 230, 258, 291–94 for a discussion of doctrinal development that reflected progressive ideas and a reliance on blending Joseph Smith's teachings with available scientific evidence. Here, individuals like Roberts, Talmage, and Widtsoe—the latter two scientists—were particularly influential.

10. To understand the shift to conservatism, see Randy Powell, "Social Welfare at the End of the World: How the Mormons Created an Alternative to the New Deal and Helped Build Modern Conservatism," *Journal of Public History* 31, no. 4 (Oct. 2019): 488–511; also, see Mathew L. Harris, ed., *Thunder from the Right: Ezra Taft Benson in Mormonism and Politics* (Urbana: University of Illinois, 2019) to understand the LDS leader most responsible for the modern form of the faith's religious conservatism.

Whatever his approach, Ivins convinced the First Presidency to hire a full-time translator for Spanish materials since the Spanish speaking were already the second-largest language group in the church, and from that group came the church's biggest challenge. As we have seen, Ivins, after taking his place in the First Quorum of Seventy, and for a time as a member of the church's Missionary Committee, wrote to Eduardo, offering him the job. "This is to be done," Ivins wrote, "on an experimental basis, at the end of which for any number of reasons it may be discontinued.... if you are interested let me know."[11] The intent of creating the position, according to the letter, was for the church and not the various missions to do the translating of church materials. This change was supposed to alleviate the burden of translation on missionaries so they could concentrate on proselytizing, though it is just as likely that church leaders were concerned about the quality of the translations and the potential of having little control over the disparate interpretations of church doctrines across the missions.

Job security worried Eduardo, given the possibility of termination after one year. What would he do in Salt Lake City if he lost his position? In El Paso, he had a job for as long as he wanted, and given the need for Mexican labor and his own clerical and administrative experience, he could find a job either there or across the border in Ciudad Juarez, where he actually worked. He had visited Salt Lake City on at least three occasions: once to visit Rhea, once accompanying Pratt, and the last time, when he drove Pratt's family there for the mission president's funeral. It is quite possible that he felt like most non-Utah saints, who saw the city as a kind of mecca with its famous tabernacle, Temple Square, and the majestic Salt Lake Temple combined with a ward or church building everywhere one turned—truly a spiritual haven from the world.

It is quite possible that like others who migrated to the Mormon center, he saw himself, at least initially, as someone on a pilgrimage. He possibly felt some part of what Simon B. Zuñiga described as his parents' reaction shortly after they arrived in the United States: "[They] thank[ed] the Lord for the great and wonderful opportunity

11. Antoine R. Ivins to Eduardo Balderas, July 3, 1939, from private collection in possession of Eduardo's daughter Ana.

to be able to come to Zion and be among Church leaders."[12] Zuñiga would go on to recall that "these wonderful neighbors ... kept us alive" during the Spanish influenza by bringing them food every day and leaving it at the doorstep for his mother to heat and keep eight members of the Zuñiga family fed.[13] Many new arrivals to Salt Lake City, if they were saints, often felt welcomed and were amazed by the cordiality and helpfulness of the people, and it is likely that Eduardo experienced that on his trips to Salt Lake City and no doubt experienced that when he arrived to be trained there, especially when he told people he would be working for the church.

Upon reporting for duty at church headquarters, President Ivins took him to meet Gordon B. Hinckley, the Missionary Committee's executive secretary and a future president of the church. "He's the one under whom you'll be working," said Ivins and then left him with Hinckley for training, most of which involved learning reporting channels, possibly setting up a working space since there were not offices, and being instructed to take "everything" to Ivins before it went out.[14] Hinckley knew no other language than English, and so he depended on Ivins's availability to look over Eduardo's work.

Eduardo's first assignment involved translating lessons to be sent out to the Spanish-language missions. Upon finishing his translation and getting Ivins's approval, he made an original copy and three or four carbon copies to be sent to the missions for further copying.[15] With no process to follow, no glossary of terms, and few prior examples of translated material, Eduardo most likely defaulted to what he learned from Rey L. Pratt. Because Pratt served for over thirty years as the mission president to the Spanish speaking in Mexico, the United States, and some parts of Latin America, he became familiar with the language and some of the cultural idiosyncrasies of the different regional Spanish spoken and became as good a translator as someone not native or academically trained could be.[16]

Apolinar, as noted earlier, believed Pratt spoke very good Spanish.

12. Simon B. Zúñiga, *From the House of Joseph to the Land of the Restoration* (Denver: Bilingual Publications, 2010), 30.

13. Zúñiga, *From the House of Joseph*, 31.

14. Balderas, Oral History, 2.

15. Balderas, Oral History, 2.

16. Zuñiga, *From the House of Joseph*, 34.

José Zuñiga, one of the early members of Rama Mexicana, remembers the mission president speaking at the reorganization of the branch in 1923. He wrote, "This brother [Pratt] was born in Mexico [no he was not], and as we would say, he was 'puro Mexicano' [100 percent Mexican]. All his words were beautifully spoken; he was a tremendous speaker in the Spanish language." According to Zuñiga, people came to hear him speak in every state he went, and not only members of the LDS church but of other religions as well. They would fill the halls to listen to the "American" speak Spanish so eloquently and clearly on any theme.[17]

Pratt was a self-trained translator, and so would be Eduardo, but with the advantage of being a native speaker and living in a Mexican household where the cultural, in addition to the linguistic, language was spoken. When it came to translating Mormon texts, however, some of which had no translation outside of Mormonism, or even any basic connection with other religious language, Eduardo relied on what he learned from Pratt. In spite of some good efforts, Pratt ended up developing what I call an English–Spanish dialect, which used English words such as *elder*, *quorum*, *Mia Maid*, *ward*, *active* and so on that had no real direct translations and gave another meaning to words like *priesthood*, *sacrament*, *deacon*, and *calling*. There were numerous other words and terms that were translated in ways in which those outside the church could not understand.[18] While Pratt and some linguistically capable missionaries could speak the language well, they often thought in English before they spoke in Spanish, which often meant a slight change of sentence structure and tone.

The first real challenge for Eduardo came when Hinckley assigned him to create a hymnal to replace the one Pratt had done of 135 translated hymns—about half of which he translated, and others probably done by white missionaries or possibly some Mexican saints. These hymnals had no accompanying music notes, so the Mexican members depended on missionaries who played the piano and knew the English versions of the hymns to know the melody.

17. Zuñiga.

18. For an explanation of the translation challenges, see John E. Carr, *For in that Day: A History of Translation and Distribution, 1965–1980* (n.p., ca.1980), 67–90, L. Tom Perry Special Collections, Harold B. Lee Library, Brigham Young University. Also, see Joseph G. Stringham, "The Church and Translation," *BYU Studies* 21, no. 1 (1981): 69–90.

The 1927 hymnal, *Himnos de Sión*, which Eduardo and Pratt translated, was an updated version from the one produced in 1912, which was an expanded version of the 1907 hymnal, *Himnario Mormón*, produced by the Mexican Mission.[19]

Singing songs of praise has been fundamental to any religious group and particularly important in the work of proselytizing, and this was no different for LDS missionaries. Unfortunately, few missionaries were trained in the language, and even Pratt, who spent most of his time in Mexico, had gaps in his Spanish language skills. Scholars Duffy and Olaiz described the earlier translated hymns as having "crude syntax, bizarre expressions, and accents forced into the wrong syllable [which made] some of the lyrics unsingable and incomprehensive."[20] The difficulty of producing hymns that met the requirement of Mormon hymnody—besides the missionaries' limited knowledge of the language—had to do with the dual mission of translating music that appealed "to the masses the church hoped to save, yet maintain[ed] the church's distinct cultural identity."[21]

It must have been surprising for Eduardo to be assigned to retranslate and replace one of his mentor's most significant works, the 1927 hymnal. Eduardo's assignment came as the church was moving toward having greater control over its music and the messages conveyed by the hymns, while eliminating native-written hymns. Duffy and Olaiz called the earlier writing and translating of hymns as a "blossoming of Spanish LDS hymnody."[22] In 1907, there were twelve original Spanish hymns and eleven more were added in 1912, making up nearly half of all the songs in the hymnal. Some of the hymns spoke directly to or about the Mexican saints. Andres C. Gonzalez, one of the earliest Mexican saints to serve a mission, did some of the earliest translations, and he also wrote a hymn.[23]

The hymns also represented a more organic gospel, whose goal was to bring the "good news" to the people of Mexico and not to create

19. John-Charles Duffy and Hugo Olaiz, "Correlated Praise: The Development of the Spanish Hymnal," *Dialogue: A Journal of Mormon Thought* 35, no. 2 (Summer 2002): 90.

20. Duffy and Olaiz, "Correlated Praise," 91.

21. Michael Hicks, *Mormonism and Music: A History* (Urbana: University of Illinois Press, 1989), 145.

22. Duffy and Olaiz, "Correlated Praise," 91–94.

23. Duffy and Olaiz, "Correlated Praise," 91–94.

what was then happening in the United States: a disciplined, orderly, and centralized membership. The mission field was a contested landscape, and the LDS missionaries competed with other Protestant groups for souls—and, of course, they both competed with the Catholic Church. This competition reflected feelings and emotions, with the emphasis on the love of God. While Protestants tended to focus on the redemption of the sinner, the LDS missionaries emphasized hope and the promises of keeping covenants.[24] Still, the latter borrowed hymns heavily from the former because the Protestants had been around longer, and their music built upon traditions of centuries of Christian traditions and also on the great European composers.[25]

It was the native-created hymns that spoke to the organic elements of Mormonism, even when the composers borrowed from the evangelical hymns they heard or were familiar with. These organic efforts reflected the richness of the conversion process and the feeling of being taken out of the world and into a new life. The gospel's strongest appeal outside the Latter-day core was not its rules, its material success, or its patriotic zeal; it was the message of heavenly beings visiting the earth, living prophets walking the earth, and the heroic—often inspiring and sometimes tragic—stories of the Book of Mormon and the other scriptural cannons.

For Mexican members, the Spanish translations of the hymns were particularly important in making them feel a part of the church, but Mexican saints and others (white Spanish speakers) had also written hymns that reflected their own feelings and interpretations of the Latter-day Saint gospel. Five Mexican saints wrote eight hymns that, ironically, focused on the gospel message itself and not on the *Lamanita*, which was a topic focused on by the three white Spanish-speaking Mormons who wrote twelve hymns included in the 1907 and 1912 hymnals, both produced by the Mexican Mission and not the church in Salt Lake City.[26]

24. "Keeping covenants" for Latter-day Saints means both obeying God's commandments and following church direction in those areas considered doctrinal.

25. Duffy and Olaiz, "Correlated Praise," 91–94. At least nine hymns were reprinted from the *Himnario Evangelico* with permission from the American Tract Society.

26. Duffy and Olaiz, "Correlated Praise," 92–93. Edmund Richardson wrote ten hymns, one on the gospel taken to the Lamanites, and the other two hymns on this topic were written by W. Ernest Young and Marion B. Naegle respectively.

Interestingly, another hymnal, *Canciones de Sión*, appeared in 1911, this one created by a woman named Samantha T. Brimhall de Foley, a native Utahn who lived in Mexico the last decade of the nineteenth century and taught in the Mormon academy of Ciudad Juarez. In it were 174 hymns either written or translated by her, of which sixty-seven were original Spanish hymns. She wrote about the Lamanites, the Mormon colonies, and about distinctive LDS doctrine such as that on the premortal existence, baptism for the dead (and against infant baptisms), as well as the Restoration. There were even two anti-war hymns (against the violence of the Mexican Revolution) included. The hymns were linguistically crude and left much to be desired when it came to Spanish translations, but like the ones written by Mexican authors, they were more reflective of the feelings and passions of the early saints in Mexico.[27]

There is no record of that hymnal ever being used in Mexico or even the Southwest, and it is possible that few, if any, Mexican or Spanish-speaking saints, ever sang any of the hymns. And yet, Brimhall's translation of "Praise to the Man," a hymn that spoke of Joseph Smith seeing the Father and the Son, was sung at the church's general conference in October 1913. Ironically, the accepted canonical translation of the hymn was done by Andres C. González for the 1912 mission hymnal, which was likely not in general circulation in Utah.[28] Its inclusion in the conference indicated that for at least some of the church authorities, a foreign-language hymn was an indication of their desire to take the gospel to the Spanish speaking.

For Duffy and Olaiz, these hymns and the hymnals, which included native-written songs and songs by white saints who proselytized in Mexico, represented the heyday of Spanish hymnody. Unfortunately, by the 1920s, church leaders were moving away from this organic religiosity that arose in the missions and toward a more centralized, doctrinally consistent message that could appear in public. This was necessitated by the need to keep a profoundly different religious movement from being "co-opted" by the world, or from

27. Duffy and Olaiz, "Correlated Praise," 94–96.

28. Duffy and Olaiz, "Correlated Praise," 94n15; also *Eighty-Fourth Semi-Annual Conference of the Church of Jesus Christ of Latter-day Saints* (Salt Lake City: The Deseret News, 1913), 24.

going into tangents that corrupted its purity. Without theologians in the traditional sense, and with so many undereducated individuals seeking to see and hear things normally left to prophets and spiritual leaders, the church found itself with a whole host of "teachers, preachers, and leaders" teaching false doctrine, promoting personal theologies, and creating their own religious communities within the larger church.[29]

In 1920, church president Heber J. Grant appointed a General Music Committee to produce a revised, standard, uniform hymnbook for the church, and this meant that hymns that did not neatly correspond with LDS doctrine were discarded, as were most of those compiled by Emma Smith, the church founder's wife, and hymns and tunes from other denominations were reduced significantly.[30] The process of deciding on a new English-language hymnal prompted the creation of a new Spanish hymnal from the one initially compiled by Rey L. Pratt. This led to most of the hymns by native Mexican composers being taken out when the new Spanish hymnal was published in 1927.

It is difficult to know if Eduardo had a chance to see any of the earlier hymnals, or Brimhall's renditions, other than the 1927 version, with which he was familiar simply by having attended a Spanish-language unit. There may have been copies available of the earlier hymnals, though the church did not then have, as it does today, a good library or museum. It is, however, quite possible that Pratt spoke to him about the process he used to develop the 1912 and 1927 hymnals and maybe shared some thoughts on the hymns he chose to keep from the earlier songbooks and his reasons for discarding some native-written hymns. Whatever discussions—if any—took place on the collection or use of hymns, there is little doubt that Balderas approached the translation with reverence both for its importance as a church assignment and because it was the work of his mentor, a man he loved dearly.

We know little of Eduardo's translation process, but there are

29. See Alexander's *Mormonism in Transition* to get a sense of the challenges the church was confronting as it sought to formalize its organizational structure and refine its doctrinal message to the outside world.

30. Hicks, *Mormonism and Music*, 28–29. See also Church Music Committee, preface to *Latter-Day Saint Hymns* (Salt Lake City: Deseret Book, 1927).

some things that we can assume. First, it took time to correct some of his former president's grammar and sentence construction, though it is likely that it was not as extensive as what would occur to his own translations in 1992, when a committee took on the task of putting out a new hymnal. This can be seen, according to Duffy and Olaiz, from the fact that Eduardo used "infinitives in Spanish in the same way" that they were used in English.[31] This again reflected the fact that Eduardo's grammar and sentence structures were learned in English—as he lacked the academic training in Spanish—and not necessarily as he learned it in the streets, at his job, or in his branch. At the same time, it was this absence of academic Spanish that made his translation so relatable to the common people coming into the church. Such was the impact of his translations that years later some members resisted replacing the 1942 Spanish hymnal with the one produced in 1992.[32]

Eduardo, whether of his own accord or from instructions from Ivins, incorporated all the 1927 hymns but doubled the number of hymns by translating 117 songs from the English hymnbook and writing four himself. Not since the early years of the church, when several general authorities translated and produced hymnbooks in Dutch, German, Italian, and other languages, did someone have such an impact on the hymnody of the church. By doubling the songs available to the Spanish-speaking saints, he further introduced them to the culture of the church and to those doctrinal phrases and sentences dear to Latter-day Saints everywhere.

Here we see Eduardo's words taking on the role of prophetic mouthpiece to his people as he translated–and thus made available in Spanish—material coming from the prophets, seers, and revelators of the church. He did so by enhancing a church Spanish language that simplified the words while providing a deeper meaning of the gospel message. Years later, Eduardo would be criticized for not strictly following a literal approach to translating the hymns and other words, but he saw the need to make things clearer for his fellow Mexican—and later Spanish-speaking—saints.[33] There is no

31. Duffy and Olaiz, "Correlated Praise," 99.
32. Duffy and Olaiz, 108–10.
33. Duffy and Olaiz, 99–103.

doubt that he learned part of this approach from Pratt, but his own familiarity with the language of *el pueblo* (the people) led him to produce the message rather than the words. This might have meant a slight change here or there, but it was meaningful, and it resonated with those who were coming into the church at the time and for many years later.

One reason the new Spanish hymnal became important was that Pratt's 135-hymn songbook had gone out of print, and the Zion's Printing Press, located in Independence, Missouri, had closed. This gave the church an opportunity to create a new, expanded version, but it also allowed for the creation of a children's hymnal, one for the MIA, and another for the Sunday School. Eventually, most of these would be combined in the Spanish hymnal.[34] This massive effort made Eduardo the most prolific and important contributor to Spanish-language hymnody in the church, a feat that has never and probably will never be surpassed or matched. While most of this addition to the Mormon Spanish hymnody came from his translations, his four MIA songs should be noted, not only because they reflected his love of the church's youth but also because they revealed the once progressive strain of the church youth programs. Eduardo had basically lived through the Progressive Era while a young man himself.

From the early part of the twentieth century, the church had been influenced and organizationally impacted by the Progressive movement, which created an impulse around the nation to professionalize, to organize, and to be concerned with the issues that affected the urban communities of the nation. It was a movement that prompted the gathering and uniting of people for social causes and for community development. In those areas, the church's women's organization, the Relief Society, flourished as it got involved in numerous social causes as well as women's suffrage and built itself into the largest and most active women's organization in the country and possibly in the world. Sunday School, which arose partly outside the church, became part of the Sunday school movement that arose among Protestant churches, and so did other organizations that later became part of the church organization.[35]

34. Duffy and Olaiz.

35. See Alexander, *Mormonism in Transition*, 133–66 for the development of church

The Young Men's Mutual Improvement Association (YMMIA)—and later the Young Ladies' Mutual Improvement Association (YLMIA)—expanded dramatically when the nation's attention turned to its youth in the later years of the nineteenth and early twentieth century. There were many urban youth who seemed lost and attracted to juvenile delinquency, and a concern also arose about the lack of masculinity among the nation's youth. For Protestants, that spurred the Muscular Christianity movement, which saw the development of recreational—particularly sport–activities for its young men at the same time they were being imbued with a Christianity that saw strength and power as a form of evangelism. There was no effeminate or weak Jesus in their theology, and while not all religious groups went along with that kind of theology, many did, and one reason was the fact that the nation's leaders and their sports figures and college athletes all clamored to protect themselves, some knowingly and other unconsciously, from the unassimilated brown and only partly integrated southern European masses in the cities.[36]

While the church was concerned about juvenile delinquency and other issues concerning urban America, their response was less about masculinity and more about making LDS youth good citizens of both the nation—which they had now embraced wholeheartedly—and the institution of the church. In Utah, the YMMIA and YLMIA engaged in all kinds of activities that ranged from sporting and recreational activities to theatrical productions, song festivals, reading literature, and in some places, participating in discussions and debates on the challenges to American society. These activities allowed the church's youth to create their own world or bubble in which they lived their religion, associated with their own kind, and avoided the evils of the world outside the church parameters.[37]

The first hymn Eduardo wrote for *Himnos de Sión* is one called "Haces falta en nuestra mutual" (You are needed in our mutual), which is a call for the youth to gather together during mutual night.

---

auxiliaries, first influenced by the Progressive Movement and then the move toward full integration in a more structured church organization.

36. For an excellent study of this Muscular Christianity movement, see Clifford Putney, *Muscular Christianity: Manhood and Sports in Protestant America, 1880–1920* (Cambridge, MA: Harvard University Press, 2003).

37. Alexander, *Mormonism in Transition*, 147–52.

"Listen youth to the call of Zion," it begins, "you are missed in our Mutual [where] you can progress incessantly with joyful resolution"; "let's expand this great association" (Asociación de Mejoramiento Mutuo), "and with courage follow the Savior; you are missed in our mutual."[38] It is a simple hymn, but it reflected the concern that church leaders had about keeping the youth in the church, and this was particularly worrying for Mexican and Mexican American local church leaders who knew that their youth lived in neighborhoods where drinking, gambling, and other vices were present. Juvenile delinquency in the Mexican barrios was a reflection of the alienation that Mexican youth felt from American society, which did not often treat them with fairness, and their parents, who often sought to keep them culturally Mexican when so much of what they saw and heard was culturally American.[39]

Eduardo understood well those concerns, having grown up in El Paso where the *pachuco* movement had its origins. Pachucos were young Mexican men alienated by American society and by their families' Mexican traditionalism. They took the style of dress of working-class Mexicans gangsters as depicted in Mexican movies, and they often listened to American music and some of the big band sounds of American and Mexican musicians. They often roamed in groups and with time became involved in drugs, petty thievery, and gang fights. They became such a problem—or at least were perceived as such—that the El Paso police ran them out of town, and many went on to develop their own subculture in Arizona, California, and even in places like Chicago.[40]

His youthful experience was not the only knowledge that Eduardo had of alienated and delinquent youth. By the time Eduardo began writing his own MIA hymns, there were already reports of police and pachuco confrontations. One year after the hymnal was

38. *Himnos de Sión* (La Iglesia de Jesucristo de los Santos de los Últimos Dias, 1942), 53.

39. For a discussion of the Pachuco phenomenon, see Laura L. Cummings, *Pachucas and Pachucos in Tucson: Situated Border Lives* (Tucson: University of Arizona Press, 2009); Javier Duran, "Border Crossings: Images of the Pachuco in Mexican Literature," *Studies in Twentieth and Twenty-First Century Literature* 25, no. 1 (2001); and Eduardo Obregón Pagán, *Murder at the Sleepy Lagoon: Zoot Suits, Race, and Riot in Wartime L.A.* (Chapel Hill: University of North Carolina Press, 2003).

40. See footnote 39.

published, the Zoot Suit Riots exploded in Los Angeles, though they were less riots than cases of American sailors beating up Mexican American youth because they wore the zoot suit and because they were seen as shirking the war effort, even though many were too young to join the military, others were denied induction, and many of them had brothers and fathers in the military.[41] That type of violence was not only in California but also in some parts of the Midwest and reflected a strong anti-Mexican strain in the Southwest and California. For many Mexican Americans like Eduardo, in places where they were a small minority, like Utah, avoiding controversy was important, and one way to do so was to hold on tightly to their membership in organizations like the LDS Church.

The second hymn that Eduardo wrote, "Luchemos por la asociación," followed somewhat the tone of his first by calling for a "fight for Zion," and for its "youth" to keep the "mantle of virtue" through "valor," a "firm heart," and "enthusiasm and fervor." "Luchemos, luchemos, todos a luchar, por la gran asociación" (let us fight, let us fight, everyone for our great association), "let us fight unceasingly, let us fight unceasingly."[42] In English it sounds rather militaristic, but in Spanish, the word *luchar*, or *fight* might be better translated to *struggle*, which according to Webster's dictionary, means to "make strenuous effort against opposition," or "to proceed with difficulty or great effort."[43] Synonymous with struggle are "endeavor," "attempt," "try" or "assay." Taken in the context of its definition and its synonyms, the word *struggle* or *luchemos* reflected Eduardo's view that the Mexican youth of the church had to struggle against habits, traditions, and even opposition from their extended families or others in their community.

"Hay gozo en la mutual" proved to be another hymn that resonated among Mexican youth and those who previously attended MIA, as it spoke of precisely that world created for the youth of the church. It spoke of memorable meetings with teachers and companions and the blessings and gifts that came with attending "la mutual."

41. See Obregón Pagán, *Murder at the Sleepy Lagoon*.

42. "Luchemos por la asociasión," *Himnos de Sión*, 57.

43. *The Merriam-Webster Dictionary*, Paperback ed. (Springfield, MA: Merriam-Webster, Incorporated, 2004), s.v. "struggle."

It prepared the youth, as the second stanza said, for the fight against vices, and declared that "with justice as its motto, [will] march the host of the MIA."[44] The fourth hymn—and we do not know in what order they were written—was called "La juventud sigue a Cristo" and brought the youth back to their purpose in the church, which was to serve a mission just as Eduardo had.[45]

The hymn begins, "Joyful today the youth, Christ they will follow. To the nations in error [or darkness], his motto they shall take. Let us take from the mutual the arms [teachings] of faith, the standards of the redeemer and king defend." The second stanza reads, "The glory of our Lord and king is intelligence [;] let us find it in mutual ... with faith and devotion."[46] Here, again, we see Eduardo's devotion to the work of the MIA and his belief that it was the MIA that could best prepare the youth to do the work of the church. It was so because it was the church entity that worked the hardest to integrate Mexican youth into American society and gave them the skills that hopefully prepared them to best navigate an often-hostile society. Mutual was no different—except in the gospel it preached—from many other Progressive Era efforts to integrate working-class and foreign youth into American society by teaching them just enough to be able to enter the job market, and for the lucky few, to rise to the middle class, though the latter was reserved mostly for white young men, native and foreign.

Yet, to many Mexican Latter-day Saint youth, the organization was also a place to find their own identity. The *mutualistas*, or mutual aid societies, had been the secular organizations that helped their immigrant parents navigate American society, and for Latter-day Saint immigrants and first-generation Americans, mutual served the same purpose. There they learned much about the American church, but in their own language or bilingually, and within the context of their own culture to the extent possible. It was there that many of them first learned to interact with white youth and white adults beyond those in school, when accompanying their parents to the store, or when encountering law enforcement. In mutuals across the

44. "Hay gozo en la mutual," *Himnos de Sión*, 61.
45. "La juventud sigue a Cristo," *Himnos de Sión*, 58.
46. *Himnos de Sión*, 58.

southwest, the youth came out of the program, if they stuck with it, more American but still Mexican enough to interact with the adults in the congregation. And for some, it was actually a way to become more Mexican because it is there where they learned to dance their native dances, learn to sing Spanish hymns, perform plays in Spanish, and associate with other Spanish-speaking adults in other wards and branches.

To the adults Eduardo gave memorable hymns that had not been available to them before, and while we have no data on what hymns the Spanish-speaking members liked, my experience in several Spanish-language units indicated that some particular hymns were sung in all of them. One particularly popular hymn was "Firmes creced en la fe" ("True to The Faith"). Another was "Oh, mi Padre" ("Oh, My Father"), and others included "Somos los soldados" ("We Are All Enlisted"), "Hoy sembramos la semilla" ("We Are Sowing"), "Con valor marchemos" ("Onward, Christian Soldiers"), and a particular favorite in all congregations I attended, "Si hay gozo en tu corazón" ("You Can Make the Pathway Bright").[47] It would take a musicologist to find the rhyme and rhythm to them and tell us what they all had in common, and we don't know whether Eduardo or someone else chose them, but it is clear that the music, not necessarily the words, brought the Mexican saints into closer proximity to their white brothers and sisters.

Most visiting authorities and English speakers, whether they knew the hymn in English or not, related to the sound of the music, and in many Mormon congregations, proximity often substitutes for mixing or integration. No doubt someone—perhaps Antoine R. Ivins or someone else who understood Spanish—checked off on the translations, though it is likely that by Eduardo's second year, this type of assignment did not bring close scrutiny. It is also possible that before the church's correlation approach, which consolidated programs and made much of the church's literature be written by committee—greatly reducing the boundaries of the creativity and ingenuity of the members' artistic efforts—a less than literal translation

47. See *Himnos de Sión*, 59, 208, 165, 225, 232, 246.

was allowed.[48] Of course, Eduardo might have simply convinced whomever reviewed his work that his Spanish "interpretation" of these favorite English hymns resonated with the Spanish-speaking members, while keeping them doctrinally in tune.

This massive translation effort helped create a Spanish-language hymnody, but one different from those earlier ones which were more organic and native to the Mexican people. This reflected Eduardo's view that Mexican saints needed to integrate into the American church while retaining a space in which Latter-day Saint words, thoughts, and music accommodated to expressions of the Mexican lived experiences. He thus translated LDS concepts into a language that the people could understand, but the translations retained some semblance to the English-Spanish language that had come from the first missionaries to Mexico and Latin America. In essence, the language that Eduardo used combined Spanish words with American concepts as well as Mexican concepts with non-translatable English words, thus creating a hybrid culture in the Spanish-language units that allowed the saints to feel part of two sometimes conflicting religious spaces.

In translating, he was Mexicanizing American concepts and Americanizing the way Mexican saints understood their religious teachings. Eduardo was becoming a translator in the way of Joseph Smith, and eventually he would serve as the model for church translation until the latter part of the twentieth century, when church committees decided to engage in a literalist approach to translation and Americanize as much as possible what non-English speaking members were learning.

---

48. See Matt Bowman, "Zion: The Progressive Roots of Mormon Correlation," in *Direction for Mormon Studies in the Twenty-first Century*, ed. Patrick Mason (Salt Lake City: University of Utah Press, 2016), 15–34. Also, see Alexander's *Mormonism in Transition*, 133, 135, 158–59. While correlation began in the early twentieth century, it was not until about the middle of the century that most church policies and programs became strictly correlated, meaning they were carefully reviewed by the highest ecclesiastical authorities and were focused on eliminating any activity or policy that might challenge church orthodoxy. This is what eventually caused a translation committee to correct what they saw as doctrinal inconsistencies in Eduardo's translations. For more on this, see Duffy and Olaiz, "Correlated Praise," 97–98.

7

MAKING THE SACRED ACCESSIBLE

TRANSLATING THE TEMPLE CEREMONY AND THE CANON

As Eduardo stood next to one of the members of the First Presidency, David O. McKay, he saw a scene inside the Arizona temple that no doubt brought a smile to his usually modest and unpretentious face and a joy deep within his heart. Sitting in front of him were nearly two hundred brown faces and bodies, some showing the strains of the long journeys they undertook to be there but all happy to participate in a solemn ceremony mostly inaccessible to Spanish-speaking saints.[1]

They had come to the temple in trucks, cars, trains, and the lucky few in buses to be "sealed" to their families and to obtain their "endowments," thus making them truly Latter-day Saints. The endowment ceremonies, for those unfamiliar with Mormon theology, are rituals in which Latter-day Saints receive special undergarments to wear for the rest of their lives and where they make covenants to keep the commandments and live a life consistent with Latter-day Saint doctrines. Sealing—whether as a couple or as a family—is the act of being ritually connected to both the nuclear family and extended family for all of time and eternity. These later ceremonies are the holiest acts of an active member of the church.

At that moment in time, these church rituals were not available in Spanish, and any Spanish-speaking person going through the temple depended on someone providing enough of a translation to get them through the ceremony. It is quite possible that this happened when Apolinar and María took their family to be sealed in the Salt Lake City Temple in 1925. While Eduardo and Guillermo

1. Eduardo Balderas, "La Conferencia en Mesa," *Liahona*, Dec. 1955.

were old enough and knew English well enough to have helped their parents, they would not have been allowed beyond the sealing room, and at their age, notwithstanding language skills, the ceremony was too difficult to understand and beyond their abilities to translate. Even today, Latter-day Saints of all stripes, going for the first time, do not fully understand the ceremony.

Lorin F. Jones, president of the Spanish American Mission (1943–1953) and his wife, Ivie, believed that the members of the El Paso Branch should go to the temple for their endowment and to seal themselves to their ancestors. On June 24, 1943, they were able to get fifteen members of the branch to go to the temple. Ivie remembered years later, "We conducted a temple excursion from [El Paso] … and were met by a number of our Mexican people from points in Arizona. We held a special meeting in the temple just prior to the night session … fifty-nine … went through the temple that night."[2] This was the first ever excursion by a group of Mexican Latter-day Saints, and while the occasion was momentous, the Joneses were saddened that the members were not able to understand much of the ceremony.[3]

Upon their return home from the temple, the president and his wife corresponded with the church authorities about the situation. Unbeknown to them, Mexican members in Mesa, Arizona, were also asking church authorities to make the ceremony and the rituals accessible to them.[4] Then in October, one of the church's apostles, Joseph Fielding Smith, came to tour the mission along with his wife Jesse. The tour was to last almost a month, and during that time they were accompanied by President Jones and his wife, who took the opportunity to press their case for Spanish-language sessions in the temple. By then, they had spoken to the Mesa Temple president, who agreed to the idea, and they approached Elder Smith with the idea of having

2. For the story of the Joneses' mission years among the Spanish speaking and the years of their mission presidency, see Janelle Brimhall Lysenko, *Mission to the Lamanites: The Story of Lorin Franklin Jones and Ivie Maude Huish Jones* (self-pub., 2008). For the information on that particular mission excursion, see page 87.

3. See Guillermo Balderas, "Historia," Balderas Family, Balderas Family Scrapbooks, 1910–1911, 315, CHL.

4. This is information that has come from those doing research on Latter-day Saints in Mesa, but who have yet to publish something specifically on the topic.

a temple day for the Spanish-speaking members where they could perform their ordinances in their language. The apostle seems to have been convinced by their tenacity and responded with, "I see no reason why the English language should monopolize the temple session."[5]

The Joneses, however, knew that they needed the full support of the church leadership, and they decided to go to Salt Lake City to present their case to the First Presidency and to other church and auxiliary leaders. They would find that the rest of the church leadership was not as sure as Smith that it was the right thing to do at the moment. In his memoir, Guillermo—who at the time was president of the Mexican branch in El Paso—recalled that several problems arose: "Could the temple sessions be held in any other language than English? Who would translate the ceremonies? Were the Lamanites ready for such a step? Who would finance such excursion[s]," and where would they stay?[6]

President Jones assured the church presidency that, indeed, the Mexican people were ready and would appreciate going to the temple for their endowments. The members, he added, would finance their own costs, but he "demanded" that not only a translation be provided during the temple sessions but that the ceremonies themselves be held in Spanish. It was a bold request, especially since some of the church leaders wondered if it was correct to translate the temple ceremonies into other languages. We do not know exactly what objections there were to translating the ceremonies, nor what the Joneses said to appease those concerns, but they convinced the First Presidency to approve a Spanish-language ceremony.[7]

The decision paid off as the number of Spanish-speaking members entering the temple increased dramatically over time as caravans came from throughout the Spanish American Mission, the Mormon Colonies in Chihuahua, Mexico, and other areas that formed part of the Mexican Mission.[8] Yet on the first allotted day, the ceremonies were still in English, as the translation took time to be completed. To alleviate the language problem and make the temple visit meaningful,

5. Lysenko, *Mission to the Lamanites*, 100–101.
6. Lysenko.
7. Lysenko.
8. Lysenko, 315–16.

Guillermo took the Mexican saints through the temple room by room the night before their temple sessions took place and explained the ceremonies and ordinances to be performed the next day.[9]

El Paso became the rendezvous meeting place for members from East Texas and Mexico. The Relief Society sisters prepared hot lunches for the travelers, while the English-speaking members provided, after promptings by President Jones, "cars, trucks, provisions and money."[10] For many Mexican saints, this opportunity to travel to the temple also provided them a chance to see their white brothers and sisters in a new light—one in which they were not leading but providing service. Mexican saints took center stage, something they rarely did, and though they were traveling with little and depended on the generosity of the white saints, their efforts to attend the temple revealed their commitment to the Mormon gospel.

For white saints, excursions allowed them to see the faith of their Spanish-speaking brothers and sisters. It also provided them an opportunity to participate in the "blossoming" of the Lamanites, who, they had been taught, were to hold a special place in the moving forward of the church. This they had heard from every mission president since Rey L. Pratt became president of the Mexican Mission, and through the dividing of that mission into two, and they no doubt heard the same message from the current leader of the Spanish American Mission, President Jones.

Possibly no other church official, besides Rey L. Pratt, did more for Mexican saints than Lorin F. Jones, and in this he was accompanied by his wife, Ivie. Rather than just preside and make sure the missionaries completed their duties, stayed safe, and converted new members—an important and heavy duty in itself—Lorin and Ivie focused on making the members of the El Paso Mexican branch self-sufficient. To prepare for the temple excursions that only two years later became "annual Lamanite conferences," they organized classes in which the Spanish-speaking saints learned about collecting the necessary information to take their ancestors' names to the temple and be sealed to them.[11]

---

9. Lysenko, 108.
10. Balderas, "Historia," 315–16.
11. Lysenko, *Mission to the Lamanites,* 110.

One of President Jones's first actions after World War II, which had depleted the mission of missionaries and Melchizedek Priesthood holders, was to call Andrés C. González as a counselor. González's life story, as written by his grandson tells us much about early Latina/o Latter-day Saint experiences and their interaction with white saints. While he was the first Mexican missionary of the church, one of the first translators of hymns and other materials, and possibly the first Mexican saint to hold some kind of leadership position beyond the local level, records indicate he never attended a Spanish-language branch.[12] One reason for this may have been that none existed at the time he came to El Paso, and another that he married a white woman.

González's first assignment was to organize quorum activities for the Aaronic Priesthood, which was the organization of the male youth from twelve to eighteen years old, and no doubt to teach the youth and their parents the role the priesthood played in the administration of the church. Seeing him organize the quorum, preside over young white missionaries, and teach members in their own language no doubt impressed the members of the El Paso Branch.[13] They had never seen Mexican leadership in the church beyond their local branch and rarely in their jobs or in their social or legal interactions outside the church.

Both González and the Joneses understood that for the Mexican saints in El Paso to take the next step in their *Mormonismo*, they needed to go to the temple and receive their own endowments, make covenants, and understand the rituals of the Church of Jesus Christ of Latter-day Saints. Both men believed in the ability of the Mexican saints to be leaders and to expand the church within their barrios, and they may have even believed them to be capable of leading those outside of their communities—if not those (white) saints at the time, at least their children. This was the reason why the temple ceremonies had to be translated and made accessible to the Spanish-speaking members.

12. Balderas, "Historia," 311. For a history of Andrés C. González, see John A. González, *No More Strangers and Foreigners, The Melding of Cultures against the Backdrop of Deep Religious Faith* (JAG Legacy Press, 2018). González was the author of one of the most popular hymns in the Spanish speaking church, *Placentero Nos Es Trabajar.*

13. Balderas, "Historia," 311.

Guillermo felt the same way, and he had the confidence of President Jones in the things he was trying to do in his branch. Thus, the mission president chose him to help facilitate the temple ceremonies for those Mexican saints who attended the temple. As mentioned earlier, on the branch members' first temple trip in 1943, which included not only the Mexican saints from El Paso but others from around the Southwest, Guillermo took the saints through the temple room by room and explained to them in Spanish the covenants they would be making and the significance of the ceremonies and ordinances they were to perform. The next day, the Spanish-speaking saints would hear the temple ceremonies in a language many did not understand, but if memory served them well, they knew what was happening.

We have no record of Eduardo's thoughts as he saw the members from throughout the Southwest and northern Mexico gather in the temple, nor do we know if he knew of Guillermo's actions—most likely he did—but standing there with a church leader, it must have dawned on him how important his translations were. Only two years before, the church, through his efforts, had provided these same members a new hymnal and some Spanish-language lesson materials, and now he stood there as an example of a committed Mexican saint, literally touching shoulders with one of God's anointed. Whether he fully understood it or not, that scene affirmed many testimonies that the "blossoming of the Lamanites" was real.

Seeing his brother as a branch president leading his flock to the temple no doubt brought Eduardo great joy. While a humble man, always appreciative of where he found himself, he indubitably felt proud of his brother's active participation in such a historic moment. It would be one of many times that he saw Book of Mormon prophecy being fulfilled, just as the prophets had foretold. No doubt, for those who knew him from his days in El Paso, him standing next to church authorities was also a testament of what could be accomplished by a devoted life.

While Eduardo had stood next to apostles and visiting authorities as they spoke to the Mexican saints, mostly during mission conferences, this was his first time translating in what was truly a historic moment: the temple adapting to a whole new constituency.

Eleven years later, in 1955, the same David O. McKay, now president of the church (1951–1970), told Mexican and other Latina/o saints participating in the tenth temple excursion, "It was because of your fidelity and diligence that we felt an impression to give to other people the [same] opportunity to receive [these] blessings in their own language."[14]

In a later session, he reiterated the importance of the excursions: "You are serving as an example to the members of the church in Europe. Their eyes are upon you."[15] He could have added that the Mexican and Latina/o saints' eyes were still on Eduardo Balderas, now in his tenth temple excursion. He and Rhea had made the commitment after the first Spanish-language temple session they had attended together to be there every year for as long as they could. During that first temple session, he had been asked to assist in the session and was called to be a temple worker and sealer, an opportunity few Mexican saints or saints of color had ever had.[16]

Four years later, in 1959, when writing about the saints who continued to come to the temple, Eduardo said, "This experience will make them better members [of the church] and they will feel like never before, to be a light upon the hill."[17] He must have been particularly impressed and inspired by a reunion of one thousand members, former Spanish-speaking missionaries, and other interested individuals who had been part of the Mesa excursions for over ten years. There, they listened to instructions by Elder Mark E. Petersen, the church's representative to the excursion and someone who later wrote about the promises of the Book of Mormon to the Lamanites.[18] No doubt he praised their fidelity and their sacrifice and reminded them of the great responsibility they had to spread the gospel to the Spanish-speaking world.

These gatherings, which became spiritual feasts for Mexican, Mexican American, and Central American saints, could only

14. Balderas, "La Conferencia en Mesa," 152.

15. Balderas, "La Conferencia en Mesa," 153.

16. Balderas, Oral History, 66–67.

17. Eduardo Balderas, "La Decimacuarta Excursión a Mesa," *Liahona*, Jan. 1, 1959, 12.

18. Balderas, "La Decimacuarta Excursión a Mesa," 13; see also Mark E. Petersen, *Children of the Promise: The Lamanites; Yesterday and Today* (Salt Lake City: Bookcraft, 1981).

continue with the formalizing of the temple ceremonies in Spanish. Consequently, the First Presidency assigned Antoine R. Ivins to have the temple ceremonies translated, and he asked Eduardo to assist. This was one assignment that Eduardo could not do on his own because he did not have the last word on the ritual's terminology, and while Ivins didn't either, the member of the Seventy did have ready access to the Brethren, who could decide theological questions.

Translation, Ivins understood, required numerous hours of meticulous and painstaking converting of words and concepts from one language to another, and he neither had the time nor the practice of such labor. By now, Ivins had seen Eduardo's work and noticed the confidence his young assistant exhibited in accomplishing the tasks set before him and his familiarity with those of his people coming to the temple. Translations of this type only worked if the translator had an audience in mind, and this was an audience few church leaders had experience with. Any initial reluctance, if there was any, most likely hinged on the church leaders' uncertainty over whether these people, or any people like them, were ready for these more complicated ordinances.

There was, however, no uncertainty in Eduardo. "It was an unforgettable experience," he later recalled about the translation.[19] The church authorities had a particular view on how it was to be done and how that translation was to be used, though we have no record of the specific instructions they gave. Eduardo and Ivins were given a year to finish the translation for the October excursion in 1945. In all, they were to translate the ritual of anointing, the endowment session, and the sealing ceremony, each of which had several parts to them that required multiple steps to perform.

Eduardo remembers having "many interesting experiences" as he and Ivins sought to understand what each ritual meant, how it could be conveyed, and how to maintain a consistency of words and ideas throughout the three different rites. He shared, "When we didn't know how to translate a certain phrase … it became necessary for us to consult the Missionary Committee or the First Presidency,

19. Balderas, Oral Interview, 66.

whoever could answer our question" and clarify the point.[20] This process not only informed Ivins and Eduardo but no doubt caused church authorities to look closely at a ceremony that had developed over time, and which no one person or prophet had been solely involved in creating.

"It was like a school to me," Eduardo told an interviewer years later, "learning just what some of the unfamiliar phrasing in the endowment ceremony entails."[21] It was also a "thrill" for him to be working closely with a man he looked up to and who was responsible for him working for the church. He admired the man, who was the son of a former apostle of the church, was a lawyer trained in Mexico, who knew the Spanish language, and who had been a mission president and now served in the presidency of the Quorum of the Seventy. The fact that he was helping the man he respected most, next to Rey L. Pratt, translate one of the utmost important ordinances that Latter-day Saints performed only made it a further momentous occasion for him.[22]

In that year, they finished a rough translation, went over it several times, clarified every word and phrase, had it typed and distributed to the Arizona temple and the church archives, and had it distributed to the temple workers to be studied. Come October 1945, the people arrived for the first official "Lamanite temple excursion" to do their ordinance work and to hear from their leaders. So many came that Eduardo was asked by the mission president to serve as a temple worker again. He accepted and was officially set apart, and that began a yearly ritual that he and Rhea undertook and because it was not an assignment from the church—he took vacation time and covered expenses from his own pocket.[23]

This kind of "after hours" religious work fed into Eduardo's own commitment to a work he saw as sacred and urgent. Just as important, it gave him an opportunity to lead his people, even though he had no ecclesiastical responsibility and he was speaking someone else's

20. Balderas, Oral History, 66. For an in-depth look at LDS temple worship, see Devery S. Anderson, ed., *The Development of LDS Temple Worship, 1846–2000* (Salt Lake City: Signature Books, 2011).

21. Balderas, Oral History, 66.

22. Balderas, Oral History, 66; Anderson, *The Development of LDS Temple Worship.*

23. Balderas, 67.

words. Still, in that world of the Spanish speaking, where so much congregational leading and spiritual growth occurred below the official surface—as has been done since the church entered spaces of color—Eduardo played an important role. He was not speaking or writing official theology, but he was further extending that "theology on the ground" that Mexican saints and other saints of color practiced in their sacred spaces, and he did this by providing Spanish words and terms that explained Latter-day Saint cosmology.

It would be almost thirty years later that the film version of the endowment in Spanish became a reality, thus allowing the endowment ceremony to be conducted in Spanish in any temple where there were enough saints requesting it. That the translation of the ceremony was only tweaked to synchronize it with the English film version attests to the quality of the translation.[24] The temple ceremonies have evolved over time, and the rituals have become less about consequences and more about promised blessings, making them more appealing to a younger generation of Latter-day Saints, but they have yet to fully become more culturally appealing to people of color. Thus, they have become rituals to practice and ordinances to remember, but meaning remains elusive to those who are not steeped in Mormon canon and attuned to traditional Latter-day Saint theological interpretations.[25]

Cultural relevancy was not an idea back then, but Eduardo nonetheless understood that for his people to "blossom" in this still predominantly American church and receive all the blessings they were promised, they had to receive their endowments and seal themselves not only to their immediate families but to their ancestors. Eduardo knew it was a way for the Spanish-speaking saints to qualify to assume leadership positions beyond their wards and branches, something that came generations later. The Spanish translation served Spanish-speaking saints around the world, including in places like the Switzerland Temple, though ironically, Spanish-language sessions were not available in Salt Lake City until shortly after

24. Balderas.

25. Temple worship, as it was once known, is in itself rather simple, and much of the meaning comes not by attending the temple but by listening to and reflecting on what church leaders say it means, which can then change when the practices and the teachings of those or future church leaders change.

Eduardo's retirement, an indication that some leaders still resisted the idea of a universal, multilingual temple worship in the church's heartland.[26]

In Utah, Mexican and Latin American saints wishing to attend the historic sanctuary on Temple Square received cards that had a Spanish translation of the temple ceremonies, and in some parts of the temple rituals, they were simply provided an explanation of what would happen, and then they listened to the ceremony in English. We have no record of how Eduardo felt about this, but it must have been perplexing to know that almost thirty years after he helped translate the temple ceremonies, his people were still using the pre-translation methods to go through the temple right across from the church's administrative building where, in the 1970s, church leaders were no doubt conscious that the Spanish-speaking membership was growing in unprecedented numbers.[27]

Though pleased with his work on the temple ceremonies, he was not content with translating manuals, letters, and other documents, which while of much worth, were not as transcendental since their content changed often. The one thing missing, which President Rey L. Pratt had surely made Eduardo aware of in his early convert years as well as after his mission, was a Spanish translation of the other Mormon scriptures. Only the Book of Mormon had been translated into Spanish, but for any LDS community to be fully versed with Latter-day Saint doctrine, it needed to be able to read the Doctrine and Covenants and the Pearl of Great Price, the two other scriptures that made up the Mormon canon.

While the Book of Mormon provided Latter-day Saints with the major basis of their doctrine, it did not provide a governance structure nor answers to particular questions in administering a church.

---

26. Balderas, Oral History, 67–68.

27. For some inexplicable reason, Latter-day Saint leaders up until almost the twenty-first century still saw Salt Lake City as a place where the English language had to dominate. I remember when the first Spanish-language stake was created in Houston, Texas, and Latina/o saints in Utah, whose numbers were more numerous than those in Houston, requested a similar organization in the state. Then church president Gordon B. Hinckley sent a clear message to a gathered group of Latina/o saints: "Not in Utah." That changed, however, in 2024 when two Spanish-language stakes were established in Utah, and more were promised. The author attended the establishment of the second in Provo, Utah, where a Latino general authority promised "more to come."

That came from the Doctrine and Covenants. From the Pearl of Great Price, saints learned deeper doctrinal points, and it provided Mormonism a distinctive version of the creation story and the essence of the Godhead that distinguished it from most other religious traditions. Lacking a translation of these two scriptural texts handicapped the Spanish-speaking leadership and might have been one reason, among others, why the Salt Lake City Rama Mexicana, and also other Spanish language branches throughout the Southwest continued to have white leadership.

Rey L. Pratt understood the importance of these two books of scripture, and he began a translation of a selection of them and soon had Eduardo, who was then on his mission, helping him with words he did not understand and acting as a sounding board. Pratt, however, died before he could finish the full translation. Ivins, who eventually took over as mission president, undertook the task to finish the translation and had it published as *Revelación de los últimos días* (revelation of the latter-days). When he first arrived in El Paso, knowing of Eduardo's assistance to Pratt, he gave him a copy of the translation.[28]

Working with Pratt on the selections provided Eduardo the first opportunity to work on scriptures, a challenging effort, but one that tied him to those men he came to admire and write about who translated God's word. Pratt, a very devout and religious man, taught him the reverence to the scriptures that became obvious to anyone who knew Eduardo. It is hard not to imagine Pratt holding a copy of the Doctrine and Covenants in his hands, softly turning the pages, and putting Spanish words on paper or dictating them to Eduardo in a reverential tone, but also with excitement in his voice because he was making God's word available to a people he loved so dearly.

Ivins seemed quite different. As a member of the First Quorum of the Seventy, he served as one of the church's general authorities, and like so many of them at the time (and since, some would say), he came across as serious, somber, and maybe even a bit aloof and related to Eduardo as a leader rather than a mentor. While he worked with Eduardo—who admired him greatly—for a number of years and was responsible for bringing him to Salt Lake City, nothing

28. Balderas, Oral History, 43–44.

indicates that they were friends. Instead, they were brothers in the faith but within a leader and disciple relationship, though Eduardo always credited him with making him the translator he became. Those feelings are a testament to Eduardo's humility and ability to forgive, because as noted before, Ivins had proven less than a friend when he tried to dissuade Rhea from marrying him.

After a few years working on translating, Ivins called Eduardo into his office and told him that under the direction of the church's First Presidency, he had finished a full translation of the Doctrine and Covenants and he wanted Eduardo to take a look at it and prepare it for publication. "Being rather new ... not sure of my ground, and dealing with a General Authority," remembers Eduardo, "I took the manuscript and kept it for a few days and returned it to him with just a note here and there. He looked over what I'd done, smiled and thanked me."[29]

It surely surprised Eduardo that nothing came of the manuscript, and it was not until three or four years later that he approached Ivins and asked what had ever happened to it. "Oh, it's still in my file," he responded. By this time, Eduardo had the hymnal and the temple ceremony translations under his belt and felt more confident of his abilities, especially since Ivins had stopped looking over his shoulder. "I wonder if I could have a second chance," asked Eduardo, to which Ivins responded, "I was hoping you'd say that."[30]

For Eduardo, Ivins's willingness to wait revealed great wisdom. He had waited until Eduardo was not only better prepared but also more willing to edit the work of one of his superiors, a rather bold move back then (and even today, among some) in a religious culture where leaders are often seen as working under the direction of the Holy Ghost, and thus their work is divinely inspired. Eduardo said, "He [Ivins] knew there was something wrong [with the translation] the first time he gave it to me, so he ... wisely kept it ... until ... I was better prepared." This time Eduardo engaged with the scripture more thoroughly as he came to understand that translation was more than changing one word with another of a different language.[31] Without

29. Balderas.
30. Balderas.
31. Balderas.

question, he now understood that translating was his profession, and while others above him knew the language and had to be consulted periodically, none of them had been given the gift of translation, which Balderas now knew he had. After all, Joseph Smith translated the Book of Mormon and the Pearl of Great Price by the power of the Holy Ghost. Why would it be any different to translate them into Spanish?

This time, as with his translation of the hymnal and unlike the translation of the temple ceremony, Eduardo worked mostly on his own, painstakingly going over Ivins's translation, correcting words, clearing up sentences, and making thoughts accessible to the people he had taught as a missionary and later led as a branch president. While always seeking to use the best grammar and to maintain a consistency with the way the church authorities taught, the audience he had in mind were people with limited schooling, not often inclined to read or understand complicated material. The Doctrine and Covenants itself promised that "every man shall hear the fullness of the gospel in his own tongue and in his own language" (Doctrine and Covenants 90:11). In his "own tongue and in his own language" meant social and cultural context, which native language provided, even if only enough to have people build upon that social frame of reference as their experience with and knowledge of the Latter-day Saint gospel grew. For the Spanish-speaking saints, this prophecy to make doctrinal matters comprehensible to them found fulfilment through Eduardo's work.

After finishing his first major revision and rewrite, he met with Ivins to discuss the changes to the manuscript. Eduardo remembers this as "a very, very pleasant and educational task."[32] Ironically, this time Eduardo did not describe it as a spiritual experience as he did with the translation of the temple ceremony—not that he doubted that translating scripture was a spiritual task, but now, after several years under Ivins's tutelage and after completing numerous translations of lesson manuals and missionary tracts, the hymnal, and the temple ceremony, he felt comfortable in his abilities and in tune with the spirit of revelation that he believed was necessary to translate. To

32. Balderas, 44.

the extent possible, within an asymmetric relationship, an equality in the process of translation now existed.

By this time, Eduardo had—in his mind if not in that of his leaders—turned his "job" into a "calling," and he saw it this way until he translated his last word. He did not need to be "set apart" as he had been and would be when called to different church callings because his work and its outward spiritual manifestations—exposing Spanish-speaking members to the fullness of the Latter-day Saint gospel—had set him apart in a way that Ivins or other church authorities never did.[33] As the Doctrine and Covenants clearly stated, "Therefore, if ye have desires to serve God ye are called to the work" (Doctrine and Covenants 4:3). Eduardo now felt as the prophet Joseph Smith, who quickly left behind the mechanics—Urim and Thummim and seer stones—of translation and began to translate through revelation.[34]

After receiving approval from Ivins to have the work printed, Eduardo asked about the Pearl of Great Price, a book with profound Latter-day Saint doctrine but one that even now is less read and understood by church members. "Oh, that can be done later," responded Ivins, which might have puzzled Eduardo, who now seemed determined to provide his people with all that the Latter-day Saint gospel offered. Possibly still thinking of this not-yet-to-be-translated book, he inquired of the printers the cost of printing the smaller book, and they informed him that it would be quite expensive and suggested he print it together with the Doctrine and Covenants.

Eduardo then went to Ivins, who sought and received approval, and he then commenced the translation of the last book of the LDS canon. This small volume, with teachings only partly found in the

33. To be "set apart" is a term Latter-day Saints use to describe the way they are called to a church position. The person is first interviewed by the bishop, stake president, or other presiding authority and then presented to the congregation for a sustaining vote. Hands are then place upon their head by a priesthood leader, and the person is given the charge and authority to perform the task to which they've been called.

34. To learn about Joseph Smith's evolution as a translator, see James E. Lancaster, "The Method of Translation of the Book of Mormon," *John Witmer Historical Association Journal* 3 (1983): 51–61; and Michael Hubbard MacKay, "The Secular Binary of Joseph Smith's Translations," *Dialogue: A Journal of Mormon Thought* 54, no. 3 (Fall 2021): 1–39. While initially depending on the Urim and Thummim to translate, he later put them aside and did most of the translation through inspiration and revelation.

other books of the canon, must have been a challenge, and it is quite possible that he had numerous consultations with Ivins, who no doubt consulted with his superiors. It is also possible that with the translations of the Doctrine and Covenants, the temple ceremony, and numerous manuals and sermons under his belt, he simply did it on his own. Unfortunately, all we know is that it took him about three months to complete his translation and get it approved.[35] By this time, notwithstanding Ivins's knowledge of the language, the Brethren had to trust Eduardo in a way they had never trusted anyone before.

The end result of Eduardo's work was that the Doctrine and Covenants and Pearl of Great Price were printed together in 1948 for the first time in any language, and both became more accessible and likely to be read more frequently than when the books were apart. I remember in my own household having several copies laying around and finding it hard to read the Doctrine and Covenants and not the Pearl of Great Price, simply because leaving one out felt like the reading was incomplete. Eduardo may well have understood something about his people that others did not: they were going to have to be encouraged to read, and many would have to learn to read or improve their reading abilities through the Spanish-language scriptures, which was the case with numerous men and women who inspired me but who struggled with reading anything beyond the scriptures.

Eduardo understood the limitations that every Mexican church leader confronted when they could not read the English language. He remembered his own father teaching only from the Book of Mormon in priesthood quorum meetings, a time when men should have been taught about their priesthood duties and about the protocol of church leadership. "Continuing revelation," a concept unique to the Latter-day Saints in the modern era, was based partly on the collection in the Doctrine and Covenants of "direct revelation"—both personal and collective—that Joseph Smith and other LDS prophets had received. No doubt that when he served as branch president, Eduardo saw the need to teach his leaders and members from the Doctrine and Covenants and the Pearl of Great Price.

He had taken care of the challenge of translating the lesson

35. Balderas, Oral History, 44.

manuals and other church literature that came to the branches, wards, and missions, and he had enhanced the Spanish-speaking members' doctrinal and theological culture by expanding their collection of hymns. Now he had completed the translated canon. Possibly no Spanish-speaking leader, since Margarito Bautista and the leaders of the Third Convention, understood the challenge that a limited canon had on Mexican and other Spanish-speaking saints. It was one reason, at least in Bautista's view, that leadership beyond the branch was out of reach for them.

Working at the highest level of the church administration, or at least being in close proximity to it, exposed Eduardo to the complexity of the church in ways that few ethnic saints and saints of color experienced. His own travels with church authorities allowed him to hear priesthood and doctrinal instruction that was not recorded. He came to learn the "language" of authority and of doctrinal instruction in a way that no other saint of color in his time ever did. Just as important, having such an efficient translator, and one who understood how to present the message to his own people, allowed visiting church authorities to be more expansive in their teachings and instructions.

The first edition of the Spanish-language Doctrine and Covenants and the Pearl of Great Price came out in 1948. Shortly afterwards, Eduardo began working on a translation into Portuguese, this time not as translator but as a supervisor of the process, which became complicated when the Brazilian woman doing the translation came into conflict with others in the Missionary Committee and refused to proceed. Gordon B. Hinckley, then the non-ecclesiastical director of the committee, asked Eduardo to take over. Though his Portuguese language skills were limited, he found himself comparing the Portuguese translation with the Spanish one and then the English, checking out the differences and asking questions about translation in Portuguese.

This was typical of Eduardo, who sought answers and solutions from any source he could find and then did his best to make sure the translations were accessible to the people who read them. As always, he remained positive about the challenges he faced as the church's first translator. He shared, "This task was very helpful to me, a great experience which I appreciated, and a wonderful opportunity to learn Portuguese."[36] Up to this point, there were few other translators, and most of them were temporary or part-time employees. All of them were untrained and solely dependent on Eduardo to learn not only the process but also the underlying philosophy of translating Mormon theology. It is unfortunate that Eduardo did not write a journal and so we do not know how he developed his approach nor his thoughts about taking the fullness of the gospel to his Spanish-speaking and now Portuguese brothers and sisters.

The effort to translate such a voluminous amount of materials and to ponder those special spiritual moments in translating Latter-day Saint canon took an inordinate amount of time, often causing him to stay late at the office, and just as often to take work home—not necessarily the physical documents, but those thoughts about a word, a phrase, or a full theological concept that were the burden of the mental work of spreading the gospel in every language. His son Daniel remembers his father rarely ever being home, coming home late, leaving early, and sometimes accompanying church leaders on trips.[37] There are few memories of his children of him playing with them.

What Eduardo's children do remember is his humble demeanor, the Mexican meals he cooked for them, and the times they went to visit him at his work and got a chance to see him with those religious giants of mid-twentieth century Mormonism. They also remembered his love for their mother. It was his beloved sweetheart, Rhea, who carried the load—a common situation among many Latter-day Saint families in which the husband carried priesthood responsibilities, or like Eduardo, worked for the church. Rhea's responsibilities, however, did not end when all the children went to bed and the chores were done.[38]

It is obvious from the early letters that Eduardo wrote to court Rhea, the pictures of them participating in branch and ward activities, and the later pictures of them growing old together, that they

36. Balderas, Oral History, 45.

37. Daniel and Christine Balderas, interview by Ignacio M. García, Cindy Perez, and Fernando Gomez, Summer 2020, Provo, Utah, recording and hard copy of interview property of author. Much of the information of the Balderas family life comes from this interview, as well as a phone conversation with Anna Balderas on December 2, 2020.

38. Daniel and Christine Balderas, interview.

forged a special bond. Very much like Mormon men of that era and many today, Eduardo needed Rhea to keep the family functioning right and to help him emotionally to carry on his work. While Eduardo comes across as a self-starter and a tenacious fulfiller of duties, he also presents a figure who was fragile and humble, seeking to accommodate others, and rarely having an opportunity to lead, even in those efforts where he was better qualified to do so than anyone else around him. Having a family to lead with kindness and humility provided him with his only "leadership" opportunity for most of his life.

This reliance on Rhea to "steady the boat" at home and to comfort him when he felt overburdened or stressed, however, took its toll on her. Her children remember her often going into her bedroom and closing the door behind her to have some moments to herself.[39] Rhea had married the kind of man every young Latter-day Saint woman was encouraged to find: one devoted to the church, seeking to learn the gospel, and giving service when called. Not only that but her husband also worked for the church, rubbed elbows with general authorities, and produced work that no one else had ever done before at that level. But she learned, as other Mormon women had throughout the church's history, that her marriage was always going to take second place to the church service of men like Eduardo. Her children remember her as being proud of his work and basking in the opportunities she had to be around church leaders she admired, but no doubt she would have loved to have had a more "normal" marriage.[40]

The one place that did provide Eduardo a chance to let loose was the Rama Mexicana that he attended for the first decade or more after arriving in Salt Lake City. There, he would serve in a variety of callings: choir director, Sunday School president, teacher, missionary, and even as a counselor in the branch presidency. Eduardo, the quiet person working in the church administration building, was someone else in his local church, particularly when it came to acting in plays and singing during the church festivals and dinners. Sometimes he took his act on the road, performing in non-church functions and

39. Christine and Daniel Balderas, phone interview with author, May 23, 2023.
40. Christine and Daniel Balderas, phone interview.

wearing mariachi and other Mexican wardrobe items, at times with his wife and at other times accompanied by other singers.[41]

He also became involved in Mexican Independence Day celebrations citywide, and there are copies of letters in which he invited church leaders, the governor, and city officials to such activities.[42] Eduardo was part of that immigrant generation that felt connected to its roots in another country, though, ironically, he never lived in Mexico for any extended time, he married a white woman, and he became an American citizen. Just as ironic, while he came to represent the Spanish-speaking church, his children rarely ever participated in these types of events.

His son Daniel remembers not learning Spanish because his father had no time to teach the children, and their mother, who spoke what Daniel described as "Tex-Mex" Spanish, did not see herself as capable. Like many first-generation Mexican immigrants, Eduardo lived a dual life. He translated all the church material into Spanish for the thousands of saints in the Southwest and south of the border but did not teach his children to speak Spanish. He also got the branch to celebrate Mexican Independence Day and became involved in his community's festivities, but his home, according to his children was American.[43] This situation would be little different for many Mexican immigrants who worked in white spaces and whose children went to school with few other Spanish-speaking children.

For families like Eduardo's, who bordered on middle-class status, theirs was going to be an American life they could not fully live in the Mexican barrios, and their children would likely find white spouses and practice their religion in white wards. This did not happen often, at least initially, to people for whom Eduardo was

41. Christine and Daniel Balderas, phone interview. Also, see Betty G. Ventura, *The History of the Salt Lake Mexican Branch, 1920–1960* (self-pub., 1998), for numerous notations of his participation not only in administrative functions but also in cultural and musical activities.

42. Private collection of letters in the Balderas family's possession to Eduardo Balderas from J. Reuben Clark, of the First Presidency (Sep. 17, 1946); Duane G. Hunt, Catholic Bishop (Sep. 16, 1946); David O. McKay, First Presidency (Sep. 13, 1946); Earl J. Glade, Salt Lake City Mayor (Sep. 11, 1946); and Herbert B. Maw, Utah Governor (Sep. 11, 1946). All indicated they received Eduardo's invitation to attend a Mexican Independence Day celebration. All expressed their regrets for not being able to attend.

43. Daniel and Christine Balderas, interview. Anna Balderas, phone conversation.

translating the Mormon canon and other material. Those people's children often found themselves in segregated schools—not always physically, because they were few in number, but surely socially and culturally—and this impacted their learning, provided them few skills, made it difficult for them to find good jobs, and limited their economic integration into American society. Many had few of the advantages that Eduardo could give his own children, simply by his working for the most important institution in Utah.[44]

The Spanish-speaking church was a help for those seeking to keep their Mexican culture at home. At the same time, it opened the door for some to an assimilation that took them away from their communities. As the Balderas children remembered it, sacrament meeting was in Spanish, but all the classes were in English. The history of the branch has the Balderas children—Samuel, Ana Rhea, Roberto, and Daniel—presenting several special musical numbers (1955) when their father spoke.[45] It would be years after the Rama Mexicana was established before it became a priority that the youth learn Spanish.[46] I remember the same thing happening in my Spanish-language ward—sacrament meeting, firesides, and leadership meetings being conducted in Spanish, but classes often in English—but my cultural advantage was living in a larger Mexican barrio and going to school with almost all Mexican kids. I also had the advantage (often a disadvantage) of my parents not speaking English, and neither did my extended relatives, so I had to keep my fluency in the language.

The Balderas children had little of those advantages, nor did they have the benefit of seeing Spanish as a foreign language to be studied and to be praised for learning, as it was for white children who now had learned another language. Speaking Spanish was a punishable offense in most of the public schools in the Southwest, but only for Mexican students, and while there were no such rules in Utah,

44. See Jorge Iber, *Hispanics in the Mormon Zion, 1912–1999* (College Station: Texas A&M University Press, 2000), particularly chapters 1, 3, and 5, for a discussion of the educational, economic, and social circumstances of the Mexican population in Utah.

45. Ventura, *History of the Salt Lake Mexican Branch*, 44.

46. See Ventura, *History of the Salt Lake Mexican Branch*, 21. In 1938, sixteen years after the branch was established, the branch president, James Vernon Graves, assigned a Sister Deifilia J. Torres to teach the children how to read, write, and speak "the language of their parents." He later served as Sunday School president and organized several programs that had the youth presenting talks in Spanish.

Mexican children were often ostracized for being Mexican, which included speaking their parents' language.[47] The Balderas children were spared that situation for the most part, and that in itself made them view themselves as being just like anyone else. It would be naive, however, to assume that the idea never crossed their minds that they were different and that other Mexican kids, less assimilated, were treated with less respect by both classmates and teachers. Being part white, having no accent, and being children of a father employed at church headquarters had its advantages but could not hide all the realities.[48]

Eduardo also provided his children with other plusses, like having family home evening—years before the church officially adopted the program—where he taught the gospel to them in English, thus affirming what the children were subconsciously learning in branch classes, and that is that the Mormon gospel was an English gospel, exactly the opposite of what Eduardo was trying to demonstrate with his translations. One only has to remember the discussion among church leaders about whether the temple ceremonies could be in a language other than English to understand how a simple class to the family in English affirmed the need to assimilate into a world foreign to many Mexican youth.

As they grew older, the Balderas children saw the disconnect between themselves and the Mexican branch as they lived in a white neighborhood, had only white friends—since they saw their church classmates only once or possibly twice a week—understood very little said in sacrament meeting, met their father's white bosses (who were also their church leaders), and were detached from the Mexican world in which their father seemed the happiest. We do not know Rhea's feelings, but she seemed, in pictures at least, to be quite happy in the Rama Mexicana, to which she had belonged almost

47. See Ignacio M. García, "'The Best Bargain … Ever Received': The 1968 Commission on Civil Rights Hearing in San Antonio, Texas," *Southwestern Historical Quarterly* 112, no.3 (Jan. 2019), for a discussion of the educational odyssey many Mexican children suffered in American schools.

48. In a discussion with a Dale Rees, a gentleman who knew Eduardo, he told me that his wife went to school with some of the Balderas children and she knew that Mexican kids were being harassed for being foreigners. Whether any of that happened to the Balderas children is unknown.

since her return from the mission field. She had also once found it fascinating to possibly live in Mexico with Eduardo when most of his family had moved south and he had worked mostly in Ciudad Juarez, just across the border from El Paso.[49]

The process to move away from the LDS Spanish-speaking world began when the children started going home by themselves, hoping to meet up with their white friends in church, and eventually convinced their parents that they should attend the neighborhood English ward by themselves. It is hard to know why Eduardo, whom his children saw as a very traditional Mexican father—what he said was the law—agreed to this arrangement. After all, for Latter-day Saints, unity of the family—including worshipping together—was and is fundamental to their religion. Eduardo, however, might have seen what he considered inevitable and that is that his children were going to live in a white world, probably have white spouses, and hopefully—the dream of many Latter-day Saint families—be called to important church positions.[50]

Eduardo, however, lived his Mexican ways in the branch that he and Rhea continued to attend for years after their children left that space. His son Daniel remembers Eduardo playing in the infield for the branch's softball team. He remembers his father as being "a good player" but admits that he was too young to make any real assessment of his father's skills. "He was big. I was little," he said, and that colored his views of his father's ability to play the softer version of America's pastime.[51]

Christine, Daniel's wife, remembers her father-in-law playing in a band and performing during the branch's *piñata* parties. Numerous family pictures attest to his love of music and theater.[52] It was there in the branch that Eduardo lived his cultural and social life, and it was the place where people understood—though not fully—his importance to their spiritual and religious lives. The branch provided him valuable time away from the office, where he had to be in a temperate mood, where the hierarchy above him had so many layers,

49. Eduardo to Rhea, Dec. 2, 1934, from private collection in possession of Eduardo's daughter Ana.

50. Daniel and Christine Balderas, interview.

51. Daniel and Christine Balderas, interview.

52. Daniel and Christine Balderas, interview.

and where he only spoke English except when reading his translations out loud or providing instruction to his mostly white assistants. In the branch, he could be his gregarious self, relax with friends, eat rich Mexican food, dance to Spanish-language music, and forget the stress at the office. All this notwithstanding that he loved his work.

On Sundays he could lead, instruct, and inspire his fellow congregants. Though he never became the branch's president—a rather strange decision by his leaders—he nonetheless had a great impact on his fellow worshippers because he knew the scriptures and church protocol better than anyone there. He could share with them anecdotes and stories about church leaders, about how decisions were made, and about how the work among the Spanish speaking was going. He would often share (sometimes in sacrament meetings) a report about his travels to Latin America, and how the work was going there. It was his personal report of what he saw as the blossoming of the Spanish-speaking Lamanites.[53]

Eduardo might not have been a church leader, but there was no doubt that to many Spanish-speaking saints, he was the closest thing to one. His daughter-in-law Christine remembers that some considered him the "thirteenth apostle."[54] This admiration would grow exponentially when he was called to be a patriarch, which will be discussed more in length in a subsequent chapter. He would probably have said, if asked, that the branch meant as much to him as he did to it. It was there where he saw the fruits of his work, and it provided him experiences important to his translation as he saw Spanish-speaking members practice their faith, heard their desire to read the works that were at the time only available in English, and understood the urgency of having his fellow Mexican saints be prepared for their missions and for future leadership positions.

His work would be appreciated within the confines of his department but never rewarded to the extent it should have been because he never rose in the ranks of his department. One former translation division head—a Latino—told me years after Eduardo had died, that maybe the church "wanted someone more assertive" to lead.[55] This

53. Ventura, *History of the Salt Lake Mexican Branch*, 44–45.

54. Daniel and Christine Balderas, interview.

55. This came from a conversation I had at grocery store with a former BYU

assessment sounds ridiculous when acknowledging that he served for over three decades, helped develop the translation department, and even taught its leaders much about the work of translation.[56]

Given his commitment to the church, the joy he took in his work, and his spiritual experiences working with church leaders and translating church canon, the temple ceremony, and the lesson manuals that went out worldwide, it is likely that Balderas might have publicly taken issue with this author's assessment that he was overlooked. In part because he stood on a perch that overlooked the institutional landscape of his people in the church, he was conscious of his responsibility to keep them believing that all things in the church were done by revelation and inspiration. There are no dissenting or critical comments to be found about his feelings toward his situation within the Mormon kingdom, but it is difficult to imagine that he never once asked himself why he never led a department he basically founded or why he never got called to lead his people in their own branch.

---

administrator who had once served in the translation department. It was not meant to be, but the comment came out as callous given how often that same administrator had talked about the unfairness of the university when it came to students and staff of color.

56. See John E. Carr, *For in that Day: A History of Translation and Distribution*, 1965–1980 (n.p., n.d., ca.1980), L. Tom Perry Special Collections, Harold B. Lee Library, Brigham Young University, for a history of the church's translation department. What stands out is the lack of credit given to Eduardo for his work in creating the need for the department.

8

THE *LIAHONA*

TAKING PROPHETIC VOICES TO THE SPANISH-SPEAKING WORLD

Eduardo's translation work affirmed the viability of taking the LDS message throughout the world while maintaining what was taught under the direction of church leaders in Salt Lake City. Before his activities established the idea of translating and disseminating a uniform gospel message, the church depended on mission presidents, missionaries, and volunteers to translate the proselyting materials, classroom lessons, and parts of the LDS canon in those places where a language other than English was spoken. While men like Pratt and Ivins were fluent enough to do somewhat accurate translations, there were others who were less prepared, and relying on young missionaries with a rudimentary knowledge of the language brought all kinds of challenges.

Unfortunately, there are no works on the challenges of translating LDS canon into other languages. Those unfamiliar with the process are apt to think that translation of religious documents might simply be the exchanging of an English word with one of another language. Eduardo found out that was not the case. In his own work, he had to understand context, receive clarification from church leaders, become well versed with two languages, all wedded together with reflection, prayer, and divine help. On more than one occasion, when he asked a church leader for clarification of a verse or concept, he was told to go back and see what church leaders had said in the past and how the concept, phrase, or word was used over time.[1] Most

1. Eduardo Balderas, Oral History, interviews by Gordon Irving, 1973, typescript, 61–62, Oral History Program, CHL. In the case discussed in these pages, there was a

mission presidents and young missionaries—even those with the best of language skills—did not have the time or training to engage in such efforts, something Eduardo did often in translating church documents and scriptural references into Spanish.

Now that the church canon had all been translated and the lesson manuals, hymns, and other church materials had been or were in the process of being translated, the messages of the Mormon prophets often used by missionaries and leaders to teach the Mormon gospel needed to be translated correctly. This need was most urgent in the mission field, not only in missionary proselytizing but also in the numerous mission publications, newsletters, and magazines that had popped up throughout the areas where missionaries wandered. These publications were particularly popular in Mexico and Latin America, where missionaries sought to connect their LDS communities with the larger church by providing messages from leaders in Salt Lake City and also providing stories and anecdotes from different areas in the mission.

In Spanish-speaking countries, two monthly magazines existed: one, the *Liahona*, was published in Mexico City by the Mexican Mission, and the other, *El Mensajero*, was produced by the Argentina Mission. There were also others that came out periodically in Uruguay and Central America. Collecting stories, articles, and sermons to translate and edit required an inordinate amount of time. A report by Gordon B. Hinckley, who headed the translation efforts for the church, indicated that in the Mexican Mission, 360 hours were required, "with one missionary spending all of his time" to produce the monthly publication.[2] In the Argentina Mission it took five hundred hours and three missionaries were assigned full time to the task.[3]

Emphasizing the demands that producing a magazine put on the missionaries, Hinckley recommended the "church publish one

question as to whether to use the singular or plural in translating a word from a passage in the Doctrine and Covenants. J. Reuben Clark sent Eduardo to the Church History Library to study a legal case in which church President Joseph F. Smith testified and used the scripture in a particular way.

2. John E. Carr, *For in That Day: A History of Translation and Distribution, 1965–1980* (n.p., n.d., ca. 1980), L. Tom Perry Special Collections, Harold B. Lee Library, Brigham Young University, 246–47.

3. Carr.

Spanish-language magazine for distribution to all of the Spanish-language missions and among the … members in [those] stakes."[4] This magazine, according to Hinckley, needed to be published in Salt Lake City, be part of the church administrative structure, and be under the editorial direction of the First Presidency and the Quorum of the Twelve Apostles. Publishing in Utah would also provide other benefits such as reduced costs, less burden on the missionaries, a lessening of worries for the mission president, better control of the content, and a unified message for the Spanish-language members, and it would also ensure a better translation.[5]

While these recommendations had merit in putting together a more professional magazine, the implementation of Hinckley's recommendations, like the retranslation and expansion of the Spanish hymnal, took away the organic aspects of the messages provided by such magazines. As regional magazines, these publications had a stronger connection to the members and nonmembers served by the missions. Occasionally, local members contributed to the content, and that allowed the magazines to be more relevant to the religious lives of the members in the area. The missionaries, most often white young men and women from the states, also benefitted from the need to interact with local members to find out about their spiritual needs and to talk about the people they were serving.

This centralization of the gospel message, however, meant greater clarity in the church's communication with its Spanish-speaking members and brought them in closer, at least emotionally, to their leaders in Salt Lake City and the rest of the church. Spanish-speaking members would learn the same things, read the same news, learn of changes occurring in the church hierarchy much sooner than before, and benefit from information and counsel of the other auxiliaries. At the same time, the centralization cemented the asymmetric relationship between the church's core and its peripheries and led to a dependence on those who came from the core to preach and proselytize. Salt Lake City became a sort of Mount Olympus—or Vatican—for most members outside of Utah and the United States, which slowed down the development of local leadership. Not only

4. Carr, 247.
5. Carr, 248.

were the "real" leaders in their localities the mission presidents and the missionaries—outsiders—but now their emotional "religious space" was somewhere else, in a space where their own religious experiences did not play out.

We have no record of Eduardo's views on the subject, though it is logical to assume that he supported the move toward a unified magazine for Spanish-speaking countries, simply because it brought to bear the resources of the core to the peripheries. His were not the thoughts of a fighter for regional autonomy because as a witness to his father's struggles to lead a congregation and as a former branch president himself, he understood that the outlying saints had few resources, were limited in their knowledge of the gospel, and often felt isolated from the rest of their fellow members. The centralization of authority was both a blessing and a challenge for Mexican and Latin American saints, remained so for most of the twentieth century, and promises to be an issue in the current century.

The responsibility to develop a unified magazine fell to the translation department, which meant that it became Eduardo's new assignment. Though overwhelmed by the work he now shouldered, he must have felt excited by this new endeavor. His fellow Mexican and Latin American saints would soon have the opportunity to read the words of the prophets and other leaders and to be informed of the many activities of the church. Eduardo, like many of his fellow congregants in Utah, lived in a social and religious bubble in which almost every aspect of their lives centered around the institutional church. This was particularly true for his Spanish-speaking brothers and sisters, who worked, bought, rented, and rubbed shoulders with white Latter-day Saints but remained segregated within their own religious space, thus spared the many conflicts that Latter-day Saints might have been confronting in the larger society.

Though Spanish-speaking members in Utah confronted an asymmetric relationship with their white brothers and sisters—if not always in church surely outside of their meetings—they saw themselves as highly blessed compared to their neighbors to the south. They were near a temple, they saw their general authorities (who often visited the Rama Mexicana), they had Eduardo Balderas—who often took it upon himself to inform them of what was going on in the church—and their children were going on missions from the earliest days of the branch. Though lumped into the pile of disliked Mexicans outside the boundaries of their chapel, as a collective group and within their religious spaces, they were seen as faithful, humble, and good citizens by white religious and political leaders.

In a meeting with Hinckley, Eduardo heard him ask, "Why not consolidate all of these publications into one?"[6] By then, the importance of having one unified magazine had become more urgent. The Uruguay Mission had requested permission to add to the magazines that the Mexico and Argentina Missions had, which would possibly open the door for other missions to request their own publications. Here is where the history of the *Liahona* gets murky, because the only history (unofficial and not distributed) of the magazine points out the early recommendation that it be published in Salt Lake City, but Eduardo remembers being assigned by Hinckley to go to Mexico City and see about publishing there.[7]

Mexico City was the second-largest city in Latin America, next to Buenos Aires, Argentina, but was closer to Salt Lake City and was more familiar to church leaders.[8] This was to be the first of many trips abroad that Eduardo undertook as church translator. Eduardo spent nearly six months in Mexico City trying to get all the details worked out to publish the new magazine.[9] We do not know anything about what he did during that time or whether he was there for six months consecutively, but he likely spent most of the time looking for print shops capable of doing such work and distribution outlets equipped to handle a large volume of magazines, figuring out Mexican post office regulations, finding translators to help with the work, and feeling out church leaders there on the idea of a church magazine for the Spanish speaking.

It is, however, probable that Eduardo spent part of this time meeting with local leaders and members who wanted to know what

6. Carr, 248.

7. See Carr, 247, for one version of the story and Balderas, Oral History, 42–43, for Eduardo's recollection.

8. See data from National Population Censuses and DEPAUL C Project in Miguel Villa and Jorge Rodríguez, "2 Demographic Trends in Latin America's Metropolises, 1950–1990," United Nations University (old website), accessed June 2023, archive.unu.edu.

9. Balderas, Oral History, 42–43.

was going on in Salt Lake City, and he most likely took time to tell them about the translation efforts the church was undertaking. He was just as likely invited to speak to small groups of members or even during sacrament meetings. No other Mexican or Latina/o saint stood as prominent in the Spanish-speaking church as did Eduardo. Even those who knew little about him could not help but be impressed with his church position—though a job and not a calling—and his proximity to the Brethren.

The time in Mexico City proved fruitful in that Eduardo found a print shop that could undertake the job, and this allowed for seven volumes of the magazine to be printed, but eventually the distance and paper shortages caused the publication of the magazine to fall behind schedule. It, in fact, fell almost three months behind. Being so far from Mexico City prevented Eduardo or anyone else from responding appropriately. Eduardo, given his tenacity and experience, could have resolved or mitigated the challenges, no doubt, but that effort would have hampered his own translation work, so the operations were moved to Salt Lake City.[10] It would be years before any church operations were again attempted outside of the country.

When the effort to publish a unified magazine began, a *consejo de redacción* (editorial advisory board) made the decisions on which articles to translate and what material to include. Antoine Ivins and Gordon B. Hinckley, along with Eduardo, served on the board, which eventually turned into the permanent editorial board. *Liahona* was chosen as the name, which was the name of the magazine published by the Mexican Mission, though earlier it had been called *El Atalaya*, or the "watchtower."

The name *Liahona* (from the Book of Mormon), had first been used by the Central States Mission for their own newsletter and magazine that later merged with the *Elders' Journal* of the Southern States Mission to become *Liahona, the Elders' Journal*.[11] That journal ended its run on February 27, 1945, at which time Arwell L. Pierce, president of the Mexican Mission, asked permission to use

10. Balderas, 42–43.

11. See "Featured Collection: Liahona, the Elders' Journal, 1903–1945," Church History, the Church of Jesus Christ of Latter-day Saints, Mar. 10, 2021, history.churchofjesuschrist.org.

the name as a replacement for the mission's own magazine, *El Atalaya*, founded in 1937.[12] It would be an easy transition, since *Liahona* could be pronounced in Spanish without any need to translate, and it came directly from the Book of Mormon, a scripture many Mexican saints still considered their own.

The first issue of the *Liahona* came out in May 1955, and the editorial board was identified as Antonine R. Ivins, Gordon B. Hinckley, Eduardo Balderas, and Arnold J. Irvine. Ivins would serve only until August, and Irvine until December, leaving Hinckley and Balderas alone until May 1956, when W. Earnest Young joined the editorial committee. He too, however, departed in November of that year. Gloria Recarte joined the staff the following October (1957) as the first woman (and one of Latin American descent), but she left the following April. Marion G. Romney joined the editorial board in 1961, most likely as the presiding authority. The following January, R. Hector Grillone became the first Latino editor—Eduardo had never been designated as editor—and he stayed for about three years.[13]

There would be other changes in the editorial board, and then the magazine stopped listing the editorial board in August 1971. During that time, Eduardo had some staff help but shouldered the majority of the translating work for the magazine. It became a particularly heavy burden as the magazine began publishing articles not only by the church's general authorities but also by auxiliary leaders and other individuals, and Eduardo not only translated their words but also ended up translating poems and hymns not in the Spanish hymnal, creating Spanish captions, and making sure that the magazine came together, thus becoming involved in the production, and assuring the magazine was distributed on time. What made it an even greater burden was that he continued to translate manuals, lesson plans, and letters to and from the church leaders. It is little wonder that he spent limited time at home.

Though Eduardo did not see himself as an author—at least outside of his work as a translator, which he considered somewhat as authoring—he did contribute four articles during his tenure on the

12. Carr, *For in That Day*, 248.

13. See *Liahona*, issues from May 1955, Aug. 1955, May 1956, Dec. 1961, Jan. 1962, and May 1963.

editorial board. Probably one of the most important in his mind and one that took research, a skill he had learned after being counseled several times to "research the item" when he had questions about the meaning of a phrase or word, was "How the Scriptures Came to be Translated into Spanish." It told the story of the two most important translators of the Bible into Spanish, Cosiodoro de Reina and Cipriano de la Valera, two Spanish monks. He told of the struggles to get the Bible translated into Spanish and the odyssey that Reina traveled to learn not only how to translate but more so to understand the Bible. Valera would be responsible for modernizing terminology and spelling and putting the books of the Apocrypha together.[14]

He then wrote about Melitón González Trejo, a former Spanish military officer who converted to the Latter-day Saint church and who told then LDS prophet Brigham Young of his desire to bring the Book of Mormon to his people and later published a selection of Book of Mormon chapters with Webster Jones. After serving several missions to Mexico, Trejo and James Z. Steward translated the whole Book of Mormon into Spanish. That translation stood until 1952, when Balderas made some minor revisions and updated the language to reflect a more modern interpretation. Unfortunately, we know no details about the work involved. Balderas mentioned the work Ivins did in the translation process and downplayed his own part.[15] He could have rightfully said that his translation work was key in taking the LDS gospel to the Spanish speaking, but he was too humble of a man to do so.

The article did, however, underscore the important work of translation and the sacrifices that were often made in order to have the Bible—and, indirectly, other scriptures—come to people who spoke and understood other languages than Latin. Translation was, in fact, the most important work in spreading the Christian gospel, and it was a difficult process that often took revision upon revision to find and refine new words for an old canon and to make it understandable to multiple peoples. Balderas could identify with Reina and Valera because he recognized the process of translation and the need, as did

14. Eduardo Balderas, "How the Scriptures Came to be Translated into Spanish," *Ensign*, Sep. 1972, 26–29.

15. Balderas.

the aforementioned, to seek biblical—or at least scriptural—expertise from those who had it.

Scriptural translation was particularly difficult for Eduardo because the LDS Church did not have trained biblical or scripture scholars who studied and researched the Mormon canon and the Bible. Rarely did those leaders and teachers who taught the Mormon scriptures have training in "biblical languages" or ancient material culture or degrees in ancient studies, and even more rare was their legitimacy in the biblical studies world, though that did not seem to bother those who taught or wrote about Latter-day Saint theology. Theirs was an insular world in which their access to "prophetic voices" and the "whisperings of the spirit" were legitimacy enough. Stepping out of the world of Catholic and Protestant biblical or scriptural studies allowed them to say things in their own way. This lack of biblical expertise was the reason, most likely, why Latter-day Saint translators and scholars did not attempt a translation of the Bible. Joseph Smith did attempt one but never finished the process.

Beyond translations, the most important topic for Eduardo were the temple trips that people from Mexico and Central America took to the Mesa Temple. This is the one topic that revealed Eduardo's views about his people and his hope for their "blossoming." In his article, "La Conferencia en Mesa," Eduardo wrote about the start of the second decade of temple trips from throughout the Southwest, Mexico, and now Central America. What had started as a small caravan of cars and buses from the border region and northern Mexico became a large undertaking that grew each year. It was evident by then that Mexican—and now Central American—saints had captured the spirit of temple worship, and their sacrifices to get to the holy place were just as great as those of the earlier pilgrimages. By this second decade of the excursions, however, the saints of Arizona, were better prepared to house, feed, and accommodate the needs of these new "pioneers" over the several days they spent at the temple.[16]

These pilgrimages of poor, devoted saints were a source of spiritual strength and motivation for both the Spanish-speaking saints and the white saints in Arizona—for the former as they witnessed

16. Eduardo Balderas, "La Conferencia en Mesa," *Liahona*, Dec. 1955, 139, 152–53.

their fellow adherents' sacrifice and saw it as reflection of their devotion, and for the latter as they saw the fervent religiosity of their religious siblings from south of the border. It was for both white and Brown saints a fulfilling of the Book of Mormon promises to the Lamanites about the "gathering of Israel" that was often preached from the pulpit. For the Spanish-speaking travelers, the pilgrimage reinforced the feeling that they were part of a brotherhood and sisterhood that extended beyond borders. Here, they were seeing white Americans in a different light.

Balderas, always conscious of the fragile relationship between whites and Mexicans and other Spanish-speaking peoples, sought to emphasize those special moments when the people gathered to worship together. He recounted how the mission presidents from both the United States and Mexico were there to receive the Spanish-speaking saints, but what made the trip particularly special to the Mexican and Central American saints was to see the president of the church, David O. McKay, receive them with a hearty welcome. Coming to the temple was a special occasion—seeing the Lord's anointed prophet was simply beyond expectations for most of these saints.[17]

During the gathering Eduardo wrote about in his article, President McKay spoke about the dedication of the first temple in Europe and how temple ordinances were given in Dutch, German, English, Swiss, French, Norwegian, and Finnish. He shared how the members attended the temple in groups, going through sessions, sealings, and proxy baptisms for thirty-six hours, some resting just enough to be able to get through the grueling hours required to do the work. He must have been thinking of the grueling schedule that the Spanish-speaking saints were about to embark on. President McKay also took time to remind them that it had been the historic occasion in 1945 when the Mexican saints first received their endowments in their own language that had led to the translating of the temple ceremonies for the rest of the foreign Latter-day Saint congregations.[18]

Eduardo, who stood next to McKay on this occasion in 1955, must have beamed with pride as he translated those words. He had translated similar thoughts years earlier from an apostle—Spencer

17. Balderas, "La Conferencia en Mesa."
18. Balderas.

W. Kimball—and now he was translating them from a prophet. This time, because of Eduardo's article, the news about the historic temple trips and their impact on the rest of the church outside the United States would circulate across the Spanish-speaking world. Just as important were the statistics available from the eleven sessions that the group attended. Eight hundred twenty-five endowments were given, seventy-eight of them for people going through the temple for the first time. Of those endowments, 500 were received by women and 388 by men. Twenty-eight couples were sealed for time and all eternity. The numbers do not match up but that is what Eduardo reported in his article.[19]

His next article, also on the Mesa excursions, was published in 1959. There, he returned to the details of the temple excursions to Mesa, which seems logical, since as translator for the visiting authorities and the temple sealer, he participated in all the activities surrounding the temple days for those who came from afar. With the temple ordinances now translated, Spanish-speaking individuals in the United States did not have to come in particular days or months, though some still came on locally planned excursions.[20]

Eduardo began his article with a quote from Joseph Smith, who spoke of having a place where the deceased could be saved, which of course meant an LDS temple, where non-LDS ancestors and recently deceased relatives could have the "saving ordinances" performed for them.[21] He followed the quote with a declaration that to save their dead, the Spanish-speaking members from four missions and several stakes had come to the temple the week of October 19–23, 1958. Two buses from the missions in Mexico arrived on the eighteenth, and so did a bus from the San Antonio (Spanish-language) branch as well as a cattle truck retrofitted to bring saints from another part of Mexico.[22]

Having once taken a bus trip from Mexico City to South Texas, I know that the journey is extremely tiring. Within a day you are soaked

19. Balderas, 153.

20. Eduardo Balderas, "La Decimacuarta Excursión a Mesa," *Liahona*, Jan. 1, 1959, 12, 13, 23.

21. "Saving ordinances" are rites and rituals performed in temples that are necessary to be accepted into God's presence.

22. Balderas, "La Decimacuarta Excursión a Mesa."

in perspiration, there are few places (even less in the 1950s than when I did it in the 1970s) in which to stop and eat, and the bus toilets stop working within a few days of the trip. My trip took eighteen hours on better roads than what these Mexican saints had and traveling at a faster speed. The saints in the late 1950s traveled in old buses with no air conditioning that carried more passengers than a normal tour bus. What might have made the trip much more bearable—and I know it did in the car convoy in which I went to the temple for the first time—was the effort to maintain a spiritual ambience.

We sang, began and ended each day with prayer, and shared spiritual messages as prompted by the Spirit. We shared the little we brought with us, as most of us had few economic resources—I had to borrow money to make the two-and-a-half-day trip—and we talked about the blessings of the temple and the religious pilgrimage and came to emotionally identify with the early Mormon pioneers who traveled the plains to get to their home in the mountains. It is likely that, cooped up in that hot bus or truck, the Mexican and Mexican American saints and the few Central Americans who might have joined them felt the same way as they focused on the experience they were to have once they arrived, which for some had the likely possibility of being a once-in-a-lifetime occurrence.

The day after they arrived, recounted Eduardo, the newly arrived saints, the local members, hundreds of returned missionaries who'd served in the four missions, and church officials gathered in a group one thousand strong to hear Elder Mark E. Petersen of the Quorum of the Twelve speak to them. Petersen, next to Spencer W. Kimball, proved the most significant proponent of the blossoming of the Lamanites, which he interpreted to be the Polynesians, Native Americans, and particularly the people from south of the United States border. He wrote a book years later (in 1981) where he declared, "The promises of old are being fulfilled, and the descendants of Lehi—the first Book of Mormon prophet—indeed begin to blossom as the rose.... Today they come to Christ by the hundreds of thousands as 'fellow citizens with the Saints and of the household of God'... they ... come into the place God designed for them."[23]

23. Balderas, "La Decimacuarta Excursión a Mesa," 13. See also, Mark E. Petersen, *Children of the Promise: The Lamanites; Yesterday and Today* (Salt Lake City: Bookcraft, 1981), 5.

Eduardo gave few other details of Petersen's talk, but the address no doubt underscored the significance of the sacrifices the saints had made to come to the temple and how that reaffirmed the blessings coming to the people of Latin America. He might well have promised the saints that more blessings were to come to them as endowed members. At the end of Petersen's own book, *Children of Promise: The Lamanites; Yesterday and Today*, he told his readers, that "the people are carrying on the work in the church under their own local leadership." Leadership, as we saw in the case of Margarito Bautista and the Third Convention, and which I have seen replayed over and over in Latina/o branches and wards, is one of the issues most discussed among Spanish-speaking saints, particularly in the United States, as most—though not all—issues of leadership have been dealt with in most Latin American countries, where native leaders administer at most levels.[24]

By the end of the temple excursion, informed the article, over fifteen hundred endowment ceremonies had taken place for the living and the deceased, and the youth of the visiting members had performed "hundreds" of baptisms.[25] Many members had also received their patriarchal blessings, an action that also served to prepare some of them for leadership, as they now felt they knew what their missions in life were. More on this will be said in the next chapter. At the end of his article, Eduardo wrote that the saints coming out of their temple experience in Arizona were now "fortified [spiritually] and felt the desire to be a 'light unto the world.'"[26] While this sentiment was no doubt true, Eduardo's reason for ending his article this way reflected his own desire for his people to take their place in the church. While he would write little on the subject, and even in his articles did not use the term, *Lamanite* (or *Lamanita*), there was no doubt that he believed in the promises that he had heard often from Rey L. Pratt, and by this time, he had also heard and translated the talk by Spencer W. Kimball in the 1947 general conference, where

24. Some exceptions to this trend are seen in the highest level of an area—the area authority presidency—which often provides administrative leadership in several countries of a region. Even there, however, if not the president, often a counselor of Spanish-speaking origin serves in the presidency.

25. Balderas, "La Decimacuarta Excursion a Mesa," 23.

26. Balderas.

he spoke about the mission of the church to the Lamanites, many of whom were in Latin America.[27]

Elder Kimball saw the blossoming already occurring among the people from Polynesia, in Native American reservations, amongst the mestizo and indigenous people from Latin America, and in the Maori of Australia and New Zealand. In his vision of their future, he saw them as educated, as professionals, and as leaders in the church and fulfilling the promises of the Book of Mormon. Unfortunately, Kimball saw the conversion and the promise coming with "whiteness," or the whitening of the skin of the descendants of those who converted, and even among those long-time converts. Interestingly, while the indigenous intellectual dissident Bautista did believe in this part of the "promise," Eduardo never mentioned it, at least not in any public interview, article, or discussion of his views on the Lamanites.[28]

It is possible that Eduardo felt the same discomfort that other Spanish-speaking saints did when it came to this type of phenotype transformation that saw indigenous-origin saints go from Brown to white. They might be willing to recognize that their children who did not work in the fields or in places where they were not exposed to the sun all day and possibly intermarried—as did Eduardo—with white individuals might change their skin tone, but it was harder to simply see a transformation in themselves over a period of time. After all, some part of Mexican philosophy, especially one that came out of the Mexican Revolution, did speak to a blending of all races into a cosmic race, and while there was no talk of color in it, it was expected that it would have an impact on a people's skin color.[29]

27. Spencer W. Kimball, *One Hundred Eighteenth Semi-Annual Conference of the Church of Jesus Christ of Latter-day Saints* (Salt Lake City: Church of Jesus Christ of Latter-day Saints: 1947), 15–22.

28. Kimball.

29. For a discussion of la "Raza Cósmica," see José Vasconcelos, *La Raza cósmica: Misión de la raza iberoamericana; Notas de viajes a la América del Sur* (Madrid: Agencia Mundial de Librería, 1925). See also Nicandro F. Juárez, "José Vasconselos and La Raza Cósmica," *Aztlán: A Journal of Chicano Studies* 3, no. 1 (1972): 51–82; and Agustín Palacios "Multicultural Vasconcelos: The Optimistic, and at Times Willful, Misreading of *La Raza Cósmica*," *Latino Studies* 15, no. 4 (Nov. 2017): 416–38. The concept was seen as an enlightened view of a future mixing of races, or a racist trope intended to "aesthetically" subjugate indigenous and other people of color. Most intellectuals and activists interpreted it according to their own political motives.

The talk of the Lamanite blossoming and their "whitening" would prove a difficult discussion for many of the groups within that term's umbrella, with some rejecting it because it wiped out their history and some considering the idea of "whitening" as racist. Many Latin American and Mexican saints, however, simply focused on the idea of the blossoming. As noted earlier, even Bautista, a strong proponent of indigenous rights, simply accepted the "whitening" as a given, possibly underscoring his idea of a "cosmic" race that would be both whiter (for indigenous people) and darker (for Europeans) than the races were before the mixing. This topic, however, will continue for years to create some profound and sometimes heated discussions.[30]

Ironically, he confronted a situation a few years after he wrote the article that tested his own views of his people's "blossoming": the rise of the Chicano Movement for civil rights. Like many in his generation—often described as the Mexican American or the G. I. Generation, who dominated the politics and intellectual thought from the 1930s to 1960—Eduardo saw the young Chicano/a activists as disruptive, unappreciative of what had been accomplished, and surely not reflective of the blossoming *Lamanitas*.

This Mexican American generation as well as many immigrants, like Eduardo, had accomplished so much but had done so mostly as individuals outside the mainstream. Rarely had any of them gone to the university, rose in the military ranks, or been significant in an organization with any other Mexican-origin person by their side. For many of them, their service during World War II had made them "American" and worthy of all the rights of a citizen. Eduardo did not serve in the military, having gotten a deferment through the church's efforts, and he was older than most of the men who volunteered or who had been drafted. Nonetheless, he felt quite American. By the mid-1960s, he no longer felt like an immigrant, though he still felt very Mexican, but by now his Mexican identity came from his work

30. In 2022, I attended a "Lamanite workshop" in which both active and dissident Latter-day Saint indigenous people came to discuss the issue of the idea of "whitening." As expected, those active members of the church had a more nuanced view of the identifier while those no longer with the church—mostly Native American but also some Polynesians—had a more negative view of the term. My own keynote address reiterated the view that most indigenous and mestizo saints from south of the border actually embraced the term, at least according to the literature available.

translating literature into Spanish, his involvement in local Mexican Independence Day celebrations, and his forays into the cultural activities of the Mexican branch, now the Lucero Ward.

And yet, unlike many in the Mexican American Generation, and even his own immigrant generation, he did not engage in civil rights activities, challenge segregation, or speak out about the unfair and racist treatment of Mexicans—many of them citizens—who were deported during "Operation Wetback" in the early 1950s. He was also not a "joiner," as many of his slightly younger cohorts had been after their military service, when they became part of self-help or civil rights organizations, nor did he have the experience of many in his immigrant generation that had defended their countrymen against the violence and racism they incurred in their new homeland.[31]

When cultural nationalism sprang up among Mexican saints in the form of the Third Convention, Eduardo did not serve as a bridge between its leaders and the church authorities. No doubt one reason for his lack of involvement was that he was fairly new in his job and had no ecclesiastical or administrative role of any significance. Unlike his brother and father, he did not know these individuals from the Third Convention well, nor had he experienced the philosophical debates on foreign influence and intervention that gripped the nation to the south and many saints there after the revolution. He saw their desire to have a Mexican mission president "as more than a request ... actually a demand ... suggesting to the First Presidency what should be done."[32]

While he might have empathized with members of the Third Convention—probably because of his correspondence and his discussions with his brother and father about the sincerity of those leaders, even if "misguided"—he accepted the church's view that it was "not the will of Heavenly Father that their proposal be done at

31. For a discussion of the Mexican American (G. I.) Generation, see Mario T. García's *Mexican Americans: Leadership, Ideology, and Identity, 1930–1960* (New Haven, CT: Yale University Press, 1989); Carlos Kevin Blanton, *George I. Sanchez: The Long Fight for Mexican Integration* (New Haven, CT: Yale University Press, 2014); and for a discussion of an earlier generation, see Cynthia E. Orozco, *Pioneer of Mexican-American Civil Rights: Alonso S. Perales* (Houston, TX: Arte Público Press, 2020).

32. Balderas, Oral History, 33–34.

that time."[33] He added, "While they may have had the ability [to lead], they would have no training, since they had no instructions given to them."[34] Yet, he had recognized that he had played it by ear when he was branch president, and had he known the Mexican Latter-day Saint history better—and he might have because of his father's and brother's acquaintance with the Third Conventionists—he would have known that the dissident saints in Mexico had already spent several years mostly guiding their own congregations with little literature and even less guidance from church leaders.[35]

What the Chicano and earlier Mexican civil rights movements attempted to do went beyond simply asking for their "rights." They sought to help the nation—and some within the barrio—to understand that Mexicans and Mexican Americans were more than just a minority. They were a people with a culture and a history and with the ability to defend the nation from foreign enemies and to serve more than adequately in its society. Chicano/as in particular sought to unify Mexican Americans into a potent public force by organizing them politically, helping them unionize in the fields and the factories, unleashing their creative talents—in art, music, and theater—and searching for and writing their history in this country.[36]

It is doubtful that Eduardo objected to any of these particular aims, but like many in his generation, he got caught up judging the Chicano Movement's militancy and questioning their terminology. "The word ... *Chicano* ... really doesn't mean anything," he told an interviewer. "I have always understood it to be simply slang." He told the same interviewer that he had spoken to the "older people" from Mexico living in Salt Lake City, and they assured him that they had no interest "to form part of this movement." He acknowledged that

33. Ironically, Andrés C. González's son "Andy" was in Mexico during the early Third Convention activities and told President Harold W. Pratt, "I sympathize with their desires but do not agree with their leaders' methods," *No More Strangers and Foreigners*, 142.

34. Balderas, Oral History, 35.

35. Balderas, Oral History.

36. See the following books by the author: *United We Win: The Rise and Fall of La Raza Unida Party* (Tucson: University of Arizona Press, 1989); *Chicanismo: The Forging of a Militant Ethos Among Mexican Americans* (Tucson: University of Arizona Press, 1997); *White but Not Equal: Mexican Americans, Jury Discrimination, and the Supreme Court* (Tucson: University of Arizona Press, 2008); *Hector P. García: In Relentless Pursuit of Justice* (Houston, TX: Arte Público Press, 2003) among others.

there were Mexican saints, mostly the "Chicanos," he argued, who felt they were not given "positions of responsibility" in the church's regional and local hierarchy, and he added disparagingly, "They think they are being discriminated against by not being given the same opportunities as the English speaking, or Anglo as they call them."[37]

Balderas then referenced his nephew, a bishop in one of the wards in El Paso, who had a "lot of trouble with some of these people."[38] This no doubt bothered him, as it was his family being criticized or challenged. El Paso was a hotbed of Chicanismo for a time, and even the local church was not spared the discussions and debates taking place among its members, especially its youth. There might, however, have been something that bothered Eduardo even more than his nephew's troubles, as revealed in something he told his interviewer. "When anyone stands up against them [Chicano/a activists], especially one of their own people, they are immediately dubbed as 'gringo-lovers.'"[39] By this time, Eduardo was attending an English-speaking ward, and these debates over Chicano/a civil rights might have been discussed among his fellow white members.

I remember that in my own ward in San Antonio, a school boycott in the local, predominantly Mexican American school where some of the ward's youth went caused a real debate about the same issues that garnered Eduardo's attention. There, a number of members in the San Antonio Fourth Ward became involved in the activism swirling around the barrios adjacent to it. Some members became part of a local organization called the Communities Organized for Public Service (COPS); others became members of the La Raza Unida Party. One young man became one of the founding members of Brigham Young University's Mexican American Club, and I became a Chicano/a historian.

Ironically, one person in the Rama Mexicana did not feel the same way about the Chicano Movement and became a leader in it—albeit a much more moderate version of the movement—and that was Orlando Rivera (whom Eduardo might have known). He was also the branch-turned-ward's first Latino bishop—the first one

37. Balderas, Oral History, 77–78.

38. Balderas, 78.

39. Balderas, 78.

in all of Utah. He saw it as his own personal and religious mission to work for his people, helping them attain better jobs, more education, and adequate housing, and getting them integrated in Utah society. He also sought to counter the negative image the church had among Mexicans and Mexican Americans.[40]

"When something as American as Mormonism is presented to us, my people do not find in it anything to embrace very readily," Rivera told a group of church leaders, adding that this was a reason why Mexican Americans were not embracing Mormonism with "much enthusiasm."[41] This is likely not something that Eduardo wanted to hear, since he saw Mormonism as extremely attractive to Mexicans and other Latina/os because it spoke to their history as Lamanites through the Book of Mormon. Rivera also believed in the concept of the Lamanite. He said, "We call ourselves Chicanos and all Chicanos think of themselves as having an Indo-Hispanic background, of having ancestral roots native to America as well as Europe. Thus, you considering us Lamanite is in no way offensive, but rather acceptable to our people.[42]

While Rivera talked about Lamanites, he was going beyond the perspective that Eduardo had about those people from the Book of Mormon. Rivera was tying that religious history that had no documentation, little material culture, and no direct descendants to the Chicano/a version of Mexican saints' heritage. His use of the term *Indo-Hispanic* was similar to a term used by an important Chicano/a activist leader of the time, Reies Lopez Tijerina, a former Pentecostal preacher who used the concept of an Indo-Hispano as an identity for New Mexican residents seeking to recover their lands from the federal government and large ranchers. His was a call to form a nation within a nation that would respect the rights of the "Mexican people" of New Mexico and across the Southwest.[43] Unlike other

40. See Jorge Iber, *Hispanics in The Mormon Zion, 1912–1999* (College Station: Texas A&M University Press, 2000), 85–114, for a short history of Rivera's activism and his coalition building.

41. Orlando A. Rivera, "Mormonism and the Chicano," in *Mormonism: A Faith for All Cultures*, ed. F. Lamond Tullis (Provo: Brigham Young University Press, 1978), 115–25.

42. Rivera, "Mormonism and the Chicano," 116.

43. See García, *United We Win*, for a discussion of Reies López Tijerina; also, see Lorena Oropeza, *The King of Adobe: Reies López Tijerina, Lost Prophet of the Chicano Movement* (Chapel Hill: University of North Carolina Press, 2019).

Chicano/as, Tijerina believed in the hybridity—*el mestisaje*—that had occurred with the Spanish conquest.

Other younger Chicano/a activists, both urban and rural—some even from Salt Lake City—came together the week of March 27–31, 1969, in Denver, Colorado, for the Chicano Youth Liberation Conference. The conference was sponsored by the Crusade for Justice—the Chicano Movement's largest urban organization, which sought to get working-class youth off the streets, to connect them back to their communities, to reintroduce them to their culture and their language, and to get them to partner with the university youth who also sought a return to their roots.[44]

The conference participants developed the concept of Aztlán, a mythical and political indigenous and Mexican homeland in the Southwest. There in Denver, the group of activists from around the country were presented with the "El Plan Espiritual de Aztlán," a guiding document that declared, "Aztlán belongs to those who plant the seeds, water the fields, and gather the crops and not to the foreign Europeans."[45] The document also rejected the borders that divided their people into Mexicans and Mexican Americans. It was boldly nationalistic, as it came out at a time when national liberation movements had arisen in Africa, Asia, Latin America, and even in the United States as the black liberation movement and the American Indian Movement sought to highlight the literature, music, art, and history of their people. The document ends, "With our hearts in our hands and our hands in the soil, we declare the independence of our *mestizo* nation."[46]

The leader of the Crusade for Justice and the premier intellectual of the Chicano Movement declared in a poem, "Yo Soy Joaquin," what many Mexican Americans felt about American society, though for many immigrants it might have seemed strange to hear their Mexican brothers and sisters speak this way.

> I am Joaquin
> I am lost in a world of confusion
> Caught up in the whirl of an Anglo Society,

44. See García, *Chicanismo*, 93–95; and García, *United We Win*, 93–95.
45. Quoted in García, *United We Win*, 95.
46. "Plan Espiritual de Aztlán," quoted in García, *United We Win*, 95.

Confused by the rules,
Scorned by the attitudes,
And destroyed by modern society,
My fathers have lost the economic battle
And won the struggle of culture survival.
I am the masses of my people
and I refuse to be absorbed.
I am Joaquin
The odds are great.
But my spirit is strong.
My faith unbreakable.
My blood is pure.
I am an Aztec Prince
And Christian Christ.
I shall endure!
I will endure![47]

It is quite unlikely that Eduardo knew of these documents or even the Chicano Youth Liberation Conferences. He might have read about the latter given Denver's proximity to Salt Lake City, but most newspaper coverage no doubt came from a hostile press. The reality is that Eduardo lived in a biosphere that stretched from his home to his office to the branch and sometimes to cultural activities in the wider city, but seemingly not far beyond that. He did not work for an entity like the University of Utah, or city government, or any agency or business that had to balance the state's religious conservative culture with the demands of disadvantaged groups and women seeking change in the 1960s–70s. He did not sit in classrooms where historical events and interpretations were being debated; he read no Marxist, socialist, or anti-colonialist materials; and he had no colleagues that we know of who could speak to those issues with any knowledge or sophistication.

Eduardo saw the political and social activism whirling around the nation and the state and no doubt heard of that young boy he had known in the Rama Mexicana—now bishop of the Lucero Ward—engaging in civil rights activism. He might have appreciated the more moderate approach, but it is likely that he was taken aback by

47. Rodolfo "Corky" Gonzales, "Yo Soy Joaquin," *El Gallo*, 1967.

Rivera's willingness to criticize the church's reluctance to respond to criticism about its own racial policies. While President Kimball now had the church's reins and had been an advocate for Native Americans and Latin Americans in the church—and would soon end priesthood and temple restrictions for African Americans—there were still powerful forces within the church hierarchy who rejected civil rights activism as communist-inspired and thus of the devil.[48]

If there was one weakness in Eduardo's life when it came to serving his people, it was his absence from the great debates taking place within his community and the larger Mexican and Mexican American community nationally on the issues of civil and human rights. His perceptions were blinded by the structural limitations that he confronted (like very conservative religious and political leaders in the state), by his having no position of authority within the church, and by his own limited education and knowledge of the history of his people. Chicano/a history was just emerging as an academic discipline, and there were few histories of his community available. These histories were only beginning to come to light in college campuses and through community newspapers that made it a point to discover bits and pieces of Mexican history in the United States.

Eduardo, while in many aspects a brilliant man, was a simple Brown man who found himself in a sea of religious whiteness, with his knowledge of the gospel, church history, and American history all coming from a community that saw American exceptionalism as unchallengeable and whose leaders believed that the only road to success (socially, economically, and religiously) for his community was assimilation. He was, after all, a prime example of someone on that path, having married Rhea and raised monolingual English-speaking children and finding himself in an English-language ward

---

48. No one better represented these ultra-conservative views than Ezra Taft Benson, apostle and later president of the church. See Mathew L. Harris, ed., *Thunder from the Right: Ezra Taft Benson in Mormonism and Politics* (Urbana: University of Illinois, 2019); see also Matthew L. Harris, *Watchman on the Tower: Ezra Taft Benson and The Making of the Mormon Right* (Salt Lake City: University of Utah Press, 2020). Finally, for Benson's own words, see Ezra Taft Benson, *An Enemy Hath Done This*, comp. Jerreld L. Newquist (Salt Lake City: Parliament Publishers, 1969); and Ezra Taft Benson, *Title of Liberty: A Warning Voice*, comp. Mark A. Benson (Salt Lake City: Deseret Book, 1964).

and working for a church that promoted the primacy of Americanism and the English language to even its international members.[49]

Still, it is hard not to imagine that he thought about some of these issues and possibly discussed them with his brother Guillermo, maybe his father, and possibly even his most trusted friend and love, Rhea. No matter his public utterances, or lack thereof, Eduardo was not blind to what went on around him. Notwithstanding all the talk of the "blossoming" and the expansion of the gospel among the Spanish speaking, prejudices existed, as he had experienced initially with his in-laws and those leaders who were uncomfortable with him marrying a white woman. And he no doubt heard many other stories of biases, prejudices and outright racism from fellow members in the Rama Mexicana. It is also likely that every time there was a new change of branch presidents someone would turn to him and say, "I thought you'd be the next one," something quite common in Spanish-speaking units when each change simply brought another white leader.

Eduardo's tenacity to get material translated and quickly disseminated to his people was his own way of bringing his people knowledge, which he must have believed brought them "rights" in the kingdom of God. After translating the LDS canon and temple ceremony, he asked and got permission to translate other non-canonical works that were seen by many as fundamental to understanding Latter-day Saint theology. Among those were *Jesus the Christ* (which at the time was the most important noncanonical book in the church), *Doctrines of Salvation*, *The Miracle of Forgiveness*, *Essentials in Church History*, *Articles of Faith*, and *The House of the Lord*. These books provided not only doctrine but also conservative Mormon theology that all Latter-day Saints were supposed to know. While most of them, with the exception of *Jesus the Christ*, would prove to be problematic over time, Eduardo saw them at the time as fundamental for the Latina/o saints to read.[50] More will be said about some of them in the next chapter.

49. For a discussion of Latter-day Saints and the idea of "America," see McKay Coppins, "The Most American Religion," *The Atlantic*, Dec. 16, 2020, theatlantic.com; Jaxon Washburn, "Mormonism, the 'Most American' Religious Other," *Harvard Divinity Bulletin*, Autumn/Winter 2022, bulletin.hds.harvard.edu; also see Marion G. Romney, "America's Destiny," *Ensign*, Nov. 1975, 35–37.

50. Balderas, Oral History, 72, 82.

Notwithstanding his qualms with Chicanismo, Eduardo was part of what historian Robert Chao Romero calls the "Brown Church," which refers to individuals and organizations within Christianity that have, in one form or another, fought for the rights of Brown people within the white religious spaces they've navigated. This Brown church goes back to the earliest days of Christianity in Latin America and extends to the more recent ones, and it includes men and women who gave their lives in the service of their fellow Brown people. Eduardo, while not an activist or someone who spoke "truth to power" in the traditional sense, did more to empower his people than any other Latina/o Latter-day Saint in history.[51]

Opening the canon to his people, bringing them to an understanding of temple rituals, developing a magazine to spread the Mormon gospel, and providing them the tools to become leaders in their congregations and among their people was just as significant for his Latina/o Latter-day Saints as those actions done by others in the Brown church. Without Balderas, there would be no Brown church within the Church of Jesus Christ of Latter-day Saints.

51. See Robert Chao Romero *Brown Church: Five Centuries of Latina/o Social Justice, Theology, and Identity* (Downers Grove, IL: IVP Academic, 2020).

9

FROM TRANSLATOR TO PATRIARCH

Once, near the end of his career as a translator, Eduardo was asked whether he thought the modern way of translating general conference and other major meetings—having speakers hand in a written talk (speech) and giving the translators time to prepare the translation—was better for him. He answered, "Definitely. I'd rather not have to retain the words in my memory, but translate them as I hear them spoken."[1] Standing next to the speaker to translate live had been his early experience, and he appreciated the challenge that had allowed him to learn to translate on his feet, forcing him to think of words and phrases at a moment's notice. There were times, however, when things did not go well, as happens to all translators, so the new method allowed him to prepare by forcing him to go back to the Spanish language dictionary and the English thesaurus, to ask advice from others who used the language, and to pay attention to how people spoke and how authors wrote.

Eduardo learned early on that translating was more than finding the adequate word or the correct phrases that communicated the speaker's thoughts accurately. With experience, he learned to convey the message in a manner that the audience could understand and feel the full significance of the talk. Whether he fully understood it at first or ever became fully aware, he was practicing the way of "Mormon translating" established by the church founder, Joseph Smith. While many Latter-day Saints believe that receiving revelation or translating sacred texts is a process of seeing, hearing, or receiving a

1. Eduardo Balderas, Oral History, interviews by Gordon Irving, 1973, typescript, 49, Oral History Program, CHL.

word-by-word transmission from heaven, records indicate that the method is more complicated. Joseph Smith often had to go over his revelations and translations to correct the words, expand the interpretation, and add new ideas.

As Joseph Smith's knowledge of and experience with the "new gospel" he expounded grew, so did the need for him to communicate it. Mormon theology prefaces its doctrines as coming from heaven but accepts that they are best understood in practice, and sometimes that practice requires adjustments to the language and an expansion of the application. It would be no different for Eduardo, because like Joseph, he was constructing and reworking a new way of talking about the gospel. He remembered that when he got stuck on a word, he would go to those—like Ivins and possibly others—who had been preaching and teaching for years to ask for advice, and there were times when he was simply instructed to research how a term, word, or phrase had been used in the church over time. At other times, he simply went to the translated Book of Mormon (maybe even the Bible) to see how others had used Spanish to discuss Christian teachings.

For the umpteenth time, we lament that Eduardo left no journal or other personal or published writings that could provide insight into what he thought as he struggled with words, concepts, or doctrinal questions. He did, however, through interviews, provide us a glimpse of the steps that he took to formalize the process of translation, first for himself and then for those who came along to help, most of whom came, like him, without formal training. He first began by hiring Betty Gibbs, a returned missionary who had served in Mexico as a stenographer.[2] This freed him from having to type as he thought about what words he was thinking of using. Having the words on paper enabled him to quickly see the totality of the translation and engage in the rewriting or revising. Dictating also allowed him to practice the kind of translating that required verbalization, which proved useful to simultaneous translation.

Shortly after World War II, he began getting help from people coming from Europe and others with experience as mission presidents. They came to replace sister missionaries and local members

2. Balderas, 39–40.

who helped carry on the work, which did not lessen with the war or the reconstruction efforts. Most, however, did not stay, especially those not native to the language they translated. One example is Ernest Young, who came to help after President David O. McKay asked Eduardo if he needed assistance. Eduardo quickly responded with, "Yes, the work is growing and I'm sure we can use his help." Young was seen as a natural, as he had served a mission to Mexico, but he lasted just a short time because he soon found the work too "exacting" and "require[ing] a lot of concentration, a lot of thought."[3]

In 1962, Eduardo began putting headphones in the tabernacle for general conference. This act served the still-small number of Spanish-speaking Latter-day Saints in Salt Lake City and surrounding areas as well as visitors who came from across the Southwest, Mexico, and Latin America. At the time, the church invited regional and local auxiliary and priesthood leaders to Salt Lake City for training on the days leading up to conference weekend. For the few Latina/o saints who came to these trainings, it was an inspiring experience to meet others such as themselves and to learn ways to better administer their auxiliary and priesthood organizations. It was particularly stirring for them to witness their language spoken. We have no record of what Eduardo did during those sessions, though we could assume that he translated some of the instruction.

Eduardo had an opportunity to extend his reach when Paul Evans of the KSL Radio Station, which the church owned, approached Gordon B. Hinkley to see if Eduardo could go to New York City and broadcast from there a session of general conference for saints in South and Central America and Mexico.[4] Eduardo knew almost nothing about radio broadcasting, so on arrival he was connected to the people in Salt Lake City and spoke with the engineers for about fifteen minutes simply to figure out how to adjust the volume. He was then instructed to wait for the red light and start translating as soon as he got the signal from one of the engineers.[5]

While translating in this way, Eduardo knew nothing about the talk or speaker. He just translated as he heard the broadcast and

3. Balderas, 40.
4. Balderas, 48.
5. Balderas.

quickly adjusted to the rhythm of the speaker as well as to the timing of each song and prayer. Whether it was during this first experience or after doing it several more times, Eduardo found this type of translation much easier than standing by the speaker, waiting for intervals so as to not disrupt, and having to remember everything that was said. It also allowed him to stop thinking of what he might say—he just "went into automatic."

Eduardo said translating simultaneously but not standing next to the speaker was helpful for those moments when a translator "hit[s] a mental block ... [and] just can't think of the word at the moment, and by the time [they] think of it, the speaker has gone on and left [them] behind."[6] He would do live transmission several more times, including for general conference, until the sessions were televised and all speakers had to turn in written talks to the translators a few days before conference began. The growth of the church worldwide required more translators, and eventually the church decided to establish a translation department and take the responsibility from the Missionary Department.

Before we go any further, we should pause to assess what this transmission meant to those saints south of the United States border. To hear the words of the prophets, seers, and revelators—even if through a translator—must have seemed like a special gift from heaven. If we simply remember what those members were willing to do to get to the temple, we can picture what they did to get to where they could hear the transmission. There are no details of how the transmission got to them (possibly through a radio station which may have been paid to transmit) or whether the Mexican government—to some extent quite anti-Catholic at the time—might have facilitated the transmission. We can assume that few of the saints outside Mexico City had radios, so they likely gathered in the homes of those who had them, even if it meant traveling a distance.[7] For

6. Balderas, 49.

7. I remember that in San Antonio, Texas, we would all gather in the chapel to hear what our leaders described as a radio transmission. As I said in my introduction, we stared at a wall and conjured up all these images in our minds of the Brethren speaking. Afterwards, we gathered in small groups or pairs and talked about what we had just heard, particularly if there had been any announcement of chapels being built, new missions opening, or any other news the church had for us.

many of them, it brought them emotionally to Salt Lake City and the tabernacle.

Ironically, the new translation department did not come about because of the overload that Eduardo faced daily in trying to keep up with material to be translated or because of the growing demands by church leaders for Balderas to travel with them throughout the Southwest and Latin America. Rather, it came about because Alvin R. Dyer was assigned to preside over a European mission and requested that translation be done in Europe, possibly because a number of those translators who came back to Salt Lake City after the war had either retired or gone to the Historian's Office, where the work was less demanding.[8]

Dyer soon found that translating took valuable missionary time, as Hinckley had found out years earlier. More so, he found himself constantly checking with church leaders in Salt Lake City about lesson manuals, courses of study, and other materials necessary to keep his mission and his missionaries in tune with what was happening in the church. Having more than one language to translate made the need for a translation department more urgent, but it also reflected a Eurocentric focus by some of the church leaders who saw conversion across the sea as much more valuable given that many had come from there (or had ancestors who came from there) and sought to have their compatriots accept the Latter-day Saint gospel.

Thomas Fyans was placed in charge of the new department, and he quickly divided work into three areas—Europe, Latin America, and the Far East and Polynesia—and chose directors for each area. Surprisingly, if not illogically, Eduardo was not chosen to head the Latin America area. Even more surprising, one may add, was that Eduardo was not called to head the department itself, since he ran all the translation efforts, not only for Spanish, but also other languages. To be fair, it is possible that he was asked and said no, though that is unlikely since Eduardo was a devoted saint who would have done anything for the church. It is also possible that the divine knew where he was most valuable, as we will see later. Still, it is odd that the man who all but created church translation efforts did not get a chance to lead.

8. Balderas, Oral History, 50.

Notwithstanding his lack of official standing, church translation was Eduardo's show to run, and early on he did. The newly hired translators often came to him when they got stuck on a word or phrase.[9] "You can't do it word by word," he taught them, "and come up with an acceptable translation. You have to get the thought in your mind, how you're going to ... express it, and then proceed from there." At the same time, a translator should always strive "to follow the text."[10] He urged them, no doubt, to use a Dictaphone effectively, a device still new to many who lacked clerical or secretarial experience before becoming translators.

In using a Dictaphone, he later counseled, "You don't have to concern [yourselves] about how you are going to say it."[11] He advised translators to concentrate on looking at the language and the phrase and to consider whether they were using good Spanish. Once a translation was typed, he would go over it, make the necessary revisions, and go back to the original English document to see if the intended message "broke through" in Spanish. Throughout this process, there was prayer and an effort to be sensitive to the "Spirit." He said, "In translating church material, I don't believe you can do it without the help of the Spirit. You are dealing with spiritual matters, spiritual materials."[12]

Eduardo identified what he called five "idiomatic and regional dialects" in Latin American Spanish: Andalusian Spanish, Mexican Spanish, Rioplatense Spanish, Colombian Spanish, and Caribbean Spanish.[13] The construction of the language was the same in most of these dialects, but each had its own particular list of words, phrases, and descriptors not used or known in another of the Spanish-speaking regions. What translated easily for one Latin American nation caused confusion in another.[14] One could translate baseball into *beisbol,* and hamburger into *hamburguesa* and be understood in Mexico but not in Bolivia. Both of those words had a history in Mexico because of its proximity to the United States, but not in Bolivia.

9. Balderas, 52.
10. Balderas, 53.
11. Balderas.
12. Balderas.
13. Balderas, 54.
14. Balderas.

Eduardo translated at a time before American products and idiomatic expressions had become loan words and had no need for translations within the receiving nations. In deciding on which term or word to use, he consulted the dictionary from the Real Academia Española (Royal Academy of Spanish) because their definitions and pronunciations were acceptable to most educated people in each country, though not necessarily the wider population. At first, there were complaints from Latin American members about the translations coming out of Mexico, though they were usually about words describing fruits, vegetables, articles of clothing, and household items. Sometimes complaints were more serious concerns with certain expressions.

"What was proper in Mexico or Guatemala," he remembered, "could be considered improper in other Spanish-speaking countries."[15] The challenge then became staying current with language changes in each region and sometimes in each country. One way he did this was by traveling often to Mexico—and with time to other Latin American countries—where he "exchange[d] views and opinions" with those who were doing their own translation for their areas.[16] He brought that knowledge back to translators in Salt Lake City and also carried the Salt Lake translators' knowledge back to these—often volunteer—translators throughout the hemisphere where he visited. During those visits, when in doubt about words, terms, or phrases, he spoke to stenographers and other translators, even though most would have seen him as the authority. For Eduardo, however, knowing the "language of the people" was as important as using the dictionary.[17] Here again, he affirmed his role as the translator of and for the people.

He finessed his translating skills by "moonlighting" with firms that did business on "different things" and where the workload required translating "letters, articles, and books," each with their particular terminology, and he later recounted, "I have had to dig in and enlarge my vocabulary by learning … technical phrases."[18] He

15. Balderas, 55.
16. Balderas.
17. Balderas.
18. Balderas, 56.

soon found that he had to be sensitive to age differences or particular "religious divisions," by which he meant the different auxiliaries or priesthood quorums. Each translation had to be understood and, to the extent possible, had to be presented in the "style" and context of the writer. Thus, some translations, he would add, sounded "almost poetic and others just plain."[19]

In his exit interview, he explained, "That's one peculiar thing about Spanish. It has to hit the ear just right. No matter how correct the word might be, if it strikes the ear wrong, you just don't use it." He continued, "There is a special ability, a feel for it, in order to be able to translate" correctly, and during his time as translator, he had multiple experiences with those who lacked the "knack" for making the translation "pleasant to the ear."[20] A translation could be accurate word for word and still not deliver the message or be understood in the proper context. When it came to matters of doctrine or church guidelines or instruction, those translations had to capture both the letter and the spirit of the message.[21]

After World War II, Eduardo assumed an even greater role as he became the lead man in trying to get new translations in European languages, since many of the standard works had been destroyed or damaged in the war. This was also an opportunity to correct and edit the work that had been done before—some quite a few years before. Since there was no master translator who knew all the languages, Eduardo, the most experienced, led the translators in two-to-three-hour sessions where each read verses from their own language and then read their own translation to English. This allowed them to see the words that they were using in English and how those might affect how they were translating them into a foreign language. Eduardo found this to be "a very interesting task."[22]

In one session, according to Eduardo's recollection, the question arose of how to translate the word *you*, which was often used in English to refer both to an individual and to a group. In the languages being discussed—except for Dutch—one word was used to refer to

19. Balderas.
20. Balderas, 57.
21. Balderas.
22. Balderas, 61.

the singular and another to the plural. To try to narrow the differences, the discussion participants listed the passages in which there was disagreement on the pronoun to be used. Eduardo prepared the list and took it to the Missionary Committee for their decision. When the list was returned, they discovered that for two or three of the words the committee had gone to the Quorum of the Twelve, and on one occasion to the First Presidency, to determine whether they should be translated as singular or plural.

Sometimes the usage could only be determined by going to the historical record. On one occasion, Eduardo approached J. Reuben Clark, a member of the church's First Presidency, for clarification and was referred to the Historian's Office, where he looked up the proceedings before Congress when Senator-Elect Reed Smoot was investigated for his earlier support of polygamy. Church President Joseph F. Smith testified and was interrogated over the allegations. "After I'd done this," Eduardo remembers, "and reported back to President Clark, I had a better understanding of why one section of Doctrine and Covenants should be in the singular in its entirety."[23]

This kind of historical research and the periodic discussions on the meaning of words and their correct translation were a part of the refining process that made Eduardo the church's most important translator. This kind of refining work went beyond the normal office hours—long as they were—and beyond the official documents he brought home. One of the few possessions his family kept was a small, black three-ring notebook with his name engraved on the front flap. We can only imagine that this was one of a number of notebooks and pads that he used to make notes, engage in trial-run translations, and possibly author some of his own poems, hymns, and other literature.

The notebook in his family's possession has a number of translations of hymns and songs, popular in the 1940s and early 1950s (and some from a few years earlier), which Eduardo might have heard and possibly performed when he was still in El Paso directing youth choirs and plays. The one translation that stands out is the one he did of "Schubert's Serenade," a song that expresses love for another

23. Balderas, 62.

person. Interestingly, however, the supposed translation has very little resemblance to its English translation of the Austrian text. It is a loose adaptation and has a particular line that is in no way representative of the original serenade: "You will dream of faithful love by one who unfaithful was born," or possibly, "was born unfaithful."[24] It is not likely that he was talking about infidelity but more likely that he was trying out words in rhythmic fashion and found it harder to do so when the text was not scripture.

Eduardo also translated "Friend of Mine" ("Mi amigo fiel"), a traditional folk song—most likely an old "Negro song of friendship"—and "Mother Machree" ("Mi madre tan tierna"), an Irish American song written in 1910 and first used for a show titled *Barry of Ballymore* and then in several movies up until 1938.[25] He also tried his hand at translating "I Walked Today Where Jesus Walked," a popular hymn written by Canadian-born composer Geoffrey O'Hara, which is still sung in Protestant congregations today.[26] The notebook also contains several smaller hymns and songs that are difficult to identify since he does not make note of which English songs they are and the titles do not provide any further clue. The number of those translations in the little black notebook—and there might be more in other, now lost notebooks—reflects a love for translation such as an artist might have for his art. An artist might carry a drawing pad and sketch whatever interests them, while Eduardo toted his black notebook around to translate whatever awakened his fancy.

He translated an old, less popular Protestant hymn, later to become a classic in LDS hymnology, "A Poor Wayfaring Man of Grief," which is said to be a hymn that John Taylor, one president of the church, sang to Joseph Smith and others captive in Carthage Jail before some of them were killed by a mob. While the version that Taylor sang, "The Stranger," was quite different from what became the classic Mormon hymn, the story of its singing on the last day

24. Eduardo's translation notes, private collection, property of the Balderas family at the time of this writing.

25. David A. Jasen, *A Century of American Popular Music: 2000 Best-Loved and Remembered Songs (1899–1999)* ([New York?]: Routledge, 2013), 137.

26. David A. Jasen, *Tin Pan Alley: The Composers, the Songs, the Performers, and their Times; The Golden Age of American Popular Music from 1886 to 1956* ([New York?]: Donald I. Fine, 1988).

of the prophet Joseph Smith's life solidified it as a favorite among Latter-day Saints.[27] The hymn also provided—for some Latter-day Saints who struggled with what they perceived as too institutional a religious life—a chance to sing and think about simply being Christian.[28] For Eduardo, it was a chance to translate a hymn made much more difficult because of its poetic nature and its length.

His translation of this hymn did not make it into the hymn book—one reason for this being that there would not be another Spanish hymnal until 1992, after Eduardo had passed away. It is impossible to know how much of his translation draft was used, but it is obvious that the newer translation was done by a committee and lost some of its biblical tone. We must not forget that Eduardo was a singer, while it is doubtful—though we do not really know—that those doing the translation were as into declamations, song, and theater as he had been. Further evaluation of his music translations and their drafts by a bilingual musicologist could tell us much more about his ability to translate hymns.

Over time, Eduardo broke away from the mundane work of translating manuals, correspondence, auxiliary leaders' talks, and other work he was constantly bombarded with and looked toward translating books. By the 1950s, he had more help, and the major canonical work had been done, though it would take years before that knowledge took hold in the small, often white-directed wards and branches that many Spanish-speaking saints attended. There were also those of his people who made the transition to English-language wards, either because of marriage or because they believed that assimilating was the only possible way forward in an area such as Utah, where the number of Mexican American and Latina/o saints remained quite small. For some, moving toward the white mainstream in the church was the only way to remain relevant in the kingdom of God and to become much more versed in the Latter-day Saint gospel.

Since Eduardo, too, had moved to an English ward and his children had assimilated into the English-speaking Utah world, it

27. Michael Hicks, "'Strains Which Will Not Soon Be Allowed to Die ...': 'The Stranger' and Carthage Jail," *BYU Studies* 23, no. 4 (1983): 387.

28. This phenomenon is particularly acute among Latter-day Saints because of the all-encompassing institutional demands the church makes of them.

is hard to know his exact feelings about this assimilative process, though we can argue that his unwillingness to fully leave behind that cultural world (he attended many Mexican cultural activities in and outside the church) kept him in a Latina/o, or at least a Mexican, cultural space that fed his passion for translating as much church literature and other English-language material into Spanish as he could. As historian Richard Bushman has written, "The place ... always makes a difference." In discussing the language of revelation, he wrote, "Those settings [spaces] mold our conduct to suit the occasion," but this framing could also apply to translating revelation.[29]

Eduardo's space (or settings) did, in fact, "mold" his conduct to "suit" his work. When he translated, there is little doubt that he thought of those saints he grew up with in El Paso, those with whom he shared space in Salt Lake City, and the many others he met in his trips to Mexico and other Latin American countries. He knew the hunger many of them had to learn the Latter-day Saint gospel and share it with their fellow Mexican friends and neighbors, and yet he understood the limitations they confronted without clarifying doctrinal interpretations, translations of the Brethren's words, and a knowledge of both the history of the church and its theological foundations. By the 1950s and onward, more and more books and articles were being produced by church authorities. As noted earlier, some of them proved problematic in the future, but at the time they were useful in understanding what it meant to be a Latter-day Saint, at least in the Mormon core of Utah.[30]

Eduardo, whatever his politics or personal views of American actions or policies, saw the need for his people to know what the Brethren were saying and writing. He quickly understood that besides the four scriptures that Latter-day Saints used—the Bible, the

---

29. Richard L. Bushman, "The Little, Narrow Prison of Language: The Rhetoric of Revelation," *Religious Educator* 1, no. 1 (Spring 2000): 90–104.

30. A lot of this literature proved problematic because it was Eurocentric, focused on American Exceptionalism, and made limited sense as a universal gospel outside the Mormon corridor. It provided values and morals and some clarification of LDS doctrine but little nuance in understanding the larger, more complicated world of the Brown saint. It had its influence, some for good. I remember being inspired by some of it, but over time I realized that it required a middle-class mindset that often resulted in a judgmental attitude against those who could not conform to the Latter-day Saint lifestyle because of their struggles as working-class, foreign, or poor people.

Book of Mormon, the Doctrine and Covenants, and the Pearl of Great Price—no other book, at the time, was seen as crucial as *Jesus the Christ* by James E. Talmage. This was the first Latter-day Saint theological work that combined Latter-day Saint teachings with historical and theological work from outside the denomination. Talmage used the most current works by social scientists and historians on Christ and the land and culture he grew up in.

Elder Marion G. Romney, apostle and member of the First Presidency during part of Eduardo's life, said of the book, "One who gets the understanding, the vision, and the spirit of the resurrected Lord through a careful study of the text *Jesus the Christ* by Elder James E. Talmage will find that he has greatly increased his moving faith in our glorified Redeemer."[31]

Eduardo no doubt felt the great responsibility that came with an attempt to translate this work, but it seems to have been his choice to do it. What more important knowledge could Spanish-speaking saints need than to know what their church believed about He whom they proclaimed to be their Savior? This book also provided the foundation—along with the canonical works—of the Latter-day Saints' difference from those who were members of Protestant and Catholic churches. Eduardo's desire to translate this work also reflected his own doctrinal and theological journey in the LDS faith.

Eduardo later admitted that *Jesus the Christ* proved a "greater challenge to translate" because it was also difficult to read in English, not so much because of the writing but because of the terminology used. For a time, Deseret Book, the church's publishing company, sold a glossary of "Elder Talmage's vocabulary."[32] At the same time, according to Eduardo, understanding the book was easier because Talmage used words with a "Latin or Greek origin" that were understood in the same way as Spanish.[33] Here Eduardo might have exaggerated a bit, as the use of such terminology by Talmage was just a small part of the work. Still, having worked on "biblical-style" language and having translated for many general authorities who

31. Quoted in Christiana Pinborough, "The Ultimate List of LDS Classics Every Mormon Should Read," *LDSLiving*, Apr. 15, 2017, www.ldsliving.com.

32. Balderas, Oral History, 61–64.

33. Balderas.

spoke about Christ, Eduardo probably found it easier than he may have imagined when first contemplating the translation.

His translation of church books actually started about a decade after he began translating for the church. His first translation was *Articles of Faith*, a short summary of Latter-day Saint beliefs, in 1951. He followed that up with *Teachings of the Prophet Joseph Smith*, a series of teachings by the church founder not included in the canonical works, in 1954.[34] Then came *A Marvelous Work and a Wonder* (1959), *Jesus the Christ* (1964), and *Essentials in Church History* (1965). To those he added *Meet the Mormons*, which he translated for Deseret Book and not the church, and during this period of intense work he also made revisions to the Book of Mormon.[35]

These latter revisions came when the publisher or church printer in Independence, Missouri, shut down and the printing work was sent to be done in Salt Lake City. Eduardo remembers that the type (lithograph) was so worn out because of constant usage that a new one had to be created. "I was authorized to make some revisions," he recalled, "because the language had changed in many respects. Some words were no longer in use, and others had quite a different meaning."[36] The last revision had been done by his mentor, Rey L. Pratt, in 1928. This brought Eduardo full circle as he helped edit and partially retranslate the book that had brought him into the LDS doctrinal world.[37]

In 1972, an area general conference was conducted in Mexico City. The intent had been for local translators to handle the Spanish transmission of the talks, but with little experience, the local coordinators did not plan the logistics well, and Eduardo had to be brought in to help. He was able to organize the local translators so they spoke "over the speakers," meaning that they translated simultaneously, the first time this was ever done in Mexico or any other Latin American country.[38] Unfortunately, and more challenging for Eduardo,

34. José Fielding Smith, *Enseñanzas del profeta José Smith: Selecciones de sus sermones y escritos; Escogidas y arregladas por el Historiador de la Iglesia de Jesucristo de los Santos de los Últimos Días, José Fielding Smith*, 2nd ed., (Salt Lake City: Church of Jesus Christ of Latter-day Saints, 1982).

35. Balderas, Oral History, 46–47.

36. Balderas, 57.

37. Balderas, 64.

38. Balderas, 69.

President Harold B. Lee liked the old system of "interpreting," and he had Eduardo translating at his side in all the sessions, which was no doubt quite an honor for him but also must have been nerve-racking. He did not want to make a mistake while translating for the man he considered a prophet, but adding to his nerves was the presence of numerous general authorities and Mexican church leaders who knew both languages and were keeping check on his ability to faithfully and efficiently act as the prophet's voice to the Spanish speaking.

Eduardo understood the joy and the spiritual lift that the seventeen thousand Mexican saints felt who came to hear their prophet in person for the first—and possibly only—time. An *Ensign* article about the event said, "They came from deserts and the industrial cities of the north, from the small *pueblitos* of the east and the west, and from the tropical coastlines and mountainous areas of the south that stretch throughout Central America."[39] Members in different LDS communities worked to save money to attend. Others borrowed money, and some even sold belongings to scrounge up the money, while in other congregations local leaders gathered their flocks to decide who would go and then come back and report on the conference. From Central America, saints took seven-to-eight-day bus trips, while others spent up to three weeks coming to Mexico City, and it cost them nearly three months' salary.[40]

These saints knew the hardships, or at least imagined them, but they were not to be deterred from this momentous occasion, to spend three days (August 25–27) listening to their spiritual leaders and hearing the famous Tabernacle Choir. Those from the surrounding area rode three hours daily, back and forth, standing in open trucks. But there was no disappointment. "It is more than we would have imagined possible," said one attendee, and another added, "This conference is like a dream to us—a dream that we did not even dare hope for."[41] The dream of seeing the famous choir, the three members of the First Presidency, other general authorities, and members of all the church auxiliaries—Relief Society, Sunday

39. Jay M. Todd, "The Remarkable Mexico City Area Conference," *Ensign*, Nov. 1972, churchofjesuschrist.org.

40. Todd.

41. Todd.

School, Primary, and the Young Men and Young Women Mutual Improvement Associations—was too difficult for the members to have imagined possible in their lifetime. And it was just as likely that the presiding authorities would never have imagined that a foreign country would be the site of the largest gathering of saints under one roof—at the *Auditorio Nacional* in Chapultepec Park—to ever come together.

Eduardo assembled eight local translators and other staff, engineers, and technicians to assure that those seventeen thousand saints could hear the words of their prophets, seers, and revelators in their own language.[42] Eduardo, while a humble and unassuming man who gave all credit to his God and his leaders, understood the significance of what was happening and the critical role he played. Many of these people in attendance had regularly sung the hymns he translated and those he wrote. It is probable that at least some in the larger metropolitan areas received or read the *Liahona*, and if not all of them, surely their leaders had read and taught from the Doctrine and Covenants and the Pearl of Great Price, and even from the revised Book of Mormon. And surely many there were familiar with his voice from listening to general conference.

There was little in the spiritual lives of Spanish-speaking members—those in attendance and throughout Latin America—that Eduardo had not influenced. All that the Church of Jesus Christ of Latter-day Saints could offer these saints came through Eduardo's translations, as well as the translations by those he trained in Utah and numerous places throughout Latin America. By the late 1960s and early 1970s, he was meeting with translators, local church leaders, and mission presidents to talk about translation and how to use the "new accessible" church literature. And though no records exist, at least not catalogued in the church archives or the Church History Library, he also recorded his own gospel-related messages that were transmitted through the radio in different cities of the Southwest and possibly the West. More will be said of this in the next chapter.[43]

42. Latter-day Saints believe that the members of the First Presidency and the Quorum of the Twelve Apostles are all prophets, seers, and revelators who hold the priesthood keys to the work of "the kingdom."

43. I learned this from a man who served a mission in Arizona and who recorded several of Eduardo's short radio messages.

His commitment to the church extended beyond his work in translating church literature. He loved preaching the word like his father, Apolinar, who became a member missionary from the moment he was baptized. In Salt Lake City, he became intensely involved in proselytizing. Before the Rama Mexicana came into the purview of the stake system, it was under the mission's direction, and missionary work was its main focus. In 1944, Eduardo was called as a local missionary in the Misión Mexicana Local. We don't know when he was released from that calling, but in 1952, he was called again, this time to serve in the Misión Regional de Valle de Salt Lake City.[44]

During the war years in the 1940s, there were numerous farm-working camps in the Salt Lake valley and further out north, and members of the Rama Mexicana went there to proselytize, but first they worked to get to know the men who worked in the fields.[45] "I was appointed to gather a group of young people and do some entertaining," remembers Eduardo, "not necessarily [to] go and immediately begin to preach the gospel."[46] Being a singer and entertainer, Eduardo found it easy to get people to see the branch members as fellow Mexicans who came to lighten their loads and not simply as missionaries who came to preach to them. Conversion to the LDS church for Utah Mexicans was still difficult in the 1940s, as it had been for the Balderas family in the 1920s. Samuel Victor Miera, a fellow branch member, told an interviewer that listening to "shaddy" stories, drinking beer, and smoking became things of the past among new converts, and soon, "you realize you are not getting invitations any more to ... go out some Saturday evenings with them ... and you're an island."[47]

For Eduardo, whose commitment to the church we've seen in the preceding pages, and for whom much spiritual growth came from both translating canon and other church literature and serving as translator for numerous church leaders, there was something else that awaited him, which began the last phase of his spiritual

44. Betty G. Ventura, *The History of the Salt Lake Mexican Branch, 1920–1960* (self-pub., 1998), 144–45.

45. Balderas, Oral History, 75.

46. Balderas, Oral History.

47. Samuel Victor Miera, interview by Gordon Irving, 1975–1976, 63–64, OH 175, CHL.

maturity. In 1965, Elder LeGrand Richards, a member of the Quorum of the Twelve Apostles, called him into the Pioneer Stake president's office—by this time Eduardo was serving as a high counselor—and informed him that the "Twelve" had felt a necessity to call a Spanish-speaking patriarch in Salt Lake City because of the number of saints from Latin America and Mexico.[48]

A patriarch is a non-administrative priesthood calling in the church. The main duty for someone who holds that position is to provide blessings to the members who request them. These blessings, unlike the priesthood blessings so common among saints (usually for health reasons or to deal with personal or familial concerns) are meant to provide the recipient guidance in navigating their earthly life. They first tell the person receiving the blessing to what tribe in the house of Israel they belong—or are adopted into—and what blessings they will receive if they remain obedient and devoted to the church. The patriarch then bestows (reveals) upon the recipient certain blessings—sometimes in very cryptic terms—that are meant to help the person know what life expects of them or why things happen to them. Sometimes these blessings are very specific about callings, marriage, jobs, and so on, and sometimes they are vague and the person interprets and reinterprets them as they experience life.[49]

As a stake patriarch, Eduardo was not to cross stake boundaries, since a patriarch from one stake did not have jurisdiction in another stake. That rule, however, soon fell by the wayside as people started coming to him from places—mostly other stakes—where no Spanish-speaking patriarch served. Then the coordinator of the Mesa Temple excursions asked the First Presidency if Eduardo could give blessings to those who traveled from so far, while also assisting with temple work. He was given permission, as long as it did not interfere with his translation work, and soon he was traveling to Mesa five or six times a year and giving fifteen to twenty blessings during each trip.[50]

48. Balderas, Oral History, 73–74.

49. For a short history and an interpretation of the practice of declaring a member's lineage, see M. Steve Andersen, "The Practice and Meaning of Declaring Lineage in Patriarchal Blessings," *Interpreter: A Journal of Latter-day Saint Faith and Scholarship* 46 (2021): 209–32. For an explanation of a patriarch's official duties, see "Stake Patriarch" in *General Handbook: Serving in the Church of Jesus Christ of Latter-day Saints* (Salt Lake City: Church of Jesus Christ of Latter-day Saints, 2022) sec. 6.6, churchofjesuschrist.org.

50. Balderas, Oral History, 75.

He started visiting other stakes without a Spanish-speaking patriarch as the demand for patriarchal blessings grew among the Spanish speaking. His opportunities increased when he traveled with Elder Spencer W. Kimball, giving blessings wherever the apostle spoke and making him a sort of "traveling patriarch." Kimball, partial to the Spanish speaking, probably encouraged it. During this period, Eduardo also traveled to Latin America, where he worked with mission presidents to train branch district presidents on the use and implementation of the translated material that came out of Salt Lake City. On these trips, he gave blessings when requested.[51]

Eventually, and we are not sure when, he did some traveling not for translation assignments but to give patriarchal blessings. We have little information about most of these trips, but we do know that he went to Uruguay, Brazil, and Argentina and gave over two hundred fifty patriarchal blessings. "It was an experience I'll remember the rest of my life," he recalled. "Had I not been blessed by … Heavenly Father, I would not have been able to do this. On some days, [I gave] thirty blessings a day."[52] On a trip to Spain, on which he took Rhea, he performed six hundred blessings.

Diane R. Tucker, wife of the mission president in Spain, remembers Eduardo and Rhea staying at the mission home, where he gave most of the blessings. "He would start very early in the morning and finish late at night," she remembered. During those times when he gave a blessing, he took time to "lovingly teach" the recipients gospel principles so they could better understand the process of a blessing and what it meant to their spiritual lives.[53] No doubt he counseled them to come back periodically to those documented blessings to better understand each stage of their spiritual life. While those blessings are unavailable to see, and we do not know who received them, it is quite likely that besides rank-and-file members, many leaders of those religious developing areas received their spiritual roadmaps from him.

We, of course, do not know what he told these members, but judging from his commitment to the Spanish speaking and the *Lamanitas*,

51. Balderas, 76–77.

52. Diane R. Tucker, "Remembering Brother Balderas: Not Only a Prolific Translator, but a Kind Teacher," *Church News*, July 14, 2017, churchofjesuschrist.org.

53. Tucker.

he must have impressed upon them the importance of their service in the church, the royal lineage they carried in their blood as descendants of the Book of Mormon people, and the necessity of building up their wards, branches, and stakes. He believed in all the promises that had been made about his people, and he saw them becoming future leaders in the church. This was something he had long believed, but during the late 1960s and early 1970s, and surely when Spencer W. Kimball became president the church, he saw fulfillment of the promises of the Book of Mormon becoming a reality for his people.

It is unfortunate that we do not have any personal writings or interviews about what Eduardo thought of President Kimball and the work that unfolded in Mexico, Latin America, the southwestern part of the United States, and among the Native American communities in the United States during his presidency. Kimball's legacy among Native Americans was complicated because of his emphasis on their "becoming white," but there is no doubt that no other church president cared more about them or defended them more against white racism. His legacy among the Spanish speaking was secure, as it would be among black saints when he ended the priesthood and temple restriction that had been in place for over a hundred years.

Just as endearing to the Spanish-speaking members was President Kimball's announcement during the April 1976 general conference that a temple would be constructed in Mexico City, the first in a Latin American country. Now, the Mexican saints and others from Latin America would not have to make as long a trek to the Arizona temple and would not have to worry about visas or collecting as much money to pay in American dollars. Then, in February 1977, he spoke to twenty-five thousand saints in Mexico during an area conference, breaking the attendance record of seventeen thousand set in 1973. He followed that special occasion with another area conference in La Paz, Bolivia, the next month.[54] Four years later, on

54. See *Official Report of the Mexico City Area Conference of the Church of Jesus Christ of Latter-day Saints, Held in the Sports Palace in Mexico City, Mexico, February 13, 1977* (Salt Lake City: Eborn Books, 1977); also, see *BYU Studies* 25, no. 4 (1985) for an extensive review of President Kimball's ministry, including the area conference in Mexico City; and *Official Report of the One Hundred Fifty-First Semiannual General Conference of the Church of Jesus Christ of Latter-day Saints* (Salt Lake City: Church of Jesus Christ of Latter-day Saints, 1981).

April 4, 1981, he called Angel Abrea, an Argentine member, to serve in the First Quorum of the Seventy.[55]

Eduardo must have rejoiced deeply about all of those experiences and many others that occurred during President Kimball's administration, but as was the case with so many other iconic moments, he left no record of his private reflections. Nevertheless, the things happening around him were part of what he expected as a child of the Book of Mormon, because they were predicted—in his mind and that of many other Latina/o saints—hundreds of years before. While others, all the way back to Joseph Smith, had spoken about the promises to the children of Lehi, the ancient prophet who started it all, few had made the theological and administrative commitment that Kimball had.[56] To be fair, however, one should also recognize that none of the early leaders had Eduardo Balderas by their side.

Without the Doctrine and Covenants, Pearl of Great Price, *Jesus the Christ*, *Teachings of the Prophet Joseph Smith*, the red hymnal, the *Liahona* magazine, and the hundreds of other materials translated, Kimball's work would have been impossible. Eduardo would never have been so arrogant as to contemplate such an idea, but his biographer should. Kimball had little knowledge of the Spanish language, and there is no record of his having studied Latin American history or having any affinity for cultural studies. Like many general authorities of his era, he depended on the Mormon canon and the writings of earlier church leaders to construct his own ministerial vision (theology). Eduardo's canonical translations and his live translations of Kimball's words and those of other leaders made it possible for church leaders to speak to the Spanish-speaking flock.

While Kimball's administration was truly the golden age of Latina/o Mormonism, Eduardo was only part of this ministry for a short period. By 1977, Eduardo was seventy years old, and he had retired two years earlier. Though he showed up the following workday after retirement to help with the "work," he did so without any official role in what was happening. While he continued to give

55. Jason Swensen, "Conference Moment: Prophetic Words," *Church News*, Apr. 8, 2006, thechurchnews.com.

56. See *BYU Studies* 25, no. 4.

patriarchal blessings, he did not travel, even to Mesa, on official business, and he had no say in what direction the translation of church materials took. By the end of his time at the translation department, the church started moving toward translation by committee.[57]

The end of an era had come.

57. Balderas, Oral History, 80–81; also, Christine and Daniel Balderas, phone interview with author, May 23, 2023.

10

TRADUCIDO POR EDUARDO BALDERAS

A LEGACY OF FAITHFUL SERVICE

Gordon B. Hinckley, Eduardo's long-time supervisor and a future church president, remembered an incident immediately after a session of general conference. Two young, Brown men, with suitcases in hand, approached a volunteer in the information booth and "inquired in broken English where they might find Eduardo Balderas," recalled Hinckley, only to be told by the attendant that he did not know the man. But what? "Everyone in the church knew Eduardo. So they thought."[1] But what they were really saying was that everyone in the southwestern part of the United States and in every country south of the border knew about him through his translations.

"All that they receive of church literature crosses his desk," wrote Hinckley, but then corrected himself by adding, "rather, it passes through his quick mind, and in doing so, that which was foreign to them becomes understandable."[2] Eduardo was more than an interpreter, he continued. To him came the widow about to be evicted, the student looking to go to school, the "zoot-suiter" in "more trouble than he bargained for," and many others who believed he could be "trusted with their problems and [could] give them counsel."[3] He spoke at their funerals, continued Hinckley, entertained them in their social gatherings, stood by them in a court of law "when prison and death have stood menacingly beside them," and spoke the language of advocacy (English) for them.[4]

But it was his skill as a translator that defined Eduardo's importance

1. Gordon B. Hinckley, "Salt of the Earth ..." *Deseret News*, Oct. 25, 1947, 5.
2. Hinckley.
3. Hinckley.
4. Hinckley.

to the church and his people. Hinckley remembered, "Somehow through the processes of his brain, grammar and syntax are taken care of, and what was English becomes smooth, fluent Spanish. That is a mean skill."[5] Few people could vouch for Eduardo as much as this future church president, who met him when he himself was young and slowly being introduced to the work of the church. In the translation process, Hinckley left Eduardo much to his own devices and soon found himself amazed by Eduardo's intellectual growth and his ability to work with others, design a church magazine, and translate for church authorities on the go, all while doing it in the "quiet way in which he goes about his work."

Hinckley worked around Eduardo long enough to notice something else that others either did not—or chose not to—talk about: his struggles as a Mexican in American society. He described him as someone whose "dark eyes reveal" a "feeling of sadness" for his people, "who were reduced to centuries of peonage."[6] And, yet, added Hinckley, he also carried the blood of the "proud conquistador" in his veins. "He has come of two great nations, and occasionally the resentment of both wells within him."[7]

Here Hinckley recognizes that Eduardo's life was anything but easy, having witnessed "the gaunt oppression of poverty" of his people, lived with his own financial limitations, and confronted, with his people, the "lash of racial discrimination."[8] Whether Eduardo ever confided in his former boss the difficulties he faced as an American citizen of Mexican descent or of possible slights from church authorities or fellow workers, we do not have any record, but it is obvious that Hinckley knew that something else besides the joy of service accompanied Eduardo on his journey.

Hinckley, however, in praising him, partly minimized the hardships by declaring that in Eduardo, "resentment rises, but does not receive voice."[9] Eduardo, said Hinckley, knows that "peace and brotherhood" do not come from contention, because "there is no discrimination

5. Hinckley.
6. Hinckley.
7. Hinckley.
8. Hinckley.
9. Hinckley.

against his people in the priesthood of God."[10] These words, published in a church-owned periodical and meant to underscore the church's openness to the Spanish speaking, sealed any opportunity Eduardo might have taken later in life to speak as frankly about discrimination he faced as his brother spoke years later.

President Hinckley opened a box but closed it before it became a Pandora's box. It is quite probable, given his humble and forgiving nature, that Eduardo accepted the praise with humility and gratitude. Eduardo was intelligent, sensitive, and perceptive, and he knew words, phrases, and the imageries they conveyed, but he chose to avoid controversies and disagreements with those with whom he served. It is also likely that, like many in his generation, any words of praise or recognition were better than the opposite, which they heard or read about often enough.

These words of praise were uttered—or written—before Eduardo was forced into retirement after thirty-eight years by laws that governed employment in 1977. However, little changed in his life after retirement, as his children remember him getting up early the morning after, dressing up, and getting ready to leave. When asked where he was going, he replied, "to the office," and he would keep going for almost nine more years, working part time and volunteering.[11]

He went to the office almost every day to help translate the enormous workload of a growing church, and he continued to interpret during general conference up until about 1986, when he received a recognition certificate from the translation department for "services" rendered at forty-two general conferences.[12] His children remember him as "restless."[13] His many years of traveling, translating, teaching people their duties, and reviewing others' translations had instilled in him a dutiful attachment to his work. The fact that he had no hobbies, possibly other than singing, meant he had little to look forward to in retirement.

10. Hinckley.

11. Christine and Daniel Balderas, phone interview with author, May 23, 2023. Also, see John L. Hart, "Translator Told Gospel in Spanish," *Deseret News*, Nov. 12, 1977, 45, newspapers.lib.utah.edu.

12. The Church of Jesus Christ of Latter-day Saints Translation Division, certificate to Eduardo Balderas, Oct. 7, 1986, in possession of author.

13. Christine and Daniel Balderas, phone interview.

His hectic schedule and his failure to take care of his health eventually caught up with him. He developed diabetes, then a congestive heart condition, and, according to his death certificate, Parkinson's disease. On January 6, 1989, he had a stroke, possibly caused by a fall he suffered while convalescing at his daughter Marta's home, and he died of aspirational pneumonia.[14] He was eighty-one years old. Rhea had died three years earlier.

Five days after his death, the family received a letter from the First Presidency, in which they expressed their "sadness" to hear about the "passing of ... our friend." The letter continued, "This noble and good man [was] well known by the leaders of the church, ... [and his] life reflected his love of the Lord and his desire to serve him." They added that the "Spanish speaking people were ... blessed as he traveled to their area to give them [patriarchal] blessings in their language."[15] It was signed by Kimball's successor, Ezra Taft Benson; Eduardo's friend and long-time boss, Gordon B. Hinckley (now the first counselor in the First Presidency); and Thomas S. Monson, second counselor in the First Presidency.

A short article in the church's newspaper, the *Deseret News*, stated, "Mr. Balderas was a prominent member of the Church of Jesus Christ of Latter-day Saints," and added that he "entertained for years as a singer," and that he traveled extensively, giving blessings to "people in their native language."[16] Mindful of his importance, nonetheless, the article writer showed little understanding of Eduardo's work. At that moment, Eduardo's journey began toward what was then "institutionalize memory"—a space in which those who served diligently and faithfully took their place behind the icons of the faith.[17] Most would have been happy to be there, but the history of an institution is skewed when only its leaders are known to its members.

14. Salt Lake County, Utah, death certificate no. 18–109 (1989), Eduardo Balderas, County Health Department, Salt Lake City.

15. First Presidency to Balderas family, Jan. 11, 1989, from private collection in possession of family.

16. "Eduardo Balderas Dies, 38-Year LDS Translator," *Deseret News*, Jan. 9, 1989, deseret.com.

17. Thankfully, this trend has changed in much of today's Mormon history, but there are many individuals yet to be rescued from that depository of incredible Latter-day Saints without whom the expansion of the Mormon gospel could not have been possible.

It would be left to Diane R. Tucker, a fellow translator and the wife of the mission president in Spain who housed Eduardo and Rhea when they were in the country for a patriarchal blessings marathon, to underscore Eduardo's value to his people as a whole and to individuals who knew him personally. In an article written thirty-six years after his death, she recounted how he had hired her as a translator when she came to thank him for the work he was doing for the Spanish-speaking members. Like many converts to the church, she "couldn't help notice"[18] his name in hymns she sang, and she later learned that the missionary literature used to convert her family had been translated by him.

"Through the years [of working with him]," she wrote in 2017, "I learned valuable lessons from a man who demonstrated the qualities of the Savior in the way he lived. He taught me humility not by word, but by his actions.... Brother Balderas always remained humble and never displayed worldly pride."[19] He also remained, according to Tucker, fully engaged in the work, demonstrating his "tireless efforts to utilize the talents and experiences" God gave him to expand the work of the church.[20]

Tucker also remembers, "In what became almost a daily occurrence, I would see him close the door to his office and utilize the lunch hour as a working hour."[21] This was the time that he used to review others' translations, proofread others' work, and just as likely review his own work before it was seen by the whole of the translation department. His early years as a church translator had been a time in which he did everything himself, and he had learned to stay busy. After receiving help with the normal workload, Eduardo used the extra time to translate books.

While Eduardo was in Spain, Tucker had the opportunity to see him outside of his "day job," and she saw him demonstrate the same tenacity in his patriarchal duties, going beyond the normal duties of

18. Diane R. Tucker, "Remembering Brother Balderas—A Kind and Gentle Teacher," *Deseret News*, July 6, 2017, thechurchnews.com. A verbatim article by Tucker was published eight days later (July 14) for the *Church News* with a different title, "Remembering Brother Balderas: Not Only a Prolific Translator, But a Kind Teacher."

19. Tucker, "Remembering Brother Balderas."

20. Tucker.

21. Tucker.

his calling. By most accounts, being a patriarch is not an intense calling because, by instruction, they are to give blessings only to those who request them. Because there were very few Spanish-speaking patriarchs, when people knew Eduardo was coming to town, they lined up to receive their blessings from him in their own language. When he accompanied Apostle Spencer W. Kimball to Uruguay, Argentina, and Brazil, Eduardo had the opportunity to give blessings, and no doubt his dear friend the apostle encouraged the members in those countries to take advantage of having Eduardo place his hands upon their heads to bless them.[22]

In that three-country, three-week tour with Kimball, Eduardo gave two hundred fifty blessings, sometimes doing thirty in one day—an exhausting effort given the mental, emotional, and spiritual preparation to give just one blessing after hours of translating for Kimball. Tucker wrote, "Through that special dimension of his life, he taught me what it means to endure and to teach in the Savior's way.... He would start very, very early in the morning and finish late at night. He not only spent time giving patriarchal blessings ... but he would take time to lovingly teach them gospel principles one by one."[23] She continued, "Those who remember Brother Balderas always say he was 'una alma de Dios' (one of God's souls). In Spanish, that saying has the connotation of being the most kind, the most honorable, the most just, the most humble person. Indeed he was."[24]

Eduardo took this gentle and mindful approach not only in his own translating and patriarchal duties but also in instructing his fellow translators about the process and preparation involved in the work. There was nothing mechanical about the way Eduardo did things. He took time while training or blessing others to teach gospel principles and church protocol because he believed that was the only way his people could understand the scriptures, their patriarchal blessings, and the purposes of the church. His words, when he instructed or when he gave talks to the members, carried a special spirit.

Flora D. Donaldson, while serving a mission in Chile, remembers attending a meeting in which Eduardo spoke, and being highly

22. Tucker.
23. Tucker.
24. Tucker.

impressed by this "humble, learned in the gospel man."[25] He spoke to "teachers and officers"[26] of a church school in Chile and afterwards had a question-and-answer session. We do not know under what circumstances he spoke, nor why. Was he assigned? Did he take time from his translation instruction to the missionaries and their leaders in Chile? Was he invited to speak when members and local leaders heard he was in town?

It would not be surprising if it was the latter. Latin American members and leaders saw him as an authority because he came from Salt Lake City, worked with church leaders, translated the materials they used in their congregations, and traveled for the church. No other Spanish-speaking saint had ever done any of the above. Additionally, Eduardo, the "silver-tongue" missionary that Rhea had heard about, had evolved into a knowledgeable man who knew the scriptures in ways few members or leaders did, knew church doctrine as it was meticulously preached by those he accompanied, and learned prophetic teachings from those called as prophets, seers, and revelators and for whom he translated. Over the years, the "great men" of the church of his generation no doubt shared gospel insights with him while he traveled as their close companion.[27]

The question-and-answer session, as remembered by Sister Donaldson, "was really good," as "lots of the questions were the same old ones, but he answered them in a new, enlightening way."[28] It is obvious from her journal entry that the people in the meeting were anxious to know when they would have the blessings of the temple, as no temple existed presently in Chile and would not for many years. In what was most likely a soft and positive manner, he promised them that one day, if they prepared themselves and remained a righteous people, they would be able "to do this great work."[29]

Sister Donaldson continued, "I was greatly uplifted by his power

---

25. Flora D. Donaldson, Mission Journal and Letters, Mar. 24, 1966, 37, box 1, fd. 2, MS 19265, CHL.

26. Donaldson.

27. I remember that as a young man, bishops and other leaders with whom I worked closely took quiet moments to teach me about church doctrine and protocol that they did not always share with the congregation.

28. Donaldson, Mission Journal and Letters.

29. Donaldson.

and knowledge. It was truly a great experience." After the session, Eduardo conversed with her, and she found out that he had lived in El Paso during the time her mom served in the Mexican Mission in 1925. "Sitting there," she continued, "watching him and listening to his prophetic words, I was thinking why wasn't he an apostle or even a mission president?" But then she acknowledged that his calling as a patriarch to the Spanish speaking and his translation work was "a great enough calling. He has done and is doing a marvelous work."[30]

There are probably many such comments written in various unpublished letters and journals in the church archives, and in many a closet, drawer, attic, or basement throughout the United States and Latin America. Many who met Eduardo in an official capacity and heard him speak or provide instruction could see that beneath that humble, often-timid appearance was a knowledgeable, perceptive, and spiritual soul.

We clearly see his spiritual soul in the radio messages he recorded that were disseminated over different stations in areas with large, Spanish-speaking populations during the 1960s. Dale Rees, who served as missionary in the West Spanish American Mission from January 1962 to July 1964, remembers that while he served in Safford, Arizona, he and his companion received a reel-to-reel tape each week from Salt Lake City. The tapes contained "half-hour radio programs with music and a message from Eduardo Balderas." The local radio station played one each week on Sunday.[31] "I liked them so much that I made copies to bring home with me," remembers Rees.[32]

While the church had radio programs since the 1920s, most of these were only transmitted in Utah. The messages that Rees remembers probably came from the Church Radio, Publicity, and Mission Literature Committee, established in 1935 under the leadership of Gordon B. Hinckley.[33] While we do not have any information on their origin, it is most likely that Eduardo wrote the

30. Donaldson.

31. Dale Rees, email message to author, June 15, 2018.

32. Rees, email message.

33. Elizabeth Mott and Sherry Pack Baker, "From Radio to the Internet: Church Use of Electronic Media in the Twentieth Century," in *A Firm Foundation: The History of Church Organization and Administration*, ed. Arnold K. Garr and David J. Whittaker (Provo, UT: Religious Studies Center, in association with Deseret Book, 2011), 339–60.

messages and was involved in their production. In providing these messages—most of them nondenominational—Eduardo became part of a religious radio ministry landscape that had its heyday from the 1930s to the 1960s.[34]

While not intended to proselytize, these messages served to make the church more mainstream and make it less foreign to those Spanish-speaking individuals who tuned in. We have no information on the messages' reach or their impact, but it is possible that those who chose to listen to the LDS missionaries heard Eduardo talk about moral and spiritual topics such as those titled, "El día de reposo" (the Sabbath day), "La trampa del pecado" (the sin trap), "El poder del ejemplo" (the power of example), "Los pensamientos" (our thoughts), "La naturaleza de Dios" (the nature of God), "Jesucristo es el hijo de Dios" (Jesus as the Son of God), and concepts more specific to the church such as "¿Hay una iglesia verdadera? (Is there a true church?), ¿De dónde, por qué, y a dónde?" (Why am I here?), and "La resurrección" (the resurrection).[35] It is unfortunate that only a small number of these seem to exist.

While I never heard Eduardo's messages as a boy, I do remember listening to Catholic Bishop Fulton J. Sheen, one of the most popular radio evangelists of the 1950s and '60s. My mother had the radio on most of the day, and around noon, the Spanish station broadcasted messages from Bishop Sheen. I remember how impactful they were to me as a young man struggling to lead a moral life. Because they were not tied to any particular church doctrine, I, as a Latter-day Saint, could listen to them without fear of deviating from my own faith.

After listening to Eduardo's radio addresses, I believe that had he had his own radio ministry, he would have been widely popular. He had a soothing voice, spoke with reverence, and articulated his message succinctly and with such calm that it is easy to see how one could become an avid listener, and just as important, be impacted

34. For an example of these ministries and others before them, see Kirk D. Farney, *Ministers of a New Medium: Broadcasting Theology in the Radio Ministries of Fulton J. Sheen and Walter A. Maier* (Westmont, IL: IVP Academic, 2022). For a short history of the LDS radio and television religious programing, see Fred C. Esplin, "The Church as Broadcaster," *Dialogue: A Journal of Mormon Thought* 10, no. 3 (Spring 1977): 25–45.

35. The titles of these radio addresses were provided by Dale Rees to the author.

by the messages. Here, rather than being a "Mormon messenger," Eduardo was a voice for a Christian morality devoid of religious substructures that could come across as strange to those nurtured in or exposed to Catholic and Protestant theology.

There is a Latter-day Saint notion that whatever men or women are called to do within the church, the Lord "raises" them up to the task by providing them talents, skills, and experiences that help them grow intellectually, emotionally, and spiritually. If one were to have come across Eduardo as a young, shy immigrant boy who had just dropped out of school and had parents who knew little English, it would have been difficult, if not impossible, to picture him at the height of his life.

An uninterested young boy became a devoted man of faith. He nearly failed high school Spanish but became the most prolific Spanish-language translator of the twentieth century, and without education, pedigree (pioneer stock), or pulpit, spread the LDS gospel to the Spanish-speaking world in a way no one before or since has done. All the while, he remained a humble, unassuming man who never took stock of what he had accomplished, even as he gloried in the work he was called to do.

Traducido por Eduardo Balderas meant something to those who converted to the Latter-day Saint gospel, those who found meaning in the Mormon canon, and those whose lives were touched by others who lived its ethics. Today, those "words in translation" by Eduardo Balderas continue to impact millions of Spanish-speaking converts and their families, neighbors, and friends and continue to grow the brown spaces within the Church of Jesus Christ of Latter-day Saints. It is in those brown spaces where Latino Latter-day Saints seek to forge a Christian gospel of fellowship that resonates with those who yearn for a better world. That was the message Eduardo saw in the Mormon gospel as he translated it line upon line and precept upon precept. And that will be his legacy.

INDEX